"This book offers us all a chance to do more tha
it shows us how to examine our lives and mak‹
discover are needed in our personal and profe؛
teach, encourage, support, and value all students in our classrooms."
—Kylene Beers, Coauthor of *Forged by Reading* and *Disrupting Thinking*

"In *Teaching for Racial Equity*, the authors brilliantly respond to systemic racism and oppression that have created inequities in our schools. Through the centering of racial literacy and critical self-work, they provide bold yet practical approaches for developing urgent pedagogies toward the necessary pursuit of interrupting the harm inflicted upon our children."
—Gholdy Muhammad, Author of *Cultivating Genius*

"Writing is one of the most intimate acts in which a human being can engage. Teachers almost always demand that intimacy from students without reciprocating. This volume is all about the mutuality and reciprocity that must occur in the midst of fighting against racism, sexism, heterosexism, classism, and any other 'ism' that oppresses us."
—Gloria Ladson-Billings, Professor Emerita, University of Wisconsin-Madison

"Teachers taking up the imperative to explore anti-racist teaching are often reminded to 'do the work' and to 'start with themselves.' But some wonder, what does that mean? This is a book that aims to show us what it means to do the work: what it means for the collaborating writers, the partnering teachers, and what it could mean for us as readers. At this moment of challenge and resistance in many communities to even broaching the topic of race in schools, this book is most welcome and needed."
—Elyse Eidman-Aadahl, Executive Director, National Writing Project

"I can't imagine a more rigorous, more detailed, more compassionate book about interrupting racist systems in both our classrooms and in the larger learning communities we serve."
—Matthew R. Kay, Author of *Not Light, But Fire*

"Teachers as interrupters do not see teaching as a process of gathering skills for cultivating heartless minds. Instead, interrupters are seen as maintaining a bold humanizing embrace among disciplinary content and racial consciousness. This book is an amazing read, setting in motion action-oriented ways for learners, teachers, and educators to augment racial equity efforts for positive change in and beyond schools."
—Dr. María E. Fránquiz, Professor, University of Texas at Austin
and President-Elect, National Council of Teachers of English

"A deeply personal book, *Teaching for Racial Equity* reminds us that transformative change occurs not in a silo or through top-down directives; this change happens through dialogue, personal reflection, and sometimes uncomfortable action. As a set of meaningful practices that can be used in schools right now, this book reminds teachers to act, to love, and—when necessary—to interrupt."

—Antero Garcia, Associate Professor, Graduate School of Education, Stanford University

"Every day is an opportunity to interrupt inequity, shout Perry, Zemelman, and Smith in their brilliant new book. And, they remind us, in a school system where 80 percent of teachers are white and only 20 percent are people of Color, the work of equity must be done together."

—Harvey "Smokey" Daniels, Author of *The Curious Classroom*

"Through their striking (and sometimes uncomfortable) 'Time Out to Talk' sections, the authors challenge us with their critical conversations, daring us to have our own as we move forward in our journey to become better allies, co-conspirators, and interrupters for change and equity."

—Cathy Fleischer, Professor of English Education, Eastern Michigan University

"*Teaching for Racial Equity* is a book that all current and future educators and teachers should read. It is full of authentic voices of educators and students wrestling with challenging, critical perspectives on race through compassionate dialogue, scenarios, assignments, and applied practice."

—Betina Hsieh, Associate Professor of Teacher Education, California State University Long Beach

Teaching for
RACIAL EQUITY

Teaching for
RACIAL EQUITY
Becoming Interrupters

Tonya B. Perry, Steven Zemelman,
with Katy Smith

Stenhouse
PUBLISHERS

Portsmouth, New Hampshire

Stenhouse Publishers
www.stenhouse.com

Credits pp. xix–xxii: "Racial Literacy and Poetics for the Academy & Beyond" from Volume 17, Issue 1 of *The Journal of Language and Literacy Education* by Yolanda Sealey-Ruiz. © 2021 Yolanda Sealey-Ruiz. Reprinted by permission of *The Journal of Language and Literacy Education*.

p. 24 Figure 1.1, Reprinted by permission of Yolanda Sealey-Ruiz.

Names: Perry, Tonya B., author. | Zemelman, Steven, author. | Smith, Katy
    A., author.
Title: Teaching for racial equity : becoming interrupters / Tonya B. Perry,
    Steven Zemelman, with Katherine A. Smith.
Description: Portsmouth, New Hampshire : Stenhouse Publishers, 2022. |
    Includes bibliographical references and index. |
Identifiers: LCCN 2021027481 (print) | LCCN 2021027482 (ebook) | ISBN
    9781625315182 (paperback) | ISBN 9781625315199 (ebook)
Subjects: LCSH: Educational equalization—United States. | Discrimination
    in education—United States—History.
Classification: LCC LC213.2 .P467 2022 (print) | LCC LC213.2 (ebook) |
    DDC 379.2/60973--dc23
LC record available at https://lccn.loc.gov/2021027481
LC ebook record available at https://lccn.loc.gov/2021027482

Cover Illustration by Grace D. Player
Cover design, interior design, and typesetting by Cindy Butler
Printed in the United States of America

This book is printed on paper certified by third-party standards for sustainably managed forestry.

28 27 26 25 24 23 22   4371   9 8 7 6 5 4 3 2 1

Tonya's dedication

To KP and KP, who have been supportive of this work
since the first day, who dream with me of a more equitable space

• • • • • •

Steve's dedication

To Gilead, who will inherit a world we hope does more
to embrace the hard but essential striving for equity

• • • • • •

Katy's dedication

To my family, by birth and by choice

Contents

Acknowledgments

Our deepest thanks first and foremost to our editor, Bill Varner, and to Stenhouse, for eagerly supporting our effort and that of other equity advocates whose work they are committed to publishing.

Our gratitude to Yolanda Sealey-Ruiz, whose thinking about how people can grow into understanding of self and take action for racial justice has so fully informed our work.

Our admiration for the risk-taking and creative teachers whose classroom work, shared in this book, shows what it really means to provide equitable support and learning opportunities for their students.

Tonya's Acknowledgments

With much love, I acknowledge my family—my husband, daughter, mom, brother, sister-in-law, brothers-in-law, "sisters"—and extended family for supporting me and pouring into me the love it takes to see the world differently and live it courageously. I know that my father, who is looking down, is dancing because he sees that the world he was championing is one step closer to the ideas that he believed in and rallied for.

He never won an election in our hometown, nor did he ever have the chance to publish a book, but he always was a fighter for justice and equity. I can remember the newspaper, *The Afro-Chronicle*, he started with other Black men when I was very young. I can remember the black and white ink on paper swaying in the wind on a string line in the makeshift shed-office space in rural North Carolina. Those were words, powerful words, flying in the wind. I can remember looking up and being proud of these freedom writer-fighters who created space for people of Color to have their voices amplified when no other outlet would allow their stories to be shared. He was not a professional writer, nor were the other men in the group, but they were like-minded servants who believed in community. So I feel compelled to give thanks here to the writers before me, like my father, who believed in the power of advocacy, storytelling, information sharing, and celebration of his people. I know, Dad, that you did not know at the time that your vigilance was actually planting a seed in your daughter.

In that same spirit of community and love, I acknowledge the spaces that have continued to fuel, educate, and support me in this journey.

Thank you to my church family at Sixth Avenue Baptist Church in Birmingham, Alabama.

Thank you to the Teacher Fellows in the UAB Red Mountain Writing Project. These are my people, and I love their courage and tenacity, their spirit and scholarship. They always show up for the communities they serve and make a difference every day.

With sincere love, I thank my sisters in the Tri-County (AL) Chapter of The Links, Incorporated, and the Omicron Omega Chapter of Alpha Kappa Alpha Sorority, Incorporated, for their unwavering commitment to excellence and sisterhood.

With utmost respect, I cannot forget my National Council of Teachers of English and National Writing Project families, who have spoken into me words of positivity and life-giving affirmations. To my Cultivating New Voices family, you are always amazing.

And thank you to my wonderful colleagues at the University of Alabama at Birmingham in the School of Education, including GEAR UP. We are committed to making a difference in this world using our scholarship, service, and teaching.

And to my sisters and brothers who send me love and build me when I need it most, I am most grateful.

Mentors in the field have lifted me and my work with love. Thank you to Dr. Ball, Dr. Frierson, Dr. Holley, Dr. Kirkland, Dr. Collins, Dr. Kinloch, and Dr. Beers.

And to all of the students in my middle school classrooms, high school Saturday rooms, and college classrooms, thank you for teaching me and shaping me into a teacher who is committed to making your world a better place for you and our communities. Deon, Jordyn, and Jaeden, you make us proud. And we know the future is in good hands with you leading the way.

Steve's Acknowledgments

To my parents, who modeled the courage and initiative and deep values that have helped me take up the challenges of advocating for social change. My father risked everything to create a toy factory out of nothing and was a model of innovative action for me in doing so. My mother had wanted to become a teacher, but the Great Depression prevented that, so it looks as though I unknowingly pursued what she could not. Unlike many people, she grew more open, more feminist, and more civically active as she grew older. She would have loved this book.

I want to honor all my teachers who each in their own way moved me toward the work I'm now engaged in. I especially recognize Janet Emig, whose work to understand students' learning and whose generous encouragement set me on my path as an educator focused on students and not just content, a path that has led ultimately to the writing of this book. I'll always remember sitting in her office, seeing all the books on teaching and writing on her shelves, and realizing that there was help for me as a struggling teacher that I had never known about.

Don Graves, whom I first met when he spoke at the university where I taught, so graciously shared his close attention to the genius of children and encouraged me to look closely myself.

My once-upon-a-time teaching partner, Marty Gliserman, showed me daily the beauty of what student-centered teaching could be.

And it was through writing alongside Smokey Daniels that I learned to write in a way that could speak to readers and not indulge in some jargon-filled academic exercise.

I realize now how important was the focus on social justice maintained by the adult leaders of the Jewish youth group to which I belonged as a teenager. As is the case for so many teachers, they'll never get to know how much their influence has stayed with me.

The teachers in the Illinois Writing Project have been my caring and talented professional family for the better part of my career.

My thanks to the young people on the student voice committees at Farragut Career Academy and Reilly School, where I'm simply Dr. Z. They challenged me to support them as they addressed the issues that mattered to them.

And thanks to Susan, my dear life partner of (at the time I write) fifty-five years, a consummate teacher beloved of all her students, who showed me how to ask questions and listen.

Katy's Acknowledgments

I am deeply grateful to Tonya and Steve for taking this journey together.

To my siblings, who have fed me, listened to me, and held me close (even in a pandemic): saying thank you is insufficient. To Sean and Kelly, Mike and Rebecca, and my Grandgirl Alida and Grandboy Artie: you give me great joy in the present and every reason to persevere toward a brighter future.

To colleagues who have walked alongside me—and sometimes carried me—through the writing of this book, especially the NEIU SCED folk: I'm honored to work with you in a program that is dedicated to preparing future teachers to become interrupters.

To my ATHS colleagues, particularly the "Women of Addison Trail" and my longtime teaching partner Ralph Feese: your friendship, intellectualism, and dedication to the profession continue to inspire and sustain me.

To my fellow teachers, leaders, and friends in the Illinois Writing Project and the National Writing Project network: you are my extended family, and I love what we do together.

To my theater and dance family: you make it possible for me to use all parts of my brain, and you inspire me to do so.

To two special mentors whose influence in my academic life reaches well into my identity as a person. Michael Apple, you have always seemed to know just when to provide a pat on the back and when to opt for a kick in the pants. Marilyn Bizar, I think I will always hear your voice in my head saying, "Of course you can do this!" Thank you both for your enduring guidance and support.

Together We Acknowledge

Our thanks to one another for not only working together but becoming partners and friends who care about and support one another. It's never been simple, considering how complicated and contradictory race is in America, but it's been a joyous learning experience we could not have imagined when we started.

Foreword

Yolanda Sealey-Ruiz

There are those wonderful moments in our work life when we get to witness how our colleagues' research aligns with our own. Such is the case with how I came to write this foreword. When I first received a copy of the manuscript and talked to the authors, I was struck by the term *interrupters* in the title, as it is a term essential to my own work; it is used to remind teachers that the work of racial literacy skill building must be intentional, action-oriented, and bold. The title immediately drew me into the book, and I am grateful for the opportunity to offer remarks for the opening of this courageous text.

The 2012 documentary *The Interrupters* (Kotlowitz and James 2012) tells a powerful story of how three violence prevention volunteers endanger themselves to protect their Chicago communities. The film offers an intimate look into the work of the interrupters, following them on their personal journeys and collective and public encounters with resistance to peacemaking. This film compels the emotions—empathy, fear, anger, outrage—when witnessing the impact of systemic racism, inequity, and inequality on communities of Color. *The Interrupters* should be viewed in all teacher education programs to offer an example of how unequal access to education and the persistence of racism threaten communities that have been marginalized by race. However, the film is also an inspiration for how communities can unite in support of the change needed for their members to thrive.

When I entered my second decade of teaching nearly eight years ago, I experienced an epiphany—an overwhelming desire to pause, reflect, and decide how I wanted to continue contributing to the field of teacher education. Around this time, I had shown *The Interrupters* in a course called Youth, Media, and Educational Justice that I was coteaching at Teachers College, Columbia University. This course asked the students to consider what it means to be an adult in the life of a young person who is tethered to the foster care system, the juvenile (in)justice system, or both. While watching the film for the second time, I suddenly realized what I needed to do: I needed to be more direct and deliberate about how I interrupted the inequality I witnessed and experienced in public schools, and devise an approach to be more effective in inviting the preservice and in-service teachers I work with to be "interrupters" in their schools. I needed to be deliberate as an English education teacher educator to help my students bear witness to issues of racism, biases, and allegiance to stereotypes living within themselves before they could even begin interrupting school conditions and curricula that improperly served children of Color. Similar to how the three Violence Interrupters in the documentary recognized the ways they perpetuated violence in their communities, so too my students needed to see how they were actors of racism through their beliefs and actions before they could effectively interrupt it. The most authentic way I could invite others into the deep work of interruption was to engage with my own beliefs and practices connected to race. I had to be humble enough to realize when I chose fear over the hope of change, when I remained silent in speaking my truth and sharing historical facts. In a process that I have come to call the Archaeology of Self™, I recognized my need to do the self-work first before inviting my students to do the same. And so I began this work. After more than two decades of teaching high school, adult education, graduate students, and in-service teachers, I began the deep excavation process into myself as a teacher.

While my practice has certainly been enhanced through this reflective and reflexive approach, it was not until three years ago that all of the deep self-work I began evolved into the language and visual of my Racial Literacy Development (RLD) model and Archaeology of Self theory. At the start of my journey, I created the Racial Literacy Project at Teachers College and centered the topic of racial literacy in my teaching, professional development work, and life. As I write this, I admit that I am still engaging with the deep work—applying the Archaeology of Self to various aspects of my personhood—as a teacher, mother, daughter, partner, and friend. I have learned that as much as the process is personal, it must also be done in community. As I guide people through the six components (Critical Love, Critical Humility, Critical Reflection, Historical Literacy, Archaeology of Self, and Interruption) and three tenets (question assumptions, engage in critical conversation, practice reflexivity) of my RLD model, I find myself constantly growing and changing as a practitioner and person in the world. I recognize how being deliberate about engaging these components and tenets has made it easier for me to interrupt inequity and racism in my professional and personal lives while inviting others to do the same. It also occurred to me that claiming to "educate" someone was at once bold and arrogant. My RLD model constantly reminds me of the humility that is required to do this work. On my best days, perhaps I can interrupt myself and others by asking questions—questions that matter for youth—specifically children of Color—who sit in classrooms and grapple with the relevance of the education they are receiving. They attempt to make sense of their racist world as they seek ways to live out their full humanity and chase their dreams.

The second viewing of *The Interrupters* led me to question how I presented myself in the field. I now found it difficult to embrace the title of teacher educator. Instead, teacher interrupter felt more aligned with what I wanted to do in my classrooms and the field at large. This title makes complete sense to me.

The unexpected invasion of COVID-19, the egregious murder of George Floyd on May 25, 2020, and the attack on the Capitol on January 6, 2021, are all events that have awakened segments of our society who believed that America had reached a postracial status after the presidential election of Barack H. Obama. This could not be further from the truth. We are currently living in an intensely racially polarized society that some compare to many of the turbulent decades of racial upheaval embedded in America's history. However, there are also stark differences between our past and our present in terms of the fight for racial justice and equality: the advent of social media; Gen Z, who appear to challenge the racial myths and lies passed down from previous generations; and the appearance of a racial consciousness awakening among many in society—particularly those in education—to face the impact of race on the lives of the students they serve. As a nation, we witness the clear role that race continues to play in voter suppression and laws being activated against the discussion of race in schools. On a hopeful note, however, educators across America continue to desire engagement in conversations about the impact of race on all of our lives. Students, teachers, educational leaders, parents, and social justice activists are learning what it means to become a coconspirator (Love 2019) to bring about positive change in our schools.

Here enters this book.

Teaching for Racial Equity: Becoming Interrupters plants a stake in the ground and gives us compelling reasons why, as educators, we must build our racial literacy. This book offers practical steps and strategies to begin addressing the essential need for racial equity, moving from talk, reflection, and inquiry to action in and beyond schools. It generously offers practices that we can initiate to address the inequities we identify in every aspect of our lives. If we realize the change that must happen in our schools, we also must have a vision for that change, methods to enact it, and courage to make it real. Healthy and productive discussions about race will allow us to dream of a day when all of us are free, but we need to create a plan now to ensure that will happen. Schools are ideal places for building the racial literacy skills of students and educators. In accordance with a concept developed by sociologist and feminist researcher France Winddance Twine and furthered by critical legal scholar Lani Guinier and other scholars in the field of education,[1] I define racial literacy as

---

[1] Allison Skerrett, Melissa Mosley, Rebecca Rogers, and Jabari Mahiri are noted literacy and teacher education scholars of racial literacy.

a skill and practice in which students probe the existence of racism, and examine the effects of race and other social constructs and institutionalized systems which affect their lived experiences and representation in U.S. society. Students with racial literacy are able to discuss the implications of race and American racism in edifying and constructive ways. A desired outcome of racial literacy in an outwardly racist society like America is for members of the dominant racial category to adopt an anti-racist stance, and for persons of color to resist a victim stance. (Sealey-Ruiz 2011, 25)

In schools, healthy conversations on the effects of racism across class, culture, race, and other characteristics of diversity are possible. Multiple texts and modalities to engage students in these conversations are readily available through digital technologies. To develop racial literacy among students, the use of historical, fictional, poetic, and digital texts is most effective. Teachers who are able to engage their students successfully in the topic of race are most impactful when they engage in self-exploration and honest assessments of their own role in perpetuating racist ideas. Once specific behaviors are recognized, racially literate persons find it easier to interrupt racist behaviors in future moments and guide others toward the same goal. Individuals who develop racial literacy can engage in necessary personal reflection on their own racial beliefs and practices and teach their students and staff to do the same. Racial literacy in schools includes the ability to read, discuss, and write about situations that address racial inequity and racial bias as part of the norm of the schooling process. According to Guinier (2004),

Racial literacy is an interactive process in which race functions as a tool of diagnosis, feedback and assessment. Second, racial literacy emphasizes the relationship between race and power. Racial literacy reads race in its psychological, interpersonal and structural dimensions. It acknowledges the importance of individual agency but refuses to lose sight of institutional and environmental forces that both shape and reflect that agency. (115)

We live in a racist society. Our schools are heavily impacted by the concept of race, and the teaching and learning that happen in our schools can influence the agency individuals enact against the forces of racism. Thus educators and students need a literacy to navigate this reality. As a poet, I use the genre of poetry to "write to heal and free myself" (Sealey-Ruiz, 2020), but also to make sense of what I am interrupting—and why I am interrupting in that moment. What follows is a poem written to understand my role in furthering racial literacy in education and to highlight what it offers those who commit to learning this critical skill.

Racial Literacy Poetics for the Academy & Beyond
BY YOLANDA SEALEY-RUIZ

Racial Literacy is a skill, a practice
that dares you to see your neighbors
as human.
To respect their existence
& support their resistance
when their humanity is at stake.

Racial Literacy
        calls you
                tells you
                        invites you
to bend towards justice
& break your silence
on isms & phobias that infect society—
It abhors the destruction of Black & Brown
bodies & uprises to a crescendo
when tasers & wallets & sandwiches & Skittles
are mistaken for guns.

Co-conspiring towards justice,
the Racially Literate put our minds & bodies
on the line while our souls march
towards freedom's destiny.

        We meet our ancestors on arrival.

Racial Literacy rejects daily police killings.
Scaling walls of justice instead of white houses—
It requires truth.
Telling of an archaeology of the
        self
                family
                        institutions
that you worship.

In the church of the Academy, Racial Literacy
is a foreign language that must be taught & learned.
It is how one begins & continues the fight
to restore what all have been given at birth.
What others have stolen away, leaving
a soul bereft of peace & a stranger to love.

Racial Literacy dreams justice,
talks about setting souls free from
      anxiety
            fear
                  uncertainty.
It leads with Critical Love,
seeking to penetrate that love through
our vocations & the masks we wear
in the face of the world's most pressing problems.
Racial Literacy talks of 400 of Years of Inequality.
It echoes the words of Baldwin:
Nothing can be changed until it is faced.
We face the truth that race is a lie;
socially constructed, not rooted in biology,
but boasting real & complete consequences
that wreaks havoc on the lives of those who built
this country out of blood & sweat;
those whose land was stolen in manifest marches
& movements towards a destiny that meant
claiming & conquering what was not yours.

      Change is inevitable.

Like
      the tides
            the seasons
                  our minds,
change will come when there is
a collective will for equity & disdain
for myths of meritocracy, false sentiments of equality

& true justice for all.

Racial Literates incite the change & bring the nation
to the tipping point of what it professed long ago—
before you or I
came to be.
Racial Literacy is a practice.
It probes the existence of racism
& examines the effects of its damage
on our experiences.
Racial Literates have the skill to discuss
& dismantle centuries' old lies of superiority.

Racial Literacy desires constructive talk—
Requires a stance that knows the difference
between being not racist & anti-racist.

      Yes, there is a difference.

Racial Literates know there is no neutrality
in the fight for humanity.
There is no sitting still or standing by,
upstanding against excuse-making &
fantasies that evoke distorted memories
of not seeing race & only seeing people—

      That sentence makes no sense.
      It never did.
      In Amerikkka, it never will.

Racial Literacy is
      reading
            discussing
                  writing
a world devoid of racism
& the myth race.
It seeks to reach truths

that help us discover
what we always knew—
Everyone is equal.

Racial Literacy implores the shift from the liberalism—
That free-thinking, non-racist, Kumbaya approach
to maintaining the status quo by speaking
in borrowed tongues; ventriloquists of radical love.

Racial Literacy rejects the mere speaking
& expects talk of freedom, dreaming the world we seek;
one we know can exist, the moment we dare
to be the light that
       haunts us
           guides us
               is us.

Racial Literacy will free us—
Eventually.
It will release us from static quoness
& shift us from the liberalism that traps us
in the quagmire that subjugates bodies
of glorious colors.

Racial Literacy activates the anti-racist stance;
the only leg on which to stand.
The only road to take & make while walking:
the path that leads to
       freedom
           equality
              & justice
for all.[2]

---

[2] This poem was originally published in *Journal of Language and Literacy Education* 17, no. 1 (Spring 2021): 1–5.

I celebrate the publication of *Teaching for Racial Equity: Becoming Interrupters*. It is a practical book, and one that I imagine will become an important reference for educators. It is a book that we need now, perhaps more than ever, to guide educators and their students in confronting today's challenges and to instill hope for the change we want to see in our world and, especially, in our world of education.

Yolanda Sealey-Ruiz, PhD
New York City, 2021

· · · · · ·

REFERENCES

Guinier, Lani. (2004). "From Racial Liberalism to Racial Literacy: *Brown v. Board of Education* and the Interest-Divergence Dilemma." *Journal of American History* 91, no. 1 (June 2004): 92–118. https://doi.org/10.2307/3659616.

Kotlowitz, Alex, and Steve James (producers). (2012). *The Interrupters*. [Frontline documentary]. Arlington, VA: PBS Distribution. Available at https://www.pbs.org/wgbh/frontline/film/interrupters/.

Sealey-Ruiz, Yolanda. (2011). "Learning to Talk and Write About Race: Developing Racial Literacy in a College English Classroom." *English Quarterly: The Canadian Council of Teachers of English Language Arts* 42, no. 1: 24–42.

Sealey-Ruiz, Yolanda. (2020). *Love from the Vortex & Other Poems*. New York: Kaleidoscope Vibrations.

· · · · · ·

Why We Are Writing This Book

Tonya

I write this book for Sharon.[1] Sharon was an African American student in eighth grade—shy, reserved, quiet. She was the only person of Color in the class. One day, a White student teacher asked her during a book discussion, "What do Black people think about this topic?"

I write this book for Linda. Linda, a White teacher in a suburban school, was a culturally conscious teacher who recognized that the school was serving more diverse students. This was a positive as far as she was concerned, but no one had talked to the teachers about the beautiful change and how to work with all families and students. She wrote, "We are changing, and we as teachers need help."

I write this book for Cornelius. Cornelius, an African American student in an urban context, wanted to know what I knew about him. He wanted me to know him before I taught him. Did I know about the school? The people? What happens at night in the neighborhood? He stated, "You don't know us. What we deal with. Who we are. How can you teach us?"

And I write this book for myself. I write this book for you.

For all of us who instruct students every day, who live in this universe and communicate with peoples who are like us and who are different, it is important for each of us to connect with the humanity we all possess. To do that, we must be willing to open ourselves to learning about one another, each person's histories, and even if we do not agree, each person's stance toward life. As a lifelong educator, I find it important to think about the role of an educator. Early in my career, my goal was purely to teach the skills. Then it was to apply the skills. Now it is to transform the skills into tools for application, transformation, and interruption. The ultimate learning has occurred when a student can use the skills to create something bigger than herself.

When a student can interrupt the status quo, speak up for equity, we are doing something right.

This is for you, Sharon, Linda, Cornelius, and every teacher who wants students to think and deliberate with care and love, and use their skills to interrupt those practices that devalue who we are as learners and global citizens.

---

[1] The names listed in this section are pseudonyms.

Steve

Can an older, White, privileged (in so many ways), middle-class man really do this? I've been handed so many privileges—growing up in a neighborhood of my parents' choice, benefiting from the family's successful toy factory, having no worry about being accepted to any college I wished to attend, and on and on. While I may rage at the injustices experienced by Black and Brown people, and enjoy learning their rich cultures, I can never fully know the hurt or the joy in their lives as they live them. So how can my voice possibly help or provide the right perspectives for truly equitable education?

The thing is, I simply cannot sit idly by in these times of brutality and discrimination and sheer meanness of spirit that are snatching opportunity away from so many Black and Brown children. We White educators cannot wash our hands of it and leave all the work of promoting equity only to people of Color. But we are not saviors. We must be coactors, cointerrupters, coconspirators, whatever term fits. White educators need to discuss the challenges with other White educators. We must learn about personal and structural racism, and talk about our part in it honestly and without defensiveness. We can help colleagues understand that while racism has a personal dimension, we all find ourselves living within larger racist structures we must learn to avoid supporting—actively or unwittingly—and instead work to undo. We can listen to and support colleagues of Color without requiring them to be our teachers. We can model and promote culturally sustaining teaching practices. We can speak out in hopefully constructive ways.

So I've written and loved working with my fellow authors of this book. Despite the weight of the injustice we are fighting, the work is deeply enriching. Not every reader will agree with all I've helped to say. No doubt not everything I contribute will have been said in just the right or most sensitive way. I accept all that. But I cannot remain silent.

Katy

For me, as for Tonya, particular students and teacher friends have been in the forefront of my mind throughout my work on this book, and I have written for them. And just as Steve has explained, this writing—especially in collaboration with these dedicated educators—has required me to confront the unearned privileges that have been granted me just because I happened to be born White. I have written for my family, especially my father, a flawed man who nonetheless was once described as a person who "would have bent over backward to stand upright." I aspire to live up to that legacy. With great humility, I know that I need to stand up, and step up; I have written so that my sons will, too.

Introduction

So loud, too loud. A Becky. Talking not listening.
Soften the language. What's the point? Not enough real
picture. Too many words. Not enough real world.

—Comments by some of this book's teacher-writers
during an initial online discussion

Tonya

This is a book that almost wasn't. It's not easy writing a book about
interrupting inequities. And it is really difficult writing a book like
this across different races and generations. I am a middle-aged Black
woman who lives every day in her skin and loves it. I am writing with
two people who are White, who are critical friends and coconspirators
in the work, but they are still White. They don't have to wonder whether
the reason that their informed decisions were overlooked was because of
their skin color. Nor do they have to think about whether they are invisible to others as
a result of race. And no matter how I explain or share my experiences, the level of understanding about Blackness is distant for them, although, I must admit, they are listeners
and learners. That helps tremendously.

Steve and Katy

And we, two White people, have benefited from the privilege of not
having to question, in the past, whether race has played a role in the
ways our voices and opinions are heard. But we cannot continue in
that state of denial, so we listen and we read, while recognizing that
neither of us will ever be in a position to fully understand what it
means to be a Black or Brown person. Each of us has grown in our
awareness of all the unearned access we were granted by society on the
basis of our race. Working extensively for two years with colleagues
who are Black and Brown on a project focused on equity has led us
to more deeply pursue our own learning about racism and antiracism.
We may have thought we knew the challenges and the strengths that
people of Color experience, but we still have so much more to learn.
Nevertheless, we've joined in writing this book as learners more than

as experts, as it's absolutely necessary for us as White educators to do the work of interrupting racism in every way we can, rather than leave it all to people of Color.

Thinking Together

Any one of us writing alone certainly would have had opportunities to say exactly what we thought, just the way we wanted to say it. But this book is different. It is not a watered-down version of the difficulties we face when we are trying to have these difficult conversations; it is quite the opposite. We still say what we believe, but at the same time, we are practicing what we urge for you, and also sharing our challenges. We try to take time to listen, share, put our biases into words, and tell our stories to one another. We listen to one another talk about teaching and our communities. We ask humanizing questions about who we are and how we have come to be. We find out about our lineages, our ancestors, the people who poured into us, and why those stories are important. So, yes, this is the work in action. And it is hard work. But the work is needed and hard not only for us but for others. Here is an example. Tonya received this email from a teacher-colleague:

* * *

The teacher-colleague:	My school is changing. I don't know what to do. The school doesn't know what to do.
My response:	What do you mean?
The teacher-colleague:	The population is changing. School is becoming more Black and Brown, and we are clueless.
My response:	I love this diversity. It will impact the culture tremendously.
The teacher-colleague:	We aren't doing so well.

We have been thinking about the preceding email exchange and our own experience and just how complex it all is. Inherent in this teacher's plea for help is a systemic problem, and although perhaps seemingly innocent on the surface, it is still a problem. The statement implies that "something needs to be done," that the Black and Brown people need to be addressed. But the implication that somehow things were just fine "before they got here" involves a mindset of "it's their fault" and causes people to think about addressing groups without thinking about the larger context. The standpoint that the people of Color are the ones causing the problem is a deficit perspective, allowing people to easily gravitate to something other than the beauty created when students of varying backgrounds talk and learn from each other. This deficit approach places the burden on the Black and Brown families—and needs interrupting. Conversely, the opposite attitude will allow schools to see the great opportunity to be found in working with a variety of students and families. But interrupting for equity takes work—we are talking about sweat, rolled-up sleeves, and sometimes tears—to think about, reflect, process, put into action, talk about, fail and try again to implement sustainable equity practices. It's not a pretty process, but it is so worth the struggle when we get it right. And we can work with our students to get it "more right" too.

So Take This Journey with Us

This is why we welcome you to *Teaching for Racial Equity: Becoming Interrupters*. In this book, we invite you to consider your stance about race in education, engage in honest conversations, and help students participate in their own conversations, leading to actions that promote equity.

> In this book, we invite you to consider your stance about race in education, engage in honest conversations, and help students participate in their own conversations, leading to actions that promote equity.

The result, we hope, is that we and our students learn about one another's identities, thoughtfully critique the racial inequities around us, and then act as interrupters for change. Interrupting, to us, means asking questions, thinking critically about issues, sharing narratives to illustrate points of view, providing innovative ways of viewing a subject, and embracing the work of equity and change. It means being courageous, doing these things strategically, and supporting one another in doing them, too.

Meanwhile, the word *equity* is on everyone's lips—in news articles, foundation grant priorities, election rhetoric, organizations' stated values and goals, and education advocacy. The Annie E. Casey Foundation defines equity as "the state, quality, or ideal of being just, impartial, and fair" (2015). This is different from equality. Equality is giving everyone the same thing, regardless of how much or little they may have already, but equity is giving everyone individually what they need to be successful. Knowing the definition of equity is a good thing, but it doesn't automatically help educators see how to work toward it, with either students or colleagues. So with this book we hope to help fellow teachers reflect on the role of race in their own thinking and experiences, in their classroom, in their curriculum, and in their school. We and our teacher contributors offer practical steps and strategies to begin addressing this essential need for racial equity, moving from talk, reflection, and inquiry to action in and beyond schools. We seek equity practices that we can put in place to address the inequities we identify in our everyday lives and beyond.

A major challenge in this effort is that race enters into all teachers' lives and work in many ways and at many levels. Yet many White educators (and White people in general) hesitate to talk about it, a silence that itself becomes a significant part of the problem, as many writers on this subject have been pointing out (e.g., DiAngelo 2018; Kendi 2019). So first and foremost, we educators—both those who are White and of Color—can examine our own history, attitudes, and awareness of the role of race in our own lives. People talk much about recognizing one's privileges or lack thereof, and that's part of it. But self-reflection also enables an awareness of how our experience and outlook may differ from those of the students we teach, no matter who they are. This awareness can enable us to create equitable learning pathways for all those students. Such awareness can be important for teachers of the same race as their students, as well as for those who don't share their students' particular backgrounds.

Along with differing kinds of support, we can help students gain awareness of racism as an issue in their lives and begin acting to interrupt it. These discussions and explorations are likely to vary widely depending on whether they take place in a classroom of students of Color, one with mostly White students, or one with students from a mix of backgrounds. We want to help all young people develop empathy for, and understanding of, those who are different from themselves, and come to appreciate the vibrancy of their cultures. We're also challenged to help students find and claim their voices and begin to act for change, not only in the classroom but in their community. Threading through these efforts is the development of our own relationships with and among our students, so they can risk their ideas in a safe and trusting environment.

This work is not easy. White teachers, who often hesitate to discuss race, work alongside teachers of Color who may have had a hard time getting their ideas heard and valued. We need to find ways to openly discuss racial equity issues and needs with our colleagues to better address them as a school community and actively work in a constructive way to tackle differences and misunderstandings that may emerge.

Moving beyond our students' voices are the larger institutional racist challenges around us. We teach from curriculums that often involve built-in biases (Schwartz 2019). Beyond the school walls, attitudes and pressures bear in on us from the communities in which our schools exist. Just a few examples from among those we outline later: school-district boundaries that ensure less funding for schools with a majority of children of Color; the policing that is more punitive for people of Color; the violence that weighs on some neighborhoods; the lack of resources for more rural spaces of Color. And elements of racism intersect in multiple ways. Segregation and related school-district boundaries affect property values, which in turn affect funding for schools. Less funding limits essential resources: technology, books and materials, availability of counselors and certified teachers, alternative discipline strategies such as peace rooms that replace suspension with more constructive interventions, and more. This, in turn, leads to more segregation across district boundaries as White people take flight when they perceive schools struggling—and the cycle continues.

Understanding this systemic web can help us determine how best to focus our interruptions for equity. Our influence may be limited, but we can ask ourselves about actions we, our colleagues, and our students can take to help reduce the larger inequities many students face. And through the process, we can examine and seek to understand our own development and the ways that race, experience, and aspects of privilege or lack thereof have impacted us. These tasks are restorative and not aimed to promote either guilt or self-congratulation. They simply ask us to clear-mindedly take account of what we bring to our work, the privileges or challenges we may not have been fully aware of, and the ways this increased understanding helps and/or complicates our efforts. Along with recognizing the challenges, however, we also need to celebrate the successes and creativity in our communities. No one book can explore all of this in depth. But this book offers stories and strategies to help open conversations on the various levels of racial inequity that need to be addressed.

> Along with recognizing the challenges, however, we also need
> to celebrate the successes and creativity in our communities.

Defining Racism and Antiracism

There is so much confusion and so many misconceptions around words such as *antiracism, racist,* and *racism* that right up front we had better clarify what we mean by these words so that we all can enter the conversation with a common understanding. When a public figure is accused of being "racist," many people picture someone with an evil mind who wakes up each morning thinking about how to hate and hurt another person or group that day. Other people think of someone who is quiet, less engaged in the diversity of the world, and more subtle with their biases and actions. Unfortunately, although racism is reflected in both images, it is also far deeper and more complex. At a systemic level, racism is present in all the structural ways that opportunity, resources, jobs, and justice are distributed along racial lines and denied to people of Color in society. At an individual level, racism is not necessarily a surface action but, rather, is rooted deeply in a person's veins. So much so, it is not always recognized, just flowing through the body; left unchecked, undiagnosed, and unchallenged, it continues to feed the entire physical being.

In her book *Caste: The Origin of Our Discontents*, historian Isabel Wilkerson helps address the continuing confusion for many Americans between the systemic and individual sides of racism by introducing a term for the systemic aspect that most of us see as applying only to places like India. *Caste* provides a separate word for the structural (even though artificial) arrangements that maintain White supremacy. As Wilkerson (2020) explains:

> Like other old houses, America has an unseen skeleton, a caste system that is as central to its operation as are the studs and joists that we cannot see in the physical buildings we call home. Caste is the infrastructure of our divisions. It is the architecture of human hierarchy, the subconscious code of instructions for maintaining, in our case, a four-hundred-year-old social order. Looking at caste is like holding the country's X-ray up to the light.
>
> A caste system is an artificial construction, a fixed and embedded ranking of human value that sets the presumed supremacy of one group against the presumed inferiority of other groups on the basis of ancestry and often immutable traits, traits that would be neutral in the abstract but are ascribed life-and-death meaning in a hierarchy favoring the dominant caste whose forebears designed it. A caste system uses rigid, often arbitrary boundaries to keep the ranked groupings apart, distinct from one another and in their assigned places. (17)

Caste also works because it brings home with a shock just how ugly is the structure that it labels. It may seem hidden to some, but it means that even if some people of Color advance themselves economically or politically, they still experience barriers and obstacles. The limitation of the "caste" concept, though, is that it seems to imply that change is impossible, which we fervently believe is not true. So for now we'll continue to use the terms *racist* and *racism* for both systemic and individual elements of this complex failing in our society.

With the prevalence of a more individualistic image in their minds, many White teachers hesitate to discuss race, fearing they'll be accused of a personal kind of racism that they don't believe applies to them. Or they worry they'll say the wrong thing and be misunderstood—again viewing the situation as a personal matter. Some teachers may have become so conditioned to the dominant individualistic narrative about race that it is difficult for them to identify their own racist thinking, particularly when it comes to honoring and welcoming students' use of their language and community practices. Let's be clear though: failing to address the issues of race makes teachers complicit in racist teaching and racist thinking. Antiracist teaching is the active stance that addresses inequitable practices, not the default passive stance. You cannot be silent when a racist comment or event happens and consider yourself an antiracist teacher. You cannot ignore people of Color at work and fail to ask for input about their perspective and consider yourself an antiracist colleague. You cannot talk about the "uneducated use of standard English" and still consider yourself an equity warrior for students and communities. Not only do White teachers need to understand this, but also teachers of Color need to be clear about their definition of racism and antiracist teaching, so they know how they will respond when racial issues come up.

> Failing to address the issues of race makes teachers complicit
> in racist teaching and racist thinking.

So what is it, this destructive, ugly thing we call racism? As Ijeoma Oluo (2019) states in her very clear and personal writing, it's "prejudice against someone because of their race, *when those views are reinforced by systems of power*" [emphasis ours] (26). In other words, it's not about individual attitudes alone. Oluo goes on to say, "Getting my neighbor to love people of color might make it easier to hang around him, but it won't do anything to combat police brutality, racial income inequality, food deserts, or the prison industrial complex" (29). Of course, personal relationships are very necessary and important, providing a place to begin talking and addressing issues; but real change in *broader equity practices will occur as these interactions multiply and grow to impact* even more lives to ultimately interrupt systemic inequitable practices.

Many of the manifestations of systemic racism and White supremacy—the unfounded idea that the White race is better than races of Color—can go almost unnoticed, especially by White people not directly experiencing them. Again, to quote Oluo's very helpful words, "The impotent hatred of the virulent racist was built and nurtured by a system that has much more insidiously woven a quieter, yet no less violent, version of . . . oppressive beliefs into the fabric of our society" (2019, 27). This condition is described very thoughtfully by a school principal, Joe Truss (2019), who has guided discussions and actions to combat racism with the teaching staff he leads:

It is the water we are swimming in. The trouble is we don't even see it. . . . We have all been conditioned through exposure to media, parenting, schooling, and our interactions with power structures. . . . Even I, a black educator who has studied ethnic studies and critical race theory, still perpetuate tenets of

White Supremacy Culture. . . . This has included making decisions about curriculum, school partnership, and hiring, without authentically involving teachers or students in the process.

The upshot is that all of us have been affected by and been part of the racism in our society—with painful awareness for Black and Brown people, often unwittingly for White people. In any case, the privileges gained by White people usually begin when they are small children, hardly responsible for and hardly aware of what surrounds them. It's the silence and avoidance of discussion later on that makes it easier for attitudes and behaviors to continue unexamined. Yet even when we come to understand this and begin addressing racism, we're still part of it—as White people retaining advantages, as people of Color not having access in many cases to the same opportunities, and all of us as citizens. All of us experience the damage created by inequitable schools, school-to-prison pipelines, biased judicial processes, and the limits on so many people's productivity, incomes, and spending. These limits reduce overall prosperity, not to mention create harm to the social and psychological well-being of all. However, it is still possible—and really essential—to examine one's experience and one's role honestly and then work toward undoing inequity.

The Prevalence of Racism in Education and Its Context

Now let's dig a little deeper to see just how pervasive racism is in our work. We see racism endlessly in the news of police shootings of Black men, harassment and fear felt by Latinx families, lack of resources in struggling neighborhoods, miscarriages of justice. But even if we're sympathetic and taking action—whether as White people or people of Color—we need to be well informed about the depth and breadth of those insults, the steady drumbeat of hurts and injustices that add up to create a structurally racist society, creating harm for people of Color. As Oluo (2019) explains,

On its own, each microaggression doesn't seem like a big deal. But just like one random bee sting might not be a big deal, a few random bee stings every day of your life will have a definite impact on the quality of your life, and your overall relationship with bees. (169)

In the face of all these racist conditions, we must greatly admire, honor, and respect how people of Color have, across centuries, shown amazing resiliency, resistance, courage, creativity, and even optimism in opposing those conditions. This is not to say that any of us should take comfort or minimize the destructive power of White supremacy culture and the many ways it manifests itself in all our lives. Indeed, we must be highly *dis*comforted, recognizing these two opposing phenomena—White supremacy culture and resistance by people of Color—along with our own necessity to step up and interrupt. Preferably, interrupting racism could and should lead to greater opportunity and fulfillment for all. In schools, for example, it could lead to advanced learning for all students who seek it, rather than forcing families of differing races to vie for the same limited placements—as has unfortunately happened so visibly in New York City for years (e.g., Shapiro 2020). However, in a social system filled with structures that exacerbate inequality by pitting groups against each other for supposedly limited resources, the struggle for equity grows more complex, larger, and more painful than we may have realized. Still, we must hold these three realizations—the strengths of people of Color, the deep forces of racism that give advantage to White people, and our need to act—in our awareness at once.

So let's look now at some of the ways that racism insinuates itself into our lives and our work at so many levels:

- Young people who may continually fear encountering prejudiced police stops.

- Teachers who hold unconscious biases or simply don't know how to create a supportive climate.

- Teachers who hesitate to demand enough of their students.

- School curricula that ignore the cultural backgrounds of particular students—or curriculum that simply fails to inspire them or to invite the self-expression and questioning that enables students to develop the agency they need to work for change for all students, not just students of Color.

- Hesitance of many schools to really address the structural biases that continue. The documentary *America to Me* (James 2018), for example, shows how even in a high school that is racially "diverse" (Oak Park River Forest High School, in a Chicago suburb), students, families, teachers, and administrators have avoided dealing with these challenges.

- Neighborhoods that are as segregated as ever, with Whites in some areas even creating separate school districts to avoid children of Color, which means that children of different races miss opportunities to get acquainted with and appreciate one another.

Here are still more examples, for which we can provide concrete data showing the extent of the problems.

- Bias in discipline: According to the US Department of Education Office for Civil Rights (2014), Black students are three times more likely to be suspended or expelled than their White peers. A recent study based on more than two thousand school districts finds racial disparities in suspension rates tightly intertwined with disparities in achievement. Every 10 percent increase in a district's gap in math and reading performance between White and Black students correlates with a 30 percent larger Black–White gap in suspension rates than the national average (Pearman, Curran, Fisher, and Gardella 2019).

- Fewer opportunities for students' more advanced learning: Black and Latinx third graders are half as likely as Whites to be assigned to gifted-and-talented programs (Grissom and Redding 2016).

- Lack of teachers of Color: The teaching force in 2016 in this country was 80 percent White, and half of all US schools did not employ a single teacher of Color. Not surprisingly, non-Whites made up 55 percent of teachers in schools where at least 90 percent of students were non-White. By comparison, across schools where at least 90 percent of students were White, nearly all teachers (98 percent) also were White. Of course, this reflects a continuing pattern of segregation (McFarland et al. 2018; Geiger 2018). Meanwhile, many studies show the positive effect on learning for students of Color when they have even one teacher who looks like them (Gershenson, Cassandra, Hart, Hyman, Lindsay, and Papageorge 2018; An 2019; Pollard 2020).

- Challenges for teachers of Color to stay with teaching for the long term: In spite of a considerable increase in minority hires—162 percent between the 2011–12 school year and 2015–16—the departure rate for minorities was 19 percent in 2011–12, compared to 15 percent for Whites (Barshay 2018). Note: departure data for more recent years are not presently available.

- Unequal resources due to segregation created in the drawing of district boundaries: Nearly nine million students in the United States, or one in five, live next door to a significantly Whiter and richer school district. Of the thirteen districts that surround Philadelphia, for example, two-thirds are at least 25 percent Whiter and have at least 10 percent more funding than the city schools—equating to an average of $5,000 or more in per-pupil funding (Camera 2019; Harris 2019).

There's plenty more, unfortunately, so we'll provide additional detail in Appendix 2—but you can see how deeply these conditions affect schools and student learning.

Examining Racism in Our Own Lives

Interestingly, once the larger social definition of racism is understood, we can begin to chip away at the blockade of defensiveness for White people around racism and privilege. Of course, this doesn't instantly solve the problems of racism in our schools, but the White participants in the discussion can grapple with the discomfort they may feel. In turn, teachers of Color can begin to feel safer expressing the frustrations and discouragements they may have had to live with. We can discover that it's not so difficult, finally, to speak honestly. This is not to avoid shared responsibility in a racist society, but the real question is, *what do we do now*?

That is what this book is about. As you read, you'll encounter more of our stories and those from all our writers, along with conversations we and they carried on as we did this work and read and learned about one another's experiences. After all, we can't try to encourage the writing and sharing of your stories without doing the work ourselves. Having done so, we can attest that once we've shared our realities and reflected on them, we begin to lose our fearfulness and discover appreciation and understanding. But it's not automatic that we all get along or understand right away. Sometimes we say words that we don't realize may be taken negatively. Sometimes we don't "hear" the other person because we are busy thinking about our next words or because we don't ask enough questions before making assumptions. This work is messy, messy, messy.

We believe it is essential to engage in this process as a first step toward becoming interrupters for racial equity. Reflecting on our own stories—and sharing with colleagues who listen with respect and speak openly themselves—enables us to become stronger and clearer in our effort. And this is a process. We can better understand the good fortune and advantages that we have benefited from—and whether you are a person of Color or White, if you have entered the teaching profession, you have inevitably experienced supports and help along the way, in addition to your own hard work and struggles. We can also better understand the hurts of racism that have affected teachers and students of Color in a wide variety of ways. And we can learn about and celebrate the joys and values and creativity of the various cultures present in our classrooms. We can begin to appreciate all sorts of experiences and ways that we're simply similar to or different from our students and colleagues. With the realizations gained from sharing our stories, we can become ready to adapt our teaching and our actions to the needs of our students and our schools. And we can strive to make changes and improvements in our teaching without feeling defensive or inadequate about it. It is a necessary, messy, and worthwhile process.

> With the realizations gained from sharing our stories, we can
> become ready to adapt our teaching and our actions to the
> needs of our students and our schools.

What You Are About to Read in This Book

A key to the thinking in this book about change that leads to racial equity is the process of Racial Literacy Development, conceived by Yolanda Sealey-Ruiz, and Chapter 1 explores this process as we see it. Chapter 2 explores the value of Sealey-Ruiz's stages of Critical Humility and Critical Reflection, developed through the writing and sharing of teachers' autobiographies and examining the role that racism has played in their lives. This chapter also offers a structure for helping you and others to write a bio, along with excerpts from several of our teacher-writers' autobiographies and the dialogue they carried on in response, to show how these can help you become more aware of your own and one another's backgrounds so as to better understand your classroom interactions. And we offer a strategy for guiding this process with colleagues.

In Chapter 3 we bring autobiography to the classroom, based on your own work developing your awareness. Our teacher contributors describe several very different ways they work to deeply understand and connect with students and engage them in serious learning. Their approaches enable them to listen to and nurture relationships with and among students, while supporting content learning by responding to various student needs and backgrounds.

The Racial Literacy Development concepts of Historical Literacy and Archaeology of Self point us toward the inquiry into and critiquing of racism in education that we and our students can do, preparing us for action as interrupters for racial inequity.

Chapter 4 provides two examples of ways that teachers of two different subjects, in very different settings, have guided students to critically question racist conditions in their school and community, while recognizing our limits: we're not telling students what to think but providing tools and building a sense of agency, even in the face of the undermining forces prevalent in schools and society at large.

Chapter 5 then moves to the stage of active interruption for students, offering ways that they can be helped to activate their own voices as interrupters. Students can speak out not only to critique racist conditions but also to celebrate the cultures and creative expression of groups and people of Color, whose developments are all too often underrepresented or even erased in and outside school settings.

But it's limiting to seek change only within the four classroom walls, since our students continue to learn in other spaces in and beyond the school. So in Chapter 6 we offer strategies for promoting change and interruption. After all, we cannot ask students to embark on this work without taking it on as adults ourselves. Interruption is needed to improve broader school policies in areas such as discipline and school culture, to develop sensitive guidance for responding to troubling events in or beyond the school, and to involve teachers and students in decision-making. Actually, this wider connection to colleagues is threaded throughout the book as well as in this final chapter, as all of the effort of interruption needs to be shared as much as possible.

Our version of Sealey-Ruiz's Racial Literacy Development progression is far from exhaustive. The fact is, we cannot tackle every aspect of antiracism in one book. Fortunately, a growing number of educator-authors are addressing the many challenges in this effort, and we urge you to continue developing your capacity for antiracism after you've finished our book. The references section, a list of influential authors (Appendix 1), a collection of online resources (Appendix 3), and a listing of books on antiracism and equity (Appendix 4) are provided at the end of this book to guide you to more help and knowledge. Meanwhile, what we can share are stories and strategies for developing our own voice and fellow teachers' and student voices for racial equity, based on the self-reflection and criticality that support them.

Our Teacher-Writers

We cannot do this work alone. It is the work of teachers in classrooms everywhere that will ultimately make the difference in schools to interrupt normalized practices and achieve equity. So we need to model this collective effort right here in this book. Therefore, let us introduce the six teachers and teacher leaders who have joined us to share their valuable stories and strategies.

Tina Curry is a teacher and mentor in Chicago. She is also an adjunct graduate education professor at National Louis University. In addition to her teaching duties, Tina guides the equity effort at her high school.

Adelfio Garcia is a former principal and has recently retired from his role as literacy coach at Gary School in Chicago. He now provides professional development on working with emergent bilingual students and their families, and participates as a teacher-leader with the Illinois Writing Project.

Brandon Hatcher is a special education teacher at an elementary school in Birmingham, Alabama. He is completing a doctorate focused on instructional leadership in social and cultural studies from the University of Alabama. He specializes in educational policy, critical race theory, curriculum theory, and critical social justice issues in education.

Vanessa Heller teaches in a suburban middle school in southern California. Vanessa has revised her humanities curriculum to focus on social issues, including a unit on race, racism, and discrimination, designed to support awareness and action for her students, who are mostly from affluent families.

Shonterrius Lawson-Fountain is a secondary literacy support teacher in Birmingham, Alabama, city schools. In addition to her classroom teaching, Shonterrius leads professional development on supporting student voice, and has led student workshops on creating poetry and music to address issues they care about. Presently, she is codirector for the Red Mountain Writing Project Summer Institute.

Christopher McDaniel is a science teacher and coach in Chicago Public Schools. He has developed innovative strategies for making science learning meaningful for students of Color and helping them realize how scientific knowledge can greatly benefit their lives and livelihood.

Where Do We Go from Here?

Building the relationships and understanding within this team has been one of the great joys in the process of writing this book—ironic, considering that the topic is such a troubling and painful one. Although not without the occasional frustration, the work is energizing, helping us as writers to understand one another and appreciate one another's background and perspective. Individually and collectively, we continue to take action for racial equity and help our students do so. This book is about communicating, gaining understanding, critiquing, and then building on that base to interrupt inequity. We challenge you not only to take in the words and ideas but to seek opportunities to reflect, and share with us and one another your stories of discovery, change, privilege, hurt, success and struggle in supporting students, and acting for equity. We need the energy that comes from banding together to address such difficulties. The work of equity must be done together.

Time Out to Talk

Tonya Asks Steve a Hard Question

From: Steve Zemelman
Date: Saturday, April 6, 2019, 4:17 PM
To: <Perry, Tonya>
Subject: First partial drafts of 2 conversations plus slightly updated notes on the book

Hi Tonya—

It felt good to get started on a bit of writing. Partial drafts of two of our conversations are attached. You'll need to add your side of the discussions. Also attached is a slightly updated version of the notes on the book.

We'll talk on Wed.

—Steve

Steve Zemelman, Director
Illinois Writing Project

• • •

From: Perry, Tonya
Sent: Wednesday, April 10, 2019, 1:20 PM
To: <Steve Zemelman>
Subject: Re: First partial drafts of 2 conversations plus slightly updated notes on the book

Hi Steve.

Before we go further, here is a question that you will need to answer in order to provide transparency about our work together.

Intentions are important. You never want to exploit or probe based on self-interested inquiries. That once again places the burden on the person of Color and opens up wounds from the past. Dignity, sincerity, and respect with earnest intentions are essential to develop healthy relationships and conversations.

Why did you reach out to me to think about writing this book?

Would you have thought about me as a coauthor for a text that was not about equity? Why or why not?

—Tonya

•••

From: Steve Zemelman
Date: Thursday, April 11, 2019, 8:14 PM
To: <Perry, Tonya>
Subject: First partial drafts of 2 conversations plus slightly updated notes on the book

Tonya—
Why did I reach out to you about writing this book? And would I have made the connection if it were another topic? This is hard.

First of all, I really didn't think I'd ever write another book after *From Inquiry to Action*. I had nothing new to share about writing or reading, and anyway it seemed like there were so many troubling problems in the country and affecting education that literacy seemed like a secondary matter.

I wrote *From Inquiry to Action* alone. As for earlier books, I didn't know you very well. It's hard to say what I might have thought—but between Smokey Daniels and then a later partner, I was pretty focused on the people I knew well. So no, I would not have thought of you, and after that I wasn't thinking about ANY further writing.

Would I have considered you in the past if I DID know you well? I can only say, now that we are working on this and having great conversations and trusting each other as we work, it would have been very tempting. It would depend on the topic, of course.

But why did I reach out now, and why you?

As I began realizing that the equity issue was so big and hurting kids and their education in so many troubling ways, I started feeling that I needed to do SOMETHING. Meanwhile, various pieces started to come together in my head. The documentary series *America to Me*, about race in a supposedly progressive high school in a Chicago suburb, reminded me of the many painful micro- and macroaggressions that students and teachers of Color experience. And this was happening at a high school where friends of mine were involved. Then an editor friend suggested some reading on race—Ijeoma Oluo's *So You Want to Talk About Race* and Robin DiAngelo's *White Fragility*.

After that I knew I needed to speak up, even if I didn't have all the answers. But I wondered, who could be a good partner? As a middle-class liberal White male, I could not possibly do the book without other perspectives. It wouldn't be fully accurate, it wouldn't be credible, and it just wouldn't be right. So the hard reality is that yes, inevitably my approach to you could not avoid being partly about your Blackness.

And, I don't know, our growing professional friendship told me you'd be the right person. The Urban Sites Conference in Birmingham that you organized, with all the testimony from now-adult participants in the Children's March, made a huge impression on me. I learned so much about what it took to make change around racial problems. You were the one who got us together with them. Then when Brandon Hatcher presented with my panel at NCTE 2017 and your mentoring for him was so clear, that stuck with me. Same with hearing Shonterrius Lawson-Fountain last November. You came to my session, and you appreciated my coming to yours. We were becoming professional friends.

It's hard to say what spoke to me! Your calm strength and good humor, certainly. Sure, our differing racial backgrounds do matter. But when we had "the talk" about hoping we could be up front on racial issues and our own thoughts and feelings, you were so very . . . "welcoming" is the best word I can think of. My instincts aren't always right, but this one was!

I hope this helps. Please let me know your thoughts.

Very best,
—Steve

•••

From: Perry, Tonya
Sent: Friday, April 12, 2019, 4:20 PM
To: <Steve Zemelman>
Subject: Re: First partial drafts of 2 conversations plus slightly updated notes on the book

We've been professional colleagues for a while, particularly after you came to Birmingham to keynote our National Writing Project Urban Sites Conference. Since then we'd been talking about issues around race. You told me you had enjoyed hearing about the work of Red Mountain Writing Project, particularly the experience you had when you were here. The small roundtable discussions that you found enlightening, for example.

I'd been following your work anyway, including your last text about inquiry. And some of the teachers we've worked with came together so well in one of your NCTE panels. Brandon Hatcher had been an undergraduate student of mine as I emphasized working with children who had sometimes been marginalized. We had lots of discussion about being the teacher they needed us to be. So I think that really meshed well with your work.

Then when we came together, I wanted us to have an honest and frank conversation about what it would take to collaborate. After all, race is an issue that I think adults should be able to discuss. So I've approached you about my role. I think that if I were not African American, I wouldn't be working with you on this project. The use of my Blackness or personhood of Color was a question in my mind, though now I'm OK with that. As time has gone on, I have gotten to know you and know your heart about the work. I've understood that this text is necessary and cannot be done without a person of Color. But the process balances out because we've had to have these conversations just like teachers need to have them. I think we are modeling and *living* the book. The things we are asking teachers to do—we are actually experiencing, ourselves. And so my Blackness or personhood of Color is important to the book. But this is also an exercise that I'm learning from, along with you, as we are constructing the text.

I don't see our discussion of this question as a negative. I see it as a growing opportunity to have these conversations so we can better inform other teachers and colleagues through our own experiences of what needs to happen and what these conversations look like. We don't always agree, because we're two different people with two different lives and two different backgrounds. But we have to give ourselves permission to work through those things so that we can hear each other and so we can be better listeners for our students in our classrooms and for the teachers we work with in our own Writing Projects.

I do not have a problem with the question, though it did give me pause in the beginning. However, there's this: the way I framed it gave you a position of power, as if **you** made the decision. Even though it was you approaching me, a better question would have been "Are WE going to work together, and why did WE decide that this should be a partnership, and how did WE choose each other to do this work?" That way it would decenter the power and make it more even, like in a balanced seesaw. How I originally asked the question wouldn't be how I'd ask it now, after all our months of talking.

—Tonya

CHAPTER 1

Racial Literacy:
A Guiding Concept

We have seen attempts at creating buy-in fail for initiatives like ethnic studies, mastery-based grading, or project-based learning. This is because we are starting with the branches of the tree instead of the roots.

—Joe Truss, San Francisco middle school principal

It's easy to look at systemic challenges, such as those we referred to in the introduction in the "Prevalence of Racism in Education and Its Context" section, and react with fight, flight, or freeze. How can we begin to undo all the conditions that have built up over many centuries? Well, we as individuals cannot do it alone, but we needn't be paralyzed by those three impulses. We can develop our resolve, our understanding of both ourselves and the world around us, and our ability to act to interrupt racial inequity, and we can encourage others to do so as well. And increasing numbers of educators are doing this, so we won't be alone.

The concept that we've found most helpful for doing this work is Yolanda Sealey-Ruiz's Racial Literacy Development (RLD) framework. The RLD framework has six levels that provide a way for us to think about how we approach our "roots not just the branches" understanding of race. These levels are actually recursive rather than hierarchical, but all build on a foundation of Critical Love (see figure 1.1).

The levels and the process of applying them in our teaching will guide the thinking and ideas explored in this book. The

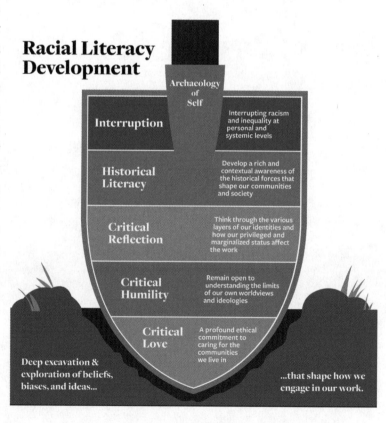

Racial Literacy Development

Archaeology of Self

Interruption — Interrupting racism and inequality at personal and systemic levels

Historical Literacy — Develop a rich and contextual awareness of the historical forces that shape our communities and society

Critical Reflection — Think through the various layers of our identities and how our privileged and marginalized status affect the work

Critical Humility — Remain open to understanding the limits of our own worldviews and ideologies

Critical Love — A profound ethical commitment to caring for the communities we live in

Deep excavation & exploration of beliefs, biases, and ideas...

...that shape how we engage in our work.

Figure 1.1. Racial Literacy Development framework

framework emphasizes the important roles of self-reflection, learning, sharing, and action, starting with examining our own lives and the impacts of racism in them. The work is grounded in the passion we have for our students, especially our students of Color, not just for them to navigate the limits that racism has imposed on them but for all of us to step up and interrupt the racist conditions they experience. Further, caring about our White students means helping them become aware of systemic racism so they themselves can act to interrupt the racism that has affected everyone and led to privileges they may take for granted. By working through the RLD framework, we can begin to critically question and understand the forces and biases in the practices in our schools so that we can act strategically as interrupters. In this chapter, we will review each level separately and describe a scenario to illustrate it in our own lives.

Before we begin, let's think more about the word *critical* in this context. Generally, one uses "critical" to describe something that is of ultimate importance, such as *critical care,* a *critical state,* or a *critical moment.* In the context of the RLD framework, we continue to view *critical* as meaning important and urgent, but in addition, critical(ity) is used as "the capacity to read, write, and think in ways of understanding power, privilege, social justice, and oppression, particularly for populations who have been historically marginalized in the world" (Muhammad 2020, 120). We will revisit this same concept in more depth in Chapter 4. As you read the descriptions of each of the six levels of the RLD framework, think about how each is viewed using a "critical" lens. For example, what does it mean to have Critical Love and not simply "love" when referring to RLD? Let's take a closer look at the six levels.

Level 1: Critical Love— the Foundation for Racial Literacy Development

DEFINITION
A profound ethical commitment to caring for the communities we work in.

SCENARIO
To begin to discuss the foundational level, let's look at a scenario involving an examination of the cover of the picture book *Only Passing Through: The Story of Sojourner Truth* by Anne Rockwell in an elementary classroom. The teacher begins with the cover of the book, allowing the students to review the illustration and characters. In this fictitious scenario, the conversation is rooted in Critical Love.

Student 1: Ms. Smith [teacher], I wanna read that one [book] 'cause she [Sojourner Truth] looks strong, and I like how she looks like she's thinking.

Student 2: Me too. She looks like me. Look at her pretty black skin.

Student 3: She looks like my grandma. Her arms. Her nose. Her lips.

Unfortunately, in the real-life version of this scenario, reported by Roberta Gardner (2016), the children of Color in the classroom reacted to the picture book quite differently: they were actually quite unaccepting of Sojourner Truth's appearance. Because we realize that the actual scene may be hurtful and could open wounds for some readers (and we want to honor you as readers), we will not share the actual transcript of Gardner's insightful work here. But in the actual discussion, the children depicted the character of Sojourner Truth as "ugly and an alien." The disheartening language, the misrepresentation of Black bodies from the mouths of young people, is devastating. But we cannot blame them for this learned behavior.

The young students, without knowing, had internalized the deficit language and images that depict Black and Brown bodies. This negativity among people of Color and White people is a learned behavior, centered in Whiteness. Therefore, the view of beauty and respect is centralized in White terms and as a result of White power, leaving Black and Brown people vulnerable to others for the definition of beauty of their own bodies. To counter this, we can teach children racial literacy as early as elementary school and younger on a foundation of Critical Love. We can teach students to love themselves as they are and help teachers show Critical Love for their students. This love is not just a feeling. As Sealey-Ruiz notes, Critical Love "means a LOVE that frees—frees the teacher from the stereotypes & biases they hold about the community of children they teach, and frees children from the stereotypes and biases the world holds about them—and they hold about themselves" (personal communication, January 2021). It's a teaching act that requires real conversations about race and who decides what is beauty, a deconstruction of ideas and norms in society, and an appreciation and celebration of all people.

WHAT COULD THIS LEVEL LOOK LIKE USING THE FRAMEWORK?

When we talk about Critical Love, we are looking at love in its purest sense, the idea of taking care of communities—their emotional, psychological, social, and behavioral well-being. We ask questions such as the following:

- In this community, who is loved?

- How do we know they are loved?

- How do they know they are loved?

- How do we as a community show love?

- Is our love consistent with uplift and empowerment?

- To whom have we not shown love in this community?

- How can we change our thinking and our behavior to better reflect inclusive Critical Love?

In the fictitious scenario here, the young students illustrate the "Critical Love story" that appreciates the beauty of all people, particularly people of Color. The book the students were reading is one of inclusion, gratitude, and awareness. However, in a classroom such as the one depicted in Gardner's research, where the language and dialogue were dominated by stereotypes and generalizations, the teacher could employ antiracist awareness strategies. Horsford (2014) suggests teaching racial literacy using *counterstorytelling* of the racialized norm as an important tool for "dismantling prevailing notions of educational fairness" (127). To support Critical Love when reading about Sojourner Truth, the teacher could lead a discussion on the many ways that people are beautiful, and continue discussion about the beauty of the inner and outer person through more stories, more dialogue, and more examples. Books such as *All Are Welcome* by Alexandra Penfold and Suzanne Kaufman, *Where Are You From?* by Yamile Saied Mendez, and *The Day You Begin* by Jacqueline Woodson may help a teacher provide a counterstory to affirm people across cultures.

At the Critical Love stage, there is a need for students to learn to love themselves and to love others. We can teach even the youngest of schoolchildren to think about the ways everyone has beauty and everyone has self-worth, especially children of Color, whose beauty is not always celebrated in "mainstream" (i.e., White) US media and culture. Horsford (2014) states that it is important to "acknowledge the pervasive role of race and racism in US society, and thus its schools, and how race operates . . . in ways that are real and powerful in the lives of the majority of schoolchildren in America" (128). It is easy for these larger forces to show themselves in students' responses to the reading of a picture book or even when they are playing games during recess. Such moments offer precious opportunities to teach students to think about others, consider the perspectives, and appreciate the differences.

- We can teach even the youngest of schoolchildren to think
- about the ways everyone has beauty and everyone has self-
- worth, especially children of Color, whose beauty is not always
- celebrated in "mainstream" (i.e., White) US media and culture.

In considering the work of Critical Love, Brandon, a teacher writing in this book, stated, "So as a White person, I've got to learn a lot of different ways that I have to act if I actually want to be antiracist and equitable instead of just a bystander who is just as guilty as a racist." Brandon realizes how big a job it is to be an antiracist teacher. The teacher is an important interrupter of racist practices and discourse in the classroom. This speaks to how we as educators need to recognize the racist acts that occur within our spaces and take conscious, actionable steps to interrupt the practices. As an example, Brandon could create space in his class for counterstorytelling to promote Critical Love. Critical Love encompasses our willingness to examine ourselves deeply and often give up or change something that we hold close to us (an idea, an approach, a way of thinking) so that others can benefit too, even when that group or person is not related to us as family by blood but connected to us as a part of the family of brothers and sisters in our human race.

Level 2: Critical Humility

DEFINITION
Remain open to understanding the limits of our own worldviews and ideologies.

SCENARIO
Here you will find a dialogue between two teachers who are selecting students for Advanced Placement for the upcoming year. They are discussing Sara, a Black student, and Lori, a White student. Both students in the scenario have B averages, but only Lori was selected for AP courses. This scenario demonstrates how access plays a role in whether students can move forward in a system of seemingly objective, fair criteria.

Teacher 1 (White teacher): I think Sara [Black student] should wait until next year to take AP Literature. She has a B average. If she makes an A this year, I think she will be ready for the challenge.

Teacher 2 (Black teacher): What about Lori [White student]? She also has a B. But I see we have admitted her to AP Literature this year.

> Teacher 1: Well, I know the family, and she will have support for tutoring and mentoring. I don't think we will need to worry about her abilities. She will make it.

In this case, because the teacher knows Lori's family, she is willing to promote her to the more challenging class; however, it appears that she does not know Sara's family or resources, so she assumes that Sara cannot do the work, although she has the same grade in the prerequisite course as Lori. The context for this discussion is in itself a significant part of the problem: a tracking system in schools has much more to do with test scores, benchmarks, and familial ties than with student resilience, ability, and school resources and support. Teacher 1 used her knowledge of Lori's family and the child's access to power (conferring with the teacher after hours, benefiting from family support, mentoring, tutoring) to propel her; whereas Sara, who apparently lacks the same access to the teacher after hours or intimate family connections with the teacher, had to fend for herself at school alone. It is quite probable then that Sara's lack of access to power left her unable to negotiate the gray spaces in school that can make a difference in a student's trajectory, a hidden type of decision-making that is only visible and available to the privileged. Critical Humility could have helped Teacher 1 realize that she didn't actually know Sara or her abilities. A discussion between the teachers using the Racial Literacy Development framework might have helped them engage in the conversation in a way that was not based on assumptions, even racist inclinations, but could be used to think comprehensively about this complex ethical stance.

WHAT COULD THIS LEVEL LOOK LIKE USING THE FRAMEWORK?

Critical Humility refers to our ability to think about the limitations of our own knowledge and worldviews. With Critical Humility, we have an opportunity to question ourselves and our decision-making. We then are able to "humble" ourselves to ask hard questions about our thinking.

- What privilege am I using here?
- Who is benefiting from my privilege?
- Who is harmed because of my privilege?
- How can I use my privilege here to provide more equity?

Rather than focusing on "playing favorites" with students' admission to higher-level courses, the teacher conversation beforehand would start with Critical Humility equity norms for discussion. Establishing these equity norms prior to the discussion sets parameters and standards that both parties agree on as they make important decisions. An example could be to set a protocol for discussion:

1. Let's take a look at the tasks we are about to do through our lens of Critical Humility.

2. What unexamined power and lack of knowledge do I have as a White teacher that we need to acknowledge? What unexamined power and lack of knowledge do I have as a teacher of Color that we need to acknowledge?

3. What power do I not have in this process as a White teacher? What power do I not have in this process as a teacher of Color?

4. How will we use our power in this process?

5. How will we limit our power in this process in order to make it more equitable?

An honest, up-front discussion about these issues before beginning a task will help preassess the work and the roles. But this is not easy work, as Critical Humility requires honesty; careful examination of one's assumptions, one's own knowledge or lack of knowledge about the situation; and truth telling about oneself and the others involved in the work. Coleman and Stevenson (2014) acknowledge the difficulty:

> In the collective research, a key theme, is how privilege, power, and fear of talking about race have prevented schools from creating an inclusive and diverse school community. . . Talking about race can be stressful. No one wants to say the wrong thing or be seen as one who always raises the issue, who challenges the dominant narrative. . . However, school communities that don't discuss racial concerns or push them under the rug undermine progress in diversity efforts. (88)

Rather than ignore that race is an issue in our schools, we must face the issues, understanding that these conversations are difficult (and can sometimes evoke strong feelings), but that they also create opportunities to have authentic discussions that move us to more equitable practices.

Level 3: Critical Reflection

DEFINITION

Think through the various layers of our identities and how our privileged and marginalized statuses affect our work.

SCENARIO

The scenario here describes a situation that placed students in potential danger. A parent has to make a decision about her child's attendance at school. She is thinking in real time about her next steps for her son, and she is afraid. Meanwhile, the teachers need to consider their own roles in the situation, the limits on their understanding of the student interactions in the school, and their ability—or lack of it—to provide safety for students of Color.

It is 7:34 p.m. I finally wind down to dinner and a chance to watch one television show before preparing for bed. After a long day at work and school, my Black teenage son walks into the den with his eyes wide and face long.

"Mom, look at this. It's another one."

I ask, "What are you talking about?"

"It is another message to us."

I take his phone and read the message that is circulating in his school and in the school system. "Tomorrow all chocolate kids will die."

My heart sinks to my stomach, and I realize what my Black son will have to face. And we have a decision to make. Will he attend school the next day? Will I keep him home? How will we face this as a family?

—Thoughts from a parent of a threatened Black son

• • • • • •

The boy's teachers then learn about this situation the next day.

Critical Reflection is thinking through the various layers of our identities and how our privileged and marginalized statuses affect our work as teachers. In this scenario, a parent has to think about who her son is as a Black male and how the marginalizing and threatening message would impact him, and also his safety. The teachers have to think in terms of not only their response to this information but also how their own identity influences their response the next day. When we critically reflect, we think about our own positions in the world and how we will be impacted by our own choices and decisions and those of others. We also have to examine our reactions and the messages we send to others. The key questions might look something like these:

- What are the layers of my identity that I bring to the table in this situation?

- How is my own life experience (with its privileges or marginalization) different from or similar to that of the student and his mother?

- How will (or did) my privilege impact my actions in this situation?

- How will (or did) my marginalization impact my actions or decisions?

- How can I respond to my students and families?

Ultimately, the mother in this scenario realized that her identity as a Black mother raising her Black son was impacting her decision significantly, as the threat of harm was against people of Color. It turned out that while she did consider keeping him home, she realized, despite her hesitancy, that the school had increased the security tremendously, and she wanted to teach her son that fear cannot triumph. She allowed him to go to school, knowing that if her son stayed home, it would give in to the conspirator's thinking and actions.

WHAT COULD THIS LEVEL LOOK LIKE USING THE FRAMEWORK?

Once teachers learn about a threat, they need to decide how to appropriately discuss the situation with the students, the class, the administration, and of course the families. However, as we live in a culturally diverse world, we must critically reflect about our roles and how we move forward: "The most socially responsible thing we can do is to prepare our students to be culturally literate in an increasingly global community and to equip them to interact with a broad range of people" (Coleman and Stevenson 2014, 87). Part of our reflection process should be a plan to improve equity and reduce hostility in our communities.

For teachers, it is important to understand the stress a threatening message like this places on families of Color. For this mother and this family, the worst scenario is that her son is in immediate danger. This is actually the scenario that she must consider seriously. The school personnel must reflect on the options for the family and create a carefully crafted response that is inclusive and allows space for the family to heal. Teachers can provide a grace period for the student to submit assignments, make a supportive telephone call to the family, and work with the students on ways to make the whole class a supportive and welcoming environment, perhaps drawing upon restorative justice practices such as those described by the International Institute for Restorative Practices in its report *Improving School Climate: Evidence from Schools Implementing Restorative Practices* (Lewis 2009).

Level 4: Historical Literacy

DEFINITION

Develop a rich and contextual awareness of the historical forces that shape our communities and society.

SCENARIO

Thinking about what we teach requires us to develop a historical literacy and contemporary understanding about our students and communities. The scenario here is a snippet of a conversation between teachers as they are choosing texts for a class to read.

Teacher 1: We need to think about books to read with our students that are inclusive.

Teacher 2: What did you have in mind?

Teacher 1: I think we should continue to read *Huckleberry Finn*. It's a classic.

Teacher 2: I know it is a classic based on your definition, but I have difficulty engaging the students in the text. And the language is difficult for my students of Color to hear. It is filled with the "N-word."

Teacher 1: Well, it is about a time period that we cannot erase. So I think they will have to get used to it. It is a part of the history of this country.

Teacher 2: Hmm, well, if we are going to keep it, to balance this, I think we should read other texts from a Black author's perspective.

Teacher 1: *Huck Finn* has a major Black character already.

The teachers in this conversation discuss literature to read with their students. However, the conversation breaks down as early as the word "classic," a code word for widely, unquestioningly accepted literature. Teacher 1 assumes that students must read the tried-and-true, time-tested classics. However, Teacher 2 is clear that the text does not work for her students. A discussion around Historical Literacy could help the teachers think together about the best reading selections for students. The teachers here could use awareness of the Racial Literacy Development framework to critique the decisions about literature choices and to ask each other the hard questions. As Tonya testifies,

> I know from my own experience that reading historical texts that use derogatory language and place marginalized groups in subhuman conditions, particularly based in slavery, can be difficult to teach. Many of the texts, like *Huck Finn* or Native American–based fiction written from the perspective of White people, can give the perception that the people of Color in the texts did not experience the struggles that were present during the time period. I consciously and intentionally create rich multicultural and multiperspective text sets using pieces of literature that provide a wide range of perspectives around the voices of marginalized characters. I make space for the voices in the curriculum. It's important.

WHAT COULD THIS LEVEL LOOK LIKE USING THE FRAMEWORK?

In the scenario here, the teachers would have benefited from a Historical Literacy discussion to set the protocols for talking about race and the history of literature instruction. It is clear that the teachers have different views about the importance of classic literature and the inclusion of foundational texts with a strong African American voice and perspective. As we look for ways to create equity spaces, having an opportunity to discuss what equitable curriculum looks like prior to talking about the books themselves, for example, might have proven helpful. To establish ways to have these hard conversations, perhaps the dialogue could address these areas:

- What is it we have traditionally done?
- Why have we participated in this tradition?
- How does that practice help our students?

- How does that practice hurt our students?

- What does our community need from us?

- How can we create a space to provide equity for the students?

- What does a new space look like if it is to address issues of equity and inclusion?

Brown (2011) states that "teachers commonly steer clear of teaching about racism, even in subject areas like social studies where the topic is relevant and appropriate" (250). She posits that according to research, teachers avoid dealing with race in the lesson and unit plans, share the topic only as an aside—referring to it in the past tense, usually in a kind, nonconfrontational manner—and discuss race without a critical lens, allowing students to accept the information without questioning it. Historical Literacy, however, invites dialogue between history and the present, confronting inequities in both subject matter and practice.

Our teacher-writer Brandon Hatcher recounted seeing a colleague reading sections of the social studies book and pausing at key points to add "Black perspectives" for the lesson. Brandon commented, "Oftentimes, our history books are whitewashed. I just found that [offering Black perspectives] to be so amazing because even the White students are learning so much about Black history in a regular history class where we usually only cater to White students."

Level 5: Archaeology of Self

DEFINITION

Deep excavation and exploration of beliefs, biases, and ideas that shape how we engage in work.

SCENARIO

Many teachers are sure that the work they do is good for all their students. They connect their students to their communities, which is always a plus, and really strive to have their students gain a better sense of the world. The teacher in the scenario here is one such educator with good intentions. But as she does this good work, we wonder if she stops to examine herself and her position in the world as a White woman, her power, and her ability to set norms without thinking about other types of identities. Here's a moment revealing that she hasn't yet fully carried out this deeper self-inquiry.

Teacher: Let's get ready to learn. Take out your notebooks and folders from yesterday.

Sasha, an emergent bilingual student: I don't have mine. Can I get it from the licker?

Teacher: Locker. Locker. I've taught you that before, remember? No, it's too late. Share.

In this short scene, we see a focused teacher publicly correcting the pronunciation of a word by a Latina student who has obviously used this same word before, while simultaneously dismissing her request to go to the locker. Instead of simply providing a response about going to the locker, which she clearly understood was the question, the teacher used it as an opportunity to "correct" language in front of the class and then add that this was not the first time Sasha used the "incorrect" word. Instead of responding this way, the teacher could have answered the question about going to the locker with a short explanation (e.g., "Remember, we cannot leave the classroom after the bell unless it's an emergency") and used a private moment to talk to Sasha, embracing her home language and letting her know she supported two ways to refer to a locker: *locker* or *casillero.*

Because all of us approach work with some bias, we have to persist in digging into ourselves to make sure that we are not taking on the role of the oppressor, even the empathetic oppressor. Rather, we need to be truly a part of the solution and the learning process. We read about and dialogue with others about race to work toward an understanding. This requires self-study and deep excavation. According to Todd Finley's (2019) "A Look at Implicit Bias and Microaggressions," there are several categories of actions that reflect deeper implicit bias to consider as we look more closely at our role. Here are three categories discussed on the website:

- A **microassault** is a "verbal or nonverbal attack meant to hurt the intended victim through name-calling, avoidant behavior, or purposeful discriminatory actions."

    Example: Students wear Confederate flag clothing.

- A **microinsult** is insensitive communication that demeans someone's racial identity, signaling to people of Color that "their contributions are unimportant."

  Example: A teacher corrects the grammar only of Hispanic children.

- A **microinvalidation** involves negating or ignoring the "psychological thoughts, feelings, or experiential reality of a person of Color."

  Example: An Asian American student from the United States is asked where she was born, which conveys the message that she is not really an American.

WHAT COULD THIS LEVEL LOOK LIKE USING THE FRAMEWORK?

We can model and explicitly teach students how to communicate while working to recognize our own biases. It is important, though, that we are equipped to help students learn the language for discussion and conversation with one another. We can only become so equipped if we constantly dig for understanding of ourselves and think about our own approaches to systematic practices. This could involve asking ourselves questions that help us really "see" what we consciously or unconsciously think, and what we do:

- How do my students feel when they are in my class?
- How can I better address areas that present cultural, social, and emotional challenges?
- What systematic practices do I need to examine to support my students?
- How am I contributing to implicit bias?
- How am I addressing these biases?

Tina Curry, a teacher-writer for this book, states that "we [too often] ask children to leave their identities at our door when they are aligned with who we think that they should be. I do think part of my work as an educator is helping my children to see who they are so they don't come to believe who others say they are [negatively]."

Level 6: Interruption

DEFINITION
Interrupting racism and inequality at personal and systematic levels.

SCENARIO
The teacher in this scenario watched a student "interrupt" normed thinking during a class discussion. Here's the teacher's report of the discussion:

In science class with my students, we discussed hair and its significance. In the racially mixed group, it was unclear to some that chemical straightening of African American hair could also be seen as changing who one is to fit into a culture. This completely baffled the White students. One African American adolescent girl spoke up, boldly yet quietly.

"I know hair doesn't seem like an important thing to you when your hair is accepted no matter how it looks. You can wear your hair in your natural state, even wet, and it is accepted." The class tuned in intently to her comments.

"But my hair does naturally things that your hair does not. My hair is very curly. Obedient hair is what I call it. If I want it to stand up, it does. But I hear some of you talk about afros like they aren't acceptable; you even laugh because your hair can't do that." Some of the children snicker, but most sit attentively listening to her points.

"Well, I may be talking about hair here, but you can substitute it for anything else. Just because I do, see, have something that you may not understand, it does not make it wrong. It just makes it different."

The teacher had clearly done some prior work creating space for the student to give input about a topic that may have seemed insignificant to others but was an important gateway to interrupting a larger issue. The student challenged normed notions of appearance and acceptability. She started with hair, but compared it to other aspects of society, causing her classmates to consider how they think of difference—not as a joke but as a serious matter.

WHAT COULD THIS LEVEL LOOK LIKE USING THE FRAMEWORK?

The teacher may have stumbled on this goldmine response incidentally, but there are opportunities in classrooms to structure protocols and thinking maps to help students inquire deeply about the roles they play in systemic and personal racism. The teacher must plan strategies to help students think through these practices and then help them move to an action or interruption phase. Creating a safe space for students to discuss issues that matter to them is essential. Matthew Kay (2018) talks extensively about the importance of "safe space" in his text *Not Light, But Fire*, arguing that "in order to nurture hard conversations about race [in the classroom], first we must commit to *building* conversational safe spaces, not merely *declaring* them" (16). It is absolutely necessary to have a place to interrupt the status quo and challenge the norms. Jamila Lyiscott (2021) advocates for "liberation literacies pedagogy," a disruption of ideological hierarchies in research and practice. Teachers are the ones who create those inclusive environments and relationships within their classrooms. We need to ask ourselves questions such as these:

- What role do I play in perpetuating inequities in the classroom?

- How do I recognize my role?

- How do I interrupt inequitable practices?

- How do I teach my students to interrupt these practices in ways that work?

- How do I model interruption for my students?

> It is absolutely necessary to have a place to interrupt the status quo and challenge the norms. Teachers are the ones who create those environments and relationships within their classrooms.

Interruption practices are important to the classroom and to spaces outside the classroom. They are the questions and comments that allow students (and teachers, too) to ask questions that can make a difference in an approach, subject-matter content, school policy, or relationships. As an important part of the RLD framework, interruption is the "action and doing" level that enables all the pieces to come together to effect change.

• • • • • •

What we learn from Sealey-Ruiz's Racial Literacy Development framework is that each of us has work to do to prepare ourselves and then take action as interrupters of inequity. In the following chapters, then, we explore explicit steps and strategies we can take to advance through this process and help our students do so as well. And as you continue to read and learn more, consider the RLD framework throughout the text. Think about how you can interrupt practices that embody racial inequities with colleagues and in your own classroom with students. Consider the different levels and your own position within the framework. Ask yourself the important questions to gauge your own development through this process. Let's do this work together.

Time Out to Talk

Adding Katy to the Team

Zoom meeting, December 19, 2020

Steve: One thing we can't overlook is that it was awkward having Katy join the team. It was hard because we were concerned not to have the Black person's voice overbalanced by two White people. It was kind of parallel to the way a teacher of Color in a mostly White school can feel isolated. The White perspective can dominate, and nobody really does anything to fix that.

Tonya: When we are in a predominantly White space, sometimes people get stuck in the idea that "quantity rules." I remember being at a board meeting in 1999 and saying to another Black person, "I guess we can't add more sessions about students of Color because the group is mostly White and they voted not to add more slots because of the volume of proposals already submitted." She said, "Quantity does not negate the quality and the importance of the voice. When you talk about race, you can't take a 'majority rules' stance, or we wouldn't ever get to know about other people." How do we get that across to people? It's a matter of perspective, and everybody's perspective needs to be at the table. Everyone should have representation. How do you make it important to infuse the voices of teachers of Color?

Katy: How do people realize the necessity of seeking out and honoring other perspectives? One question that occurs to me in our situation is, "What has a third voice contributed in this process?" Has it been worth it to have a third person join the writing team without upsetting the balance? And beyond our own situation, how do you incorporate another voice but not overpower others?

Tonya: I have been in situations with people discussing equity to find that the White people in the room believed that they were the experts without the input of people of Color. In those instances, I have been infuriated that the voice of the person who lived the experience, and even studied the experiences, then became the one whose perspective was dismissed. In a room of White people in an academic setting, I had someone tell me that she, a White woman, was the critical race expert, and imply that my input was not welcome. My research, practice, and lived experiences did not matter. And although I believe someone White can be a critical race expert, I question if one is really a critical race expert when openly dismissing an important critical perspective. Seems contradictory to the nature of the work. Naturally, I must admit, I expected it to be the same way to some degree with the three of us, particularly when Katy joined the group—two against one. I expected yet another instance of marginalization and pushing for my perspective to be heard.

Katy: Is that how you thought this would be? Is this what it turned out to be for you?

Tonya: At first I expected it to be that way. Then we began to develop some patterns that led me to believe that this would be a different experience from some of the other negative ones I had faced before.

Steve: Tonya, I think part of it is that you calmly but firmly provide ideas and perspectives that we may not have realized because we of course do not automatically see a particular point from the experience of a Black or Brown person. You don't *let* us overpower you.

Tonya: I think we acknowledge the different perspectives that we place on the table and actually ask for them. We try to make sure that we constantly take a pulse on how everybody else is feeling, thinking, reasoning through situations, which I appreciate. I think a pulse check has been helpful to all of us. The other thing we do, it seems like it takes a lot of time, but we check in with one another and continue to establish the relationships. Every meeting begins with a check-in with one another as people, humans who navigate this world, in addition to being writers and researchers. I believe we buy into who we are as individuals. This adds to the trust, being able to feel as though we can discuss difficult topics without feeling marginalized. Having Katy join has been an asset, but initially, it was something I thought was going to water down the text and make it more the voice of White people and just a smidgen of the voice of a person of Color. That's not what I wanted for this book or our experience, and that's not what this book has turned out to be.

CHAPTER 2

Starting with Ourselves

As I began exploring my own cultural identity, I saw the radical difference between my upbringing and that of my students. I had to come to the revelation that they were born and raised in Chicago, not Mississippi where I grew up, and not during the 1970s and 1980s.

—Tina Curry

In one way or another and often unwittingly, all of us participate in and are affected by the racism built into our colonized society. By this we mean that we take on the view of race that has been adopted by society without questioning how it has become a part of the interwoven fabric of our society. We accept the racist beliefs as truth. Thus, we are colonized, taken over, ruled by these thoughts that seem authentic, but they are not. We take on racist views if we are not careful and diligent, so we're in need of constantly asking ourselves about our perspective and beliefs. If we confront these conditions with clarity, we can take positive action. Telling our own story, reflecting on our own history and experiences while acknowledging strengths as well as issues, is an important step to begin or continue our journey toward teaching for racial equity. While our own past provides knowledge and experience that help make us effective teachers, at times we may also need to understand how our past might be getting in the way so we can move beyond it.

> While our own past provides knowledge and experience that help make us effective teachers, at times we may also need to understand how our past might be getting in the way so we can move beyond it.

Another reason for writing our own stories is that it's the start of activating our voices and being recognized for who we are. Once we do this for ourselves, we can help our students do so as well. Telling one's story provides a grounding for the sense of agency that enables students to speak out and advocate for themselves. This is where we gain strength to act as interrupters for equity. And it's just as important for us as the authors of this book to do this so we can write with clarity and perspective. We hope our stories can help you recognize some of the complex and widely varying experiences that make up a life, shape points of view, and hold aspects of race. That is why this book includes excerpts from our teacher-writers' autobiographical narratives, along with moments from dialogues we and they have held to better understand one another.

As we contemplate our stories, it's important to ask ourselves about privileges and disadvantages that might be somewhat hidden. However, it's easier to invoke the word *privilege* than to actually think carefully about it. Ijeoma Oluo (2019) insightfully observes that many people demand that others "check their privilege," but as she explains,

> It is a phrase most likely to be met with dismissal and derision. It's a phrase viewed as an ineffective weapon hurled at someone with no other purpose than to win an argument or at least silence the opposition. . . I've found . . . that very few people actually know what privilege is, let alone how they should go about checking it. (58–59)

Oluo (2019) goes on to provide examples of privilege from her own life experience as a Black woman:

> I have a college degree in political science. I worked very hard for my degree, studying at all hours of the night while also taking care of a small child . . . While I do have a right to be proud of my degree, it would be dishonest of me to pretend that this degree is 100 percent owed to my efforts. I was raised by a college-educated mother who taught me that a degree was important. I grew up as a neuro-typical, nondisabled child whom school was designed to serve and for whom teachers were willing and trained to dedicate their efforts. (60)

Finally, Olou lists the many benefits she has gained from that degree—not just gaining good jobs but also "the ability to yell, 'I HAVE A DEGREE IN POLITICAL SCIENCE!' during arguments about politics" (61).

Yolanda Sealey-Ruiz's Racial Literacy Development framework helps us see how essential the examination of our own privileges is in supporting equity in our students' learning processes. Critical Humility tells us we can't make assumptions about our students. Critical Reflection reminds us that we need to look at ourselves honestly and clearly. Archaeology of Self can take us into a deeper understanding of the ideas and beliefs that shape us. Let's examine two of the authors' personal histories to show how some realities of racism can be acknowledged.

Tracing the Many Elements of Race in Two Lives

STEVE'S HISTORY

I grew up in several different neighborhoods in the St. Louis area as my family grew more prosperous, but all of them were exclusively White. As a kid I almost never thought about that. The populations in the schools I attended were all White, with no teachers of Color. This meant that all my friends were White as well. My father started a toy company making kaleidoscopes, and this required annual loans, since stores wouldn't pay for shipments until after the Christmas season. It's hard to imagine that at that time, in the fifties, he could have gotten the loans if he had not been White. The factory had just one Black employee, whose job was to clean the place and operate the paint spray booth that was filled with fumes. As a little kid, I noticed this but didn't understand the implications. The profits from my family's business paid for my piano lessons, summer camps, college, and the many comforts I enjoyed.

In college at Washington University (which was not the high-flying place it is now), I started in engineering and then physics, but gravitated to English literature. And what authors did I study? Old White European and American men of course. I came to love jazz and improv performance, though the places that featured these in St. Louis were in "bad" (i.e., Black) neighborhoods. I went there anyway, but I admit I was maybe a bit nervous. When I taught at Livingston College, a new branch of Rutgers University established to serve "inner city" and "alternative" students, neither I nor many of my colleagues had ANY knowledge of the lives, experiences, strengths, or needs of the students. I don't believe I did a very good job supporting those students. My education simply hadn't equipped me for that. At Livingston there were some outstanding Black faculty—author Toni Cade Bambara; Barbara Masekela (who headed the college's writing program); and for a couple of years poet Nikki Giovanni. I stood up for them as the politics of the place grew intense. As a result, I was denied tenure—i.e., I was fired. I'm proud of what I did.

It's sad and unfortunate, though, that there were so many ways I could have had richer experiences that would have equipped me to be a better teacher for all those students early on. Even though I'd known my various experiences before, I hadn't fully considered all their implications. I hadn't taken account of how different my opportunities were from those of the students I work with in some urban, underserved schools. I hadn't thought about how my advantages continued to play out in my life. Not that I would now claim to be perfectly aware. But I hope maybe I can reflect on the reality of my early childhood, which affects who I am today, and understand more of the depth of racism in this country, so perhaps I'm better equipped to act and interrupt where I can. I'm so very thankful for the chance to work with my fellow authors now, who bring such wide and varied experience to this effort. If only I had had it long before!

TONYA'S REFLECTION ON STEVE'S HISTORY

Steve's upbringing reminds me of someone who grew up in a bubble, an insular circle of people. Not that he did not experience childhood and young adult difficulties, but the larger world and its struggles were not something he had to be aware of as a part of his existence. It is through his own curiosity that he learned about the larger world and its inequities. Steve has chosen to see the world through the critical lens; I had no choice. I recognize that his experiences as a young adult were ones that allowed him to develop a more critical eye about the larger society—asking questions about the world and who has access and why some things are available to some and not others. It has been eye opening to work with Steve through this book, as he is clear about who he is and what he has done to be an interrupter. I remember once asking him about an experience he had, and I wrote the episode from a lens of privilege based on my understanding of Steve's experience, but he was not having it. He did not want to be misrepresented at any time, always careful to own up to his own shortcomings but not take on any new ones that were not his! Part of what I get a chance to do with every piece of writing or dialogue is to think about my own positionality and how to think about how we see the world—sometimes alike, sometimes differently. That is the beauty of being ever-evolving interrupters.

TONYA'S HISTORY

I grew up in one neighborhood, a farming community, with all people of Color. People who worked all types of jobs lived in the same neighborhood. That was a beautiful blend of all working-class people working side by side, contributing to one another and offering our gifts and talents to one another as support. This is how I learned the spirit and power of true collaboration and community collectivism. My dad would do taxes, and neighbors would trade eggs or carpentry services. The entire community existed and flourished as a result of collective support for one another.

I attended schools in the 1980s with Native American, Black, and White students. My friends were mostly Black, though. Integration during school was widely accepted, but integration outside of school activities was rare. We schooled together well, but we did not socialize outside of school-related events—social circles were racially divided. Several of my teachers were of Color. And although I had teachers who were different races, my Black teachers poured into me tremendously, even beyond the school day. I can remember winning my first oratorical contest after grueling hours of practice in the evening in the class of my eighth-grade English teacher, which propelled me to other district-level competitions. My science teacher drove me to engineering competitions on the weekends. My advanced math teacher would not let me leave her class, and made me return at lunch time, until I understood major concepts. And I had White teachers who were just as dedicated to my success during the working hours; my English, band, world history, and Algebra I teachers supported my efforts and pushed me beyond my comfort level. In college, I studied English, mostly White

European and American men, but was exposed to elective courses in African and African American Studies for the first time.

My father and mother were educators who had additional talents they contributed to the community. My father, a math teacher, also wrote a newspaper with his Black friends so that we as people of Color could have representation in the local news. He wrote this in his spare time. I also considered my parents activists, as they sued the White school board so that my mother could keep her job after she publicly supported and campaigned for the defeated superintendent candidate. I can vividly remember at the age of ten having education attorneys in my home talking strategy about race, civil rights, liberty, and the individual's voice. My parents also contributed to the larger extended family, taking care of my grandmother and my uncle in our home. My uncle could never be left alone, so arrangements were made constantly for his supervision, with each of us taking our turn when we could. It was in the fabric of my family to make sure we took care of others. It was our responsibility.

I have taught in many different environments. I taught students from all different ethnic groups. In every environment, building community, empowering others, and tying learning to the real world have been extremely important to me. As a result of these principles, I've dealt with experiences of being devalued, and persevered through acts of resistance and advocacy, despite the name-calling and unprofessionalism of those in power. As I reflect on all of this, I feel that despite the inequities I experienced, I am thankful for the experiences that have continued to build perseverance and provide perspective about race and equity. These are opportunities to talk and really work through the experiences. I have become more resilient and more discerning.

STEVE'S REFLECTION ON TONYA'S HISTORY

It's striking that even though we grew up in very different settings, we both had parents who acted assertively in the world and served as models for us. Actually, my mother had wanted to become a teacher, but the struggles of the Depression made that goal impossible for her. Of course, my father's success in the business world created privileges for me, but even without those, Tonya's growing-up experiences gave her a wider perspective on race that I sure could have used in my teaching. I was a good student, which my teachers appreciated, but I never received the kinds of support she describes. At the same time, Tonya was devalued in ways that I never would have experienced, though I did have my own struggles as a geeky intellectual kid who was no good at sports. Yet she was able to develop strength and perseverance—and I would add grace, as I've seen in our work together. I wonder whether I could have grown like that.

Moving Forward

Your autobiography is certainly for yourself, to develop your own understanding of what you bring to the classroom. But hearing each other's stories helps both the sharer and listener understand the depth and subtlety and variability of privilege, along with the drumbeat of racism. Sharing can help people realize that change is not easy, as racism is deeply intertwined into so many aspects of our lives. Of course, trust is obviously essential for sharing with others. However challenging it may be to share, it can be encouraging and uplifting to discover that we are not alone in our efforts to understand our histories, move beyond them with care, and promote a more equitable education for our students.

Now let us take you through a sequence of autobiographical writing. We'll work from writing your own bio to sharing bios with fellow teachers, and then (in Chapter 3) guiding your students to write and share their own stories as well. Following are step-by-step strategies for helping you with the process of prewriting, drafting, reflecting on your bio through an equity lens, and then considering actions and interruptions to advance equity in your school. Examples from several of our teacher-writers offer an idea of what this work can look like.

Composing Your Autobiographical Narrative and Viewing It Through an Equity Lens

For autobiographical writing that supports and leads to interrupting for equity, we envision four main steps:

1. First, just as good teachers help students write by engaging them in prewriting to prime their mental pump, it can be invaluable for you to engage in some prewriting yourself. We'll provide an activity for this in a moment.

2. Next comes drafting. As you write, consider how you can recover some of the details in the key life-experience moments you decide to write about. You can visualize a scene, recall characteristics of people who were important to you, remember feelings you experienced.

3. Once you have written, we encourage you to reflect on your history through an equity lens—that is, identify roles that race has played in your life. These roles may not be overt or personal. For example, wherever you went to school, district boundaries and neighborhood conditions determined what resources your school had or lacked, with implications for maintaining White supremacy. Data we quoted in the introduction

(Harris 2019) show that many under-resourced districts exist right next to more affluent ones with much larger budgets.

4. Finally, you can consider actions to take as an educator, in light of what you have discovered through this process.

For prewriting your autobiography, here is a thinking-drawing-jotting activity that many writers young and older have appreciated:

1. Create a timeline for a chunk of your life, either drawing a literal line by hand or, if you like to work digitally, laying out a vertical chronology. List important events and dates, all sorts of moments that stand out in your memory. As you jot and record your own story, you needn't look just for moments when race played an overt role, but include whatever seems important to you. In one way or another, race will very likely be lurking there anyway. The makeup and resources of your school or community, for example, were determined by decisions and actions of home loan lenders, community leaders who drew school attendance boundaries, politicians whose policies kept people of Color out of some neighborhoods and grouped them in others, widely shared racist biases, and more.

2. Now add important people to the items on the timeline. Then add feelings that you experienced at the time of various events or that you experience now as you look back.

3. Pick one or several moments from the timeline and picture some of the details—the scene, the people, your feelings around what took place.

4. Now give yourself time to write about these moments or the period of time that you chose.

5. Finally, if you haven't already, you can begin to examine events on your timeline through an equity lens.

AN EXCERPT FROM CHRISTOPHER MCDANIEL'S BIO: YOUTHFUL ACTING OUT

Here's a timeline (figure 2.1) and bio composed by science teacher Christopher McDaniel. His timeline focused on one aspect of his life—his struggles with school. Then he chose specific aspects of that struggle to write up in more detail.

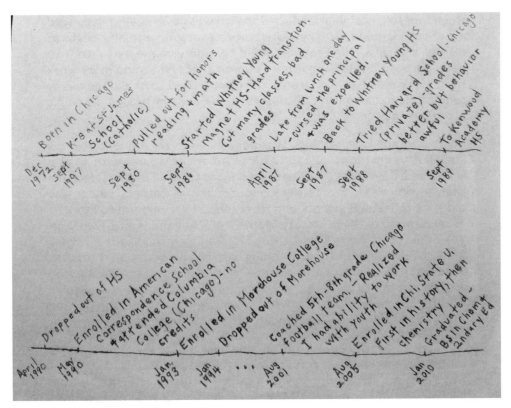

Figure 2.1. Christopher McDaniel's timeline

My name is Christopher McDaniel. I was born on the Southside of Chicago in the early 1970s. My mother was a department manager for Catholic Charities and my father was a vice president at Blue Cross Blue Shield. I have a sister nine years older than me. In my early childhood we were the ideal Black family. My mother was the assistant choir director and secretary of the church. My dad was a member of the usher board and a Sunday-school teacher. We lived in a townhouse on Michigan Avenue near downtown. My neighbors were multiracial and included judges, politicians, and doctors. My sister and I both attended Catholic schools and were involved in many after-school programs and activities. I had a wonderful early childhood.

Educationally I had always scored in the top 97% on standardized tests. I started elementary school early; my birthday was after December 1st. I should have been held back a year. I truly feel this made me more immature than my peers. I was always one of the shortest in my class and the least mature. Socially, I was always trying to prove myself, which led to me having poor behavior marks, and it kept me off the honor roll most years. Educationally I was never really challenged in school. I would finish my work before everyone else and begin to disrupt the class. The teacher would try and give me extra work to keep me busy, but I thought it was unfair that I had to do more work than everyone else. My parents constantly tried to challenge me by sending me to computer camps, chess clubs, and any type of academic programs they could find.

My fifth-grade teacher, Mrs. Washington, was very influential in my life. Mrs. Washington was a tall African American woman with an afro like Angela Davis. Mrs. Washington did more to instill Black pride in me than anyone else in my life. My school, for a small Catholic school, also did a lot to instill Black pride in its students. We celebrated liturgies in celebration of Black History Month, MLK's birthday, and Kwanzaa. We would start every day reciting the Pledge of Allegiance, singing "America the Beautiful," and finishing with the Black national anthem. In addition to all of this, there was Mrs. Washington. Mrs. Washington introduced me to my favorite poem, "We Real Cool" by Gwendolyn Brooks. She taught me to have pride in myself and my people, and that I had worth, which was probably the most important lesson of all.

Whitney M. Young Magnet High School was one of the top academic schools in the country, and I attended Whitney Young for my first two years of high school. It was a huge culture shock coming from a small Catholic grammar school. The high school structure, with its bell schedule and changing classrooms every period, was too much for me. Academically, I was unorganized and unmotivated. Socially, I worked so hard to fit in and failed so miserably. I left Whitney Young after my sophomore year with a GPA well below 2.0.

My junior year I transferred to a small private school close to my house. I only went because I knew I could make the basketball team. At Chicago Harvard High School (now closed), I had average grades for the first time in my high school career. However, I did pick up an affinity for cutting class and as always was very disruptive in classes where I wasn't being challenged. There was one African American dean/history teacher, Mr. Burton, who understood me and spent a lot of time helping me mature. Mr. Burton left Harvard at the end of my junior year.

My senior year I transferred to Kenwood Academy. This was the Chicago Public School closest to my house. I broke my ankle the summer before my senior year and was unable to play football or basketball. I started gang-banging, using drugs, and drinking heavily. I eventually dropped out of school. My mother enrolled me in American Correspondence school where I would graduate a year later. I took the entrance exam at Olive-Harvey City College and received an honors scholarship. I did two semesters in city colleges, then applied to Morehouse College in Atlanta. I would attend Morehouse for two semesters before I dropped out of college.

In my late twenties I became a football coach for Chicago Public Schools, and my teams won several city championships over the next four years. I realized that the children respected me but more importantly listened to me. I returned to college as a history/secondary education major, but switched my major to chemistry at the behest of a good friend who informed me science and math teachers were in high demand.

Getting my chemistry degree was rough for me. I had never studied before. I got a zero on an organic chemistry exam and almost lost my mind. I went outside, smoked three cigarettes and contemplated my life. When I returned to class it was over. I gathered my things and began to head home. My chemistry class was from 6 p.m. to 9 p.m., so it was about 9:15. I saw a 54-year-old lady who was also working on her chemistry degree and a 19-year-old girl working on her physics degree, both in the computer lab studying. I asked them how long they were going to be there. They replied "Until 11:30 p.m. or so." I looked at them stunned and said goodnight. I walked to the elevator telling myself it was late, I was tired, and I was going home. I got to the elevator and pressed the button. I thought to myself, "They are about to stay and study until 11:00 p.m. and you are about to go home at 9:30 because you're tired." At that moment I made up my mind that I had to work harder and stop being so soft. I stayed and studied with them until 11:30 p.m. that night and almost every night for the next three years until I graduated.

Christopher's Reflection

When I did the timeline, it gave me a better idea of what events in my life actually affected my education. After reviewing the timeline, it became clear to me that particular events in my life truly impacted my education. Starting school a year early played a major role in my educational and social development. I do give credit to my parents and the African American teachers and community members who were role models and mentors. When I decided to do something positive with my life, it was their advice over the years and the examples they set that gave me the blueprint for turning my life around. I think it is important as a teacher that I show my students examples of people who look like them that have achieved at high levels in the field of study I am focusing on.

AN EXCERPT FROM VANESSA HELLER'S BIO: OUTSPOKEN YET SECRETIVE

Here you will read an excerpt from Vanessa Heller's autobiographical narrative. (Figure 2.2 shows her timeline.) Her experience growing up differed from Christopher's in many ways, not only as a young White student but also as someone dealing with a complicated home life. Yet as you will see, once they talked together, they discovered many shared attitudes, along with their understandable differences.

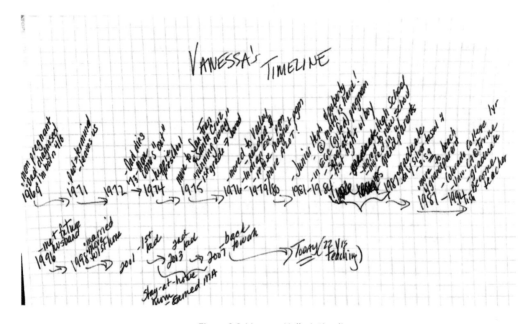

Figure 2.2. Vanessa Heller's timeline

I've always been interested in people generally and I graduated with an undergraduate degree in comparative cultures. I just find folks interesting and always have. What I haven't really done until now is purposely reflect on how racism, sexism, and privilege impact me personally.

My father died of cancer just before I turned four, so I do not remember anything about him that I recall with clarity. I only know that he was a heroin addict, artist, and eventually a wallpaper designer. My mother and I moved all the time as she had to support me and refused to accept help from her parents for many years. We moved to northern California to get away from her parents, who did not approve of her lifestyle and how she was raising me.

I spent my entire childhood moving often and living with a variety of women. I could never understand why my mom could not be happy with just me and why we had to live with these women whom I as a child considered to be strangers who were now bossing me around as if they were another parent. There were a few whom I absolutely adored as well as some I will always hate. I didn't know what gay was back then, only that my home situation was something I knew others did not and would not approve of. At the time I felt homosexuality was something to hide and so I did. Upon years of reflection, I realize my mom was trying to get by to raise me and, simply, that she was gay. However, I always resented being forced to live in situations I wasn't happy with and had not been consulted about. Needless to say, I constantly let her know what I thought about every home and every situation. To this day, I speak my mind, hate rules, and hate being cornered into situations where I feel powerless and ignored.

I also hate to lie. I always find it ironic and sad that as a child, I willingly chose to lie to my friends and others that I was so poor that we had to share a house with someone else. During the 1970s, being gay was not as widely accepted as it is now. I grew up feeling embarrassed about my situation and angry that I felt I needed to lie about being raised so differently. To this day I believe I became extroverted and open because I grew so tired of lying and being secretive.

My mom could not earn a living up north, so we moved to the San Fernando Valley, a suburb of Los Angeles, where we lived from about the mid-1970s through the 1980s. The San Fernando Valley had a large immigrant population for many decades (Kotkin and Ozuna 2002). There were always White and Latinx kids in classes together but very few Black students. My friends were all White and the closer ones were Jewish like me.

As a student, I prided myself on doing well in school, and I loved to read. Academics was the one area I could totally control when I was unhappy at home. I was placed in the gifted program in junior high called EGC or Enriched Gifted Curriculum. During my junior high days, I assumed placement in this program was academically rigorous, though I understand now that this was another form of systemic racism, as there were few kids of Color—as if kids of Color could not possibly be gifted. My gifted classes were actually physically separated from other students and buildings—as designed by the school system itself. The EGC kids were labeled as the "goody two-shoes" and "geniuses," and we regularly fought (verbally) with the kids whom we stereotyped as not smart enough to join our classes. At the time, it never occurred to me how White the population of gifted students was. All I saw then was competition and prestige.

I was never given detention because I was generally well behaved at school . . . but not quiet and docile like a "good girl" should be. I was always outspoken, often questioning and correcting my teachers. I finished my work quickly and often did all the work in my group, too. I was the kid who read with her book hidden under her desk to make the most efficient use of class time. Needless to say, I did not connect with my teachers and cannot think of one I admired or who ever tried to connect with me. School was a box to check—a thing to suffer through.

The advantage of my being a White gifted student even carried through to school discipline. On one occasion in English class, a boy and I got into a fight—a desk-clearing, kids-lining-the-walls-out-of-safety kind of fistfight. I was not given detention nor was my mother called. I was simply sent to another room until class was over. I cannot imagine another student getting away with a huge fistfight like this gifted White girl did.

The advantage of being gifted and White carried through to high school as well, where I had access to any honors and AP classes I was interested in. Again, the population in these advanced classes was predominantly White. However, right before my senior year ended, I had Black students in a class. It was an elective—ceramics. Years later, I learned what tracking was.

Vanessa's Reflection

In creating this autobiographical narrative, the overwhelming thought I had was "don't make me think about all this again . . . ," and I still feel that way. My childhood was stressful and depressing, so to look back on it makes me uncomfortable. What I also see, though, is a bright and bored little girl who had no control over her situation—and who later became a control freak because of this. I see an outgoing kid who didn't understand why her mom had been married to a man but now lived with women—and that girl believed she had to keep secrets. I didn't understand that my mom was "open" and also needed help to support herself and me. All I knew was I wasn't enough for her so she needed attention from others. My grandparents were all about me, thank goodness, and I don't think I would have come through my depression if they had not been a constant support and source of attention for me growing up. They provided the environment that I recognize now as having provided me access to privilege. The privilege of a middle-class two-(grand)parent household afforded me opportunities to attend music lessons, summer camps, travel, etc. I was an only child, White, middle class, gifted . . . The world was mine. Even though

I grew up in an area with a large Latinx population and had Hispanic friends, the impact of racism on me or my friends was not something I had considered—or even realized I had to consider. The privilege I have as a White adult—and even as a child—is that I did not and do not have to look at racial issues because of my privileged place in society . . . which can be a problem as a White teacher and the larger issue of interrupting for equity in education and beyond—thus the need for self-examination, reflection, and then action. As the writer Maya Angelou said, "Do the best you can until you know better. Then when you know better, do better."

> The privilege I have as a White adult—and even as a child—
> is that I did not and do not have to look at racial issues
> because of my privileged place in society . . . which can
> be a problem as a White teacher and the larger issue of
> interrupting for equity in education and beyond—thus the
> need for self-examination, reflection, and then action.

Sharing Autobiographical Narratives with Fellow Teachers

Sharing biographical stories, along with reflecting on the classroom situations they may influence, can help teachers support one another in addressing equity in their teaching. To make the process safe and constructive, a number of valuable protocols are available on the National School Reform Faculty (NSRF) website (https://nsrfharmony.org/). They are designed to enable a teacher (or any organization staff member, for that matter) to present an issue or challenge and get feedback from a supportive group of colleagues through a carefully structured process. For example, the "Inquiry Circles" protocol guides team members to hear one another's stories, retell them, and reflect on them to help the original tellers look deeper, see patterns, and pose questions (Bisplinghoff 2004). The full protocol is time intensive, but the steps in the process essentially look like this (based on the NSRF "Inquiry Circles" protocol, https://nsrfharmony.org/protocols/):

1. Provide writing time—unless teachers have written their bios on their own. (15 minutes)

2. In pairs, participants take turns, each listener jotting notes while his or her partner shares their story. (10 minutes)

3. Pairs join together to form groups of four. Each person retells *their partner's story*. It is especially affirming for a person to hear their story retold in another voice. (15 minutes)

4. Each participant writes a note to the partner, summarizing their thoughts and posing questions to help the original teller reflect on their story—in this case, inquiring into the role of race in their life experience. (10 minutes)

5. Debrief—each participant shares something they have discovered through this process. (5 minutes)

When your fellow teachers are ready to share autobiographies, to enjoy the power of the telling and hearing and discussing what they reveal, give it a go. Even if that readiness does not yet exist, this strategy can be a powerful tool for beginning to build trust. In Chapter 6 you will read about two of our teacher-writers' efforts to do just that.

Christopher and Vanessa Dialogue About Their Respective Histories

To illustrate the kind of relationship building through autobiography that can take place, here's an excerpt from a dialogue between Christopher and Vanessa. As a pair, they did not employ the protocol we've described, but their conversation accomplished the same purpose. Their conversation was recorded online—Christopher in Chicago, Illinois, and Vanessa in Thousand Oaks, California.

Christopher: So did you have any thoughts or questions or anything about my bio?

Vanessa: Well, I'll tell you my reactions. One of the first things that I noticed was that you're clearly gifted. And what happened—I'm a former gifted child, and now I specialize in gifted education. What is so clear to me is what we have in common is that dissatisfaction with people who don't deliver.

Christopher: Definitely.

Vanessa: And it made me giggle, but like not in a funny way, because you are so clearly born unsatisfied that you were disruptive, and I am no different. I was a pain in the ass to my teachers—not one teacher liked me. I didn't like them. I would raise my hand and correct them. I called a conference with my teacher and my mother to tell the teacher what she was doing wrong. I mean that was like in fifth grade! That didn't go over very well with anybody.

Christopher: That was me all day!

Vanessa: Yeah, nobody really liked me, but I also didn't really care because I had to get what I needed. I had to let the teacher know that "you are not giving me the education that I needed, so I would make your life freaking miserable."

Christopher: I went to a Catholic grammar school, and it was hard to ditch, you know what I mean? Then when I went to high school, with the transition between classes, I think that it was too much for me. High school was too much for me especially since I went to grammar school with the same thirty-two kids from kindergarten to eighth grade, with a transfer student here or there. But with high school with thousands of kids, I didn't know anybody. So I cut school. I wanted to cut so much in grammar school, and I couldn't. When I got to high school, I could actually pull it off. Once I learned I could go home and not answer the phone, my parents had no idea that I had been cutting.

Vanessa: I always went to a big elementary school. My high school had three thousand people.

Christopher: OK.

Vanessa: But I hated high school, and it's the same thing as being anonymous. I just chose not to participate. I just wasn't rich like the other kids. I didn't drive the same cars, and, you know, I just—I couldn't deal. High school was just something to get done, get over with. Yeah.

Christopher: I didn't like high school either, but I was popular. I was the little guy everyone liked to pick on and hang around because I was funny . . .

Christopher: Just to summarize: there are similarities between the two of us even though we grew up in different environments, you know what I mean?

Vanessa: Yeah, what I would say is—and I don't know if it's the circumstance, if it's a nature versus nurture thing—it's this inherent dissatisfaction with the way things are.

Christopher: Definitely.

Vanessa: I'm going to say for me, I know it's a control issue, and just reading your bio, I think there are some things you were not in control of either. I think luckily for both of us we do something for a living that is positive.

Christopher: Definitely.

Vanessa: . . . I wrote a note to myself about you and me being disruptive and dissatisfied. We get in trouble a lot, but it's how we use that disruption and dissatisfaction that matters. Knock on wood, we both chose education, you know, because we could have done other things. I mean I could have chosen to give in to my depression and become a totally different person, but I didn't. I mean, yeah, I'm a stereotypical teacher, but you know I don't hate what I do. Think about what I could have been. Just consider my father, back when he was a heroin addict. I didn't know that until later . . . I had lots of choices to go in a very negative direction. I think it's my inner drive, and I'm going to say perfectionism, and I have a feeling you might have that same drive, to just do more than what has been done to us, if that makes sense.

Christopher: It seems like, in a lot of ways, we are very, very similar. I get that from our conversations—again, though we came from two different upbringings. It's not even socioeconomics. It was just different. That normalcy that you speak of is kind of what was necessary. When I lived with my father, he was able to spend more time with me, so there was structure and discipline. My mother worked three jobs all the time, so I would be on my own. It wasn't that one was a better parent than the other.

Vanessa: Yeah, like my grandparents.

Christopher: So you understand what I mean? I would be interested in a conversation with you about how you became a teacher, because I had no idea. It was not something that I was looking to do, and you're similar in how we both wound up here. I would love that conversation one day.

Vanessa: Mine's really easy: I looked in the catalog and tried to find the major with the least amount of math. That's the one I took.

Christopher: Wow, OK.

Vanessa: Yeah, there was no divine calling. My parents weren't teachers. All my friends are like, "Oh, I always wanted to be a teacher," and I'm like, "Oh my God, no." To me, it's karma because I was such a pain in the ass to my teachers, and look at what happened to me.

Christopher: That's exactly how I feel about it. All of the teachers that used to hate me so much—I laugh. Here I am. Ha-ha, I'm you.

Vanessa: If I ever ran into any of them, I would never ever tell them what I do for a living. They would all laugh.

Going Deeper with a Racial Lens

These two educators speak and listen with intensity but also with such good humor, comparing their respective upbringings, so different and similar at the same time! The truth is that the first time they spoke together, on a conference call among a number of us, it did not go smoothly at all. Christopher had questions for Vanessa that she took as criticisms, which led to his feeling unheard. But now they've discovered that they are the two wisecracking humorists of our team, interested in understanding each other's roles as teachers.

Both Christopher and Vanessa reflect on how much they were similar in their behaviors—pushing back on rules and creating their own paths, of sorts, to move forward. As they advanced through school, however, one may notice that Vanessa as a White young adolescent and Christopher as a Black young adolescent were perceived quite differently. Vanessa stated in her bio that she was not punished at school, and her parents were not called after she participated in a classroom fistfight. Christopher recounts, though, being judged as a poor student for a less offensive infraction, skipping class. Although they were at different schools in different states, one has to wonder, did race play a role in the response of the schools and, as a result, in how each of them experienced schooling?

Vanessa and Christopher were both smart, but Vanessa was accepted for her intelligence. She remembers being admitted to gifted courses and was automatically allowed to be smart and somewhat noncompliant—reading under the desktop and ignoring other requirements after finishing assignments early. Christopher, though, was unable to ignore the rules without consequences. As a result, he used humor and other nonconforming antics to survive and fit in spaces that did not appreciate or perhaps expect his intellect. He got in trouble.

Vanessa could hide the one aspect of her life that she thought would make her different from her classmates. She covered up a lifestyle that her mother quietly lived. But Christopher came to school every day as a Black male. And if someone treated him differently or expected little from him, there was no lie he could tell to hide his Blackness. He lived it outwardly every day.

Christopher believes that his desire to fit in socially played a significant role in how he was positioned in school. His negative behavior no doubt impacted the opportunities he was given in school. But if Christopher had been White, would he then have been received by his teachers, classmates, and other educators as the smart, witty adolescent that he was, rather than as a disruptive, smart-alecky troublemaker? According to the National Education Association (2011), Black boys are three times more likely to be suspended or expelled from school than their White peers, missing valuable learning time in the classroom. Young Black adolescents are asked to give up their language, gestures, and cultural norms of their home community to move forward and fit in. Clearly, interruption is needed so that schools recognize the strengths that students like Christopher bring to the classroom.

We as educators need to look critically at the opportunities and actions in our own lives and how they came to be. Did everyone have the same access as I did? Who did not have access? How did I benefit from access due to my race? How were others unable to leverage access because of race? If we carefully start with ourselves, we can then begin to see how we developed our own racial literacy profile, helping us examine our own perspectives and dig deeply into our understanding of racial development and identity. But until we do this work for ourselves, it will be difficult to help students grapple with and develop their own racial literacy profiles.

Sharing Autobiographical Narratives with Colleagues

With fellow teachers, just the simple acts of sharing and reflecting can help build trust and understanding, which in turn can serve as the basis for deeper work on equity down the line. You may want to start simply over coffee with a colleague you trust. If there is a sufficient level of trust, teachers can move ahead to talk about what their stories mean for their teaching and their understanding of their students, and ways they may want to make changes in that work. Certainly for all the writers of this book, hearing the stories in this chapter (and many more over coffee and at dinners and online discussions together) has helped us cherish our relationships—along with realizing how diverse are our backgrounds—as we have grown from working together on this book.

As Yolanda Sealy-Ruiz's RLD framework reminds us, we consider the sharing of these stories essential for stepping up to interrupt for equity in our classrooms. So we're eager to hear how your autobiographical inquiry helps you advance learning equity with your students. Perhaps it will have helped you more fully understand your own history and the harm or benefit you experienced from racism, and how your history is similar to and different from theirs.

> Does your history play a role in how you approach a particular instructional strategy or classroom management practice, or the way you relate to students? Might it impact students of various backgrounds in different ways? Is there something in your own practice that you now see you need to interrupt?

Once you have written, reflected, and shared, a question to consider is how your growing understanding of your experiences may help deepen your classroom work. Does your history play a role in how you approach a particular instructional strategy or classroom management practice, or the way you relate to students? Might it impact students of various backgrounds in different ways? Is there something in your own practice that you now see you need to interrupt? Christopher explains that he makes sure to share his past struggles with his students, to show them they can overcome difficulties they may face.

> At the beginning of every school year, I pose a question to my class: What does a scientist look like? The response would always be "An older White male, with a lab coat, and glasses." I then explain that I have a degree in chemistry and used to work in a lab. I tell them it took me five years to graduate from high school and I did not receive my undergraduate degree until my thirties. And I am your chemistry teacher. I explain, "This is proof that no matter who you are or what you have been through, you can do whatever you want."

Vanessa's reflections and discussions with our group of writers led her to develop an entire unit on racism for her middle schoolers, which you can read about in Chapter 4 of this book. And then, during the antiracist actions and growing national awareness of the summer of 2020, she started Teachers for Equity, a discussion group of concerned fellow teachers from her district and others nearby.

Here are two additional suggestions for thinking through your process of autobiography and reflection.

- There are all sorts of ways racism exerts its influence on us. For White folks, the most important forces may be less visible without some reflection. As Lisa Delpit reminds us, those who have power rarely think about others who may not be in power situations. Once you have a chunk of the story written down or told, it can take some reflection to uncover what was involved, racially. Vanessa, for example, realized that no students of Color ever appeared in the gifted classes she was placed in. The follow-up questions for her could be "Why?" and "How could this be allowed to happen?"

- Keep your larger purpose in mind and use your reflections to enrich your teaching. This work is not about proving our stance. Rather, the knowledge can help us approach our students with fewer assumptions and more openness, either informed by or less limited by our past experience.

Though we've shared several pieces of our widely varied history and thoughts about our experiences of racism, privilege, and disadvantage, we don't claim that doing this makes us completely bias-free. But it does help us work more equitably with students, and it has been essential for building trust and understanding with one another, uncovering how our own and one another's perspectives on life and learning have been shaped. We hope this can encourage you to try the process yourself.

Much of what we have experienced in our lives comes unbidden from the world around us. Of course, many of us could have done more in the past to stand up to and interrupt racist actions and conditions. As our bios show, all of us are learning. But the more important question is what we do now, enlightened by understanding more of what we and our fellow teachers have experienced.

Time Out to Talk

Discussing Challenges
in Writing a Book Together

Transcribed and edited from an online discussion, July 1, 2020

Steve: You mentioned that writing a book with two White people is hard. I wish that didn't have to be true.

Tonya: Writing a book about *equity* with people who are White—it's difficult! That's not a slight. It's somewhat like, as a woman, if I were writing with a man, but really talking about a woman's perspective, and there were some things about it that were a little difficult. But I couldn't ask for a better team to work with.

So I can't help thinking about April Baker-Bell's book that just came out. You saw her at NCTE. She talks about linguistic justice, and says it just the way she wants to say it: "If y'all actually believe that using standard English would dismantle White supremacy, then you're not paying attention. . . Eric Garner was choked to death by a police officer while he was saying 'I cannot breathe.' Wouldn't you consider 'I cannot breathe' standard English and syntax?"

Katy: Something I was reading the past few weeks made that exact same point about writing by yourself, rather than in collaboration.

Tonya: A statement like Baker-Bell's—that's pretty forceful! That's really a strong statement that she could say however she wanted. And I know that a couple of times you've wanted to revise something I've written just because it was really intense, like April's statement, or was said as a negative, and to tell the truth, that's the way I wanted it. I admire April for her work!

But there are some things that, if I were writing by myself, I would not say in the same way as we might as a group. That makes sense, though. I don't know that you and Katy feel comfortable saying some of the things that I might put out there that might be really assertive or may not seem really collaborative. At the same time, you can't say everything the way I would say it, right? And there are some things that you could say to a particular audience that I can't say and get away with. So how does each of us manage that when you're writing something and you don't want your voice stifled?

Steve: Actually, when I worked with just one partner, whoever felt the strongest would "win." Because it was more important to get a book written than to agree perfectly on everything.

Tonya: But is that really what we want? When we write about some things, I think "winning" can be an appropriate approach, but maybe not in this case. We don't need a win. We need more dialogue, more conversation. In writing about equity and race, a lot of people tend to write by themselves, or they write with partners of their same ethnicity or race. Our being able to do it together is different, right!? When you two push back and ask, "Well, what are White people to do?" does that mean that nobody can write with anybody else who's different? My answer would be, "No." I just think we have to be able to have conversations and get through whatever those tough spots are, and think about how we want to say something that will be helpful for our audience collectively.

Katy: Although it's been hard, we've wrestled with questions of representation and voice: having an author who is Black and two who are White has meant we have had to pay very close attention to balance. What does it mean to have a second White author who was on the periphery of the project when it began—me!—come into the work in progress? I sure hope that we've worked those questions through, and I think—and hope—that as the quintessential "middle child," I've added to the process mindfully. But yes, it's challenging.

Steve: This does put me in mind of one passage in the manuscript where I was proposing that we tone down what you had said, Tonya. But if you felt strongly enough and said, "Steve, it's got to be said this way," I would say "OK," partly because what you said was true. You had charged that teachers aren't really seeing kids of Color for who they are. I was thinking that the teachers who will read the book might not be the ones with the problem. On the other hand, I know that when I read statements like that myself, I might think, "Well, I'm doing OK, but I don't blame the writer for saying that about other teachers." So I'm counting on both of you to speak up. Actually, Tina Curry once very rightly called me out for silencing her when I was being too insistent about something, so I know that I can be argumentative.

Tonya: Sometimes as a Black woman you have to fight to get a platform to be heard. Sometimes there's not the respect for your work, and it's constantly being looked at through other people's eyes and being evaluated. Our voice has meaning and is valuable. I think we actually get to share our thinking, and I don't feel like I'm working under any kind of silencing.

Katy: Here was my takeaway from what you said last week, Tonya. One piece of it that really resonated for me was that this *is* hard work. And we've tried to engage in it in honest and open ways, right?

Tonya: I think these conversations—I think they are important for our text, that we really need to get in and look at ways of being and have these kinds of conversations ourselves. Because the teachers we serve are going to have to do it for themselves and for the people in their buildings. And with their students. And you had best believe they'll have questions—"How can I have this conversation?" "This is really hard work!" "I'm Black, and I don't want to give up my voice in this space!" "Is it my responsibility to teach everybody about racial inequity?" Those are things that come up. You two read for yourselves. It's not that you need to understand everything in the world, but you don't come to the table with zero knowledge. You do some work, and you will see injustices in the world, and you're trying to figure it out. And we come to the table and we talk about it. But there are spaces where people come to the table asking people of Color just to tell them what to do. That's not fair. So I think it's important that we model these conversations.

CHAPTER 3

Helping Students Teach Us About Who They Are

I feel pretty good at educating kids, but how do I know if I am good at teaching to all of my students? How are students—of any color and class—receiving me as a person who is like or unlike them in color, in socioeconomic status, in gender, in religion, and even political viewpoints?

—Vanessa Heller

This is a gatekeeping society. Predetermined obstacles exist everywhere and dictate entry and nonentry into pathways. Those in power, primarily those who have money and make decisions, have held the keys to the doors of opportunity throughout US history, and this pattern continues to this day. Standardized markers such as test scores or other labels determine which students are admitted and which are denied entry into almost every sphere of society. In turn, students unfortunately internalize these scores and other markers to limit who they are and what they can do.

Many teachers do a great job of looking at their students as individuals, but sometimes we may all be guilty of referring to young people in terms of numbers. This is a reductionist approach to teaching. We have become colonized to think about students in ways that do not allow us to see fully who they are and what they can do. Just think about how we sometimes talk about students' successes: they become letter grades, standardized test numbers, "standard" language patterns, and IQ scores. Using external indicators to take the place of the special gifts, talents, and traits our students possess can be limiting for us and debilitating for them; and even the most caring of us can fall into doing this. We must remember that our students' hidden treasures are more important than the standardized markers placed on them, particularly for our students from historically marginalized populations. We know we must help students see the duality in the system that uses these indicators, but we can also help them recognize that these shortsighted markers are short-lived space holders and not interwoven into the fabric of who they are. But to do this, we need to get to know who they are at a deep and meaningful level.

> We must remember that our students' hidden treasures
> are more important than the standardized markers placed
> on them, particularly for our students from historically
> marginalized populations.

Learning to Listen to Students

Tina Curry, one of our teacher-writers who teaches in a Chicago high school, discusses how she works with her students to help them think about who they really are and how they exist in this world as people, learners, family members, readers, and writers. This helps them see their greatness and then think critically about how and why systems exist that exclude them from entry. One valuable strategy Tina uses is holding individual conferences with students about their reading—and learning to really listen to them. For example, in her conferences, students are allotted time to talk one-on-one about books. Many teachers use reading and writing conferences; here is how Tina Curry learned to use conferences to discover what motivated her widely diverse students' reading and writing.

I knew I had readers and writers when no one else did. A few years ago, when I began teaching at the high school level, I designed and taught a reading course for ninth-grade students who did not perform on par with their peers in reading. The students in my class scored at the bottom percentiles, putting them several years below grade level. I knew I had to get books in their hands that they could read, and allot time for them to read every day. Independent reading time, a part of the day dedicated to my students to read materials they chose, became sacred time in my classroom, and we did not sacrifice it for anything. I filled my bookshelves with all kinds of books.

Once I began to hold weekly reading conferences with all of my students, I always looked forward to talking with them about the books they had chosen to read. It was the highlight of my week. One weekend in reviewing my conference notes, I noticed that Christian was reading Suzanne Collins's *The Hunger Games* for the third time. I made a note to confer with him first thing Monday morning. During our conference, I encouraged him to push himself to read something else and asked why he was not interested in reading other genres and other authors. He looked me right in my eyes and said with such confidence, "You are asking me the wrong question. You should be asking me why am I reading *The Hunger Games* for the third time." And so I asked. What came out of his mouth transformed my teaching. He said, "Because Katniss defies everything and everyone. She doesn't let anyone put her in a box." I started wondering how many other students in the room had their own feelings about what they were reading and how their identities were connected to what they read. I also wondered how their reading identities actually defied the labels they had been given. This was their way of finding themselves.

Both Tina and Christian were operating in what Sealey-Ruiz's RLD framework describes as the Critical Reflection stage. Their conversation led Tina to consider the multiple layers of all of her students' identities and the ways that society's labels impacted them. Her book conferences became an equity practice through which she learned more and more about her students' life experiences, talents, expectations, dreams, interests, desires, abilities, language, history, family, and challenges, enabling her to center those attributes in her interactions with her students. Tina found that sharing reading, writing, and talking about books helped her and her students learn more about one another in ways that test scores cannot. If we are honest with ourselves, we may find through Critical Reflection that no matter how much we care about students, we sometimes define children's performance through grades and not who they are as people, not by the other more important attributes that create a person. As she describes here, Tina further discovers the complexity of their identities as she interacts more with her students.

As a teacher, I found to my surprise that all of my students had a reader's identity that I had not realized. Derrick wanted to read books about Black empowerment because he wanted to learn to navigate the world successfully as a Black man. Destiny wanted to read novels because as an emerging reader she was determined to one day read a novel independently. Dianna was drawn to poetry—more specifically poetry written by Maya Angelou, because she said she likes the way Maya Angelou's poems make her feel about herself. Trevon loved adventure stories because he found the plots to be exciting. Adrian would read anything he could get his hands on because he was thankful to have a class where he could read anything he wanted. Adrianna loved fantasy and fairy tales because of the happy endings.

This was quite a revelation for me, learning that my students each had a reader's identity. I began to see my teaching in a whole new way. I imagined who my students could be if I fostered and cultivated their reader's identities. I wanted to know more about how they identified themselves as readers, especially since what I saw in them each day when they picked up their books to read stood in contradiction to their test scores. Although my students seemed to love independent reading, they would say they couldn't read and they couldn't write.

Tina believed that her students were capable of success; however, her students believed they could not read and write because their school experiences had taught them to value only school-based reading and writing. We as teachers too often judge students based only on academic assignments, while devaluing other kinds of reading and writing that students do. Through one-to-one conferences in which we ask thoughtful questions and really listen, we can discover, as Tina did, the reality that students have their own literacies, their own ways of reading and writing the world that are connected to their identities. We do not always value these literacies in school spaces. Yet those hidden ways that students come to be are very valuable and are windows into learning more about how they learn and what they value. If we can learn from students, not judge them or change them, we also help them learn more about themselves and the world. Teachers like Tina who are able to do this type of important work can find gold. Having opened this door, Tina begins to build on the hidden literacies students possess. She discusses her process to learn more about her students, a practice that all of us as teachers can use.

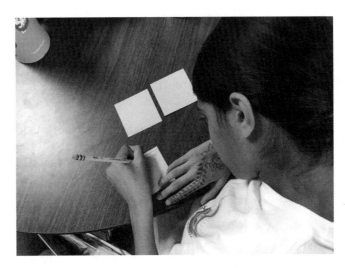

I began a quest to change my students' inner dialogue about themselves. Each year, I inherit students who believe in their minds that they are not capable and that they are "less than." That's what their test scores are telling them. That's what their poor relationships with teachers and other adults are telling them. That's what their failures are telling them. As a result, they begin to believe they do not have the intellectual capacity to read and write well. So, one of things I implement is to have my students create readers' and writers' identities by reflecting on their reading and writing histories, something I adapted from the Reading Apprenticeship Framework [Schoenbach, Greenleaf, and Murphy 2012]. To assist students in reflecting on their reading history in order to develop their reading identities, I ask them to consider how they might respond to the following questions:

- When and how did you learn to read?

- What has supported your comprehension and engagement with reading?

- What has helped you to build knowledge about text and language?

- What kinds of books are you drawn to? Why?

- What kind of books do you avoid reading? Why?

- Who is your favorite author, or what is your favorite book or story?

- How have the things you have read influenced your way of thinking or your view of the world?

- If you had a platform to talk about reading, what would you say? Why?

To assist students with creating their writing identities, I ask them to reflect on the following questions:

- How do you feel about writing?

- What do you like to write about?

- What is challenging for you when it comes to writing?

- Who is your example for good-quality writing?

- Whose writing do you find yourself trying to emulate or mimic?

- If you had a platform to talk about writing, what would you say? Why?

The answers to these questions become their narrative, which in turn becomes the catalyst for developing how they view themselves as readers, writers, and critical independent thinkers. This information empowers me as a teacher to help my students create a narrative different from the one that others have created for them, a narrative they may have participated in creating themselves, knowingly or unknowingly. I explicitly model how to change the way we talk about ourselves. Believing that our talk and thoughts have influence, I teach them to speak and think power into their lives.

I have realized they will not let me teach them unless I teach them in the context of their lives. I have decided that my curriculum has to follow their lives and that I need to honor their reading and writing identities in every question I ask, in every assignment I give, every task they engage in, and every time I listen to them.

Students Writing Their Own Autobiographical Narratives

As Tina was discovering, teaching from the center of students' humanity builds confidence and honors their histories. Cheryl Matias, editor of *Surviving Becky(s)* (2019), discusses the importance of building humanizing relationships—not relying on generalized checklists or other easy ways to teach—and learning more about individual students, especially students of Color. Teaching from this equity stance means there will be some rejection of norms that define dominant society and instead embracing ways of looking at students that go against those norms. As teachers come to realize the need for change, they can then help students develop their own questioning and positioning. A strategy to enact this is to invite students to write autobiographical narratives, just as we encourage teachers to do, as shown in Chapter 2. Both teacher and student can learn from a student's autobiographical narrative. However, it takes some reflection to make use of it, as we will explain. Let's look at one as an example.

> Teaching from this equity stance means that there will be
> some rejection of norms that define dominant society and
> instead embracing ways of looking at students that go
> against those norms.

Morgan's Autobiographical Narrative

My name is Morgan and I am currently a high school senior. My story is very short but it shows how I got to be the person I am today. I was born in June 2002, in IL. My parents were married and were financially stable. I am also a triplet. I have two sisters.

I can't remember much, but I know I switched schools after the 4th grade. I went from a generally all African American Christian school to a diverse public school. I noticed there were students of different races, but I never thought race was that important then. When I got to the school on my first day of 5th grade, I found out I had a Caucasian teacher, but I didn't think much of it and she turned out to be one of the nicest teachers I have ever had. But I understand that not everyone's experiences are like that.

At my current school, I am a part of a program called Dual Enrollment. We take classes at a local college and receive college credit. In May I am scheduled to graduate with an associate's degree in computer science. I was fortunate enough to be able to participate in this program by successfully passing some very challenging tests. Being in the program does give the students who participate in the program certain privileges. For example, if you drive to the college, you can pick yourself up some food on your way back to school instead of eating the school lunch. Also, when it is known by your teachers that you take college courses and you're doing well, they think very highly of you.

I am also a part of many other programs in our school. I have been in the National Honors Society (NHS) for the last three years of my high school career. This program is looked upon positively by colleges and universities. Being a part of this program allows me to have a bigger part in the school and is another way to have my voice heard within the school. I am also a part of the honor society at the college.

Last but not least, I attend club meetings for a club called BOSS, which stands for "Black Organization of Successful Students." It was created by some students, with the help of Dr. Curry. The club was created so students could have a safe space to discuss certain issues, for example, race or social issues. This club is also a big deal so our African American students may have a safe space to voice their concerns, as African Americans are a minority in the school.

An analysis of Morgan's writing offers an example of how to look at an autobiographical narrative as a way to see who the students are, what they value, and how they look at the world around them. Morgan, for example, has adopted an antiracist practice in joining a group; she has found a space to be herself and express her views through the BOSS club. That allows her to be appreciated and move toward another antiracist practice: acceptance and appreciation of self. Through the welcoming BOSS space, Tina has created for her and other students of Color a space where they can experience Critical Love for self. At the same time, Morgan has a double-consciousness—her identity as a successful student (a reader and a writer) in the larger society and her identity within a group that understands her challenges. It is in BOSS that Morgan has an opportunity to sift through her multiple roles as a student of Color. Creating a space to claim one's own racial identity is an antiracist practice that allows students to find where they can feel safe, and it also enables them to bring up challenges that can be difficult to address as we seek to achieve equity.

In addition to essays, autobiographical timelines can also give teachers a window into the lives of students, authentic entry points to honor their histories and teach them to identify growth moments in their lives. Here Morgan identifies some very specific entry opportunities into her life: the importance of learning, basketball, computer science, being a triplet, and friendships. You will also see that she hints at some other important decisions she has to make that are pivotal to her development and growth.

Morgan's Timeline

June 24, 2002—Born in Illinois

My parents are married and have always been in my life. I have two twin sisters. We are triplets.

September 2014—I switched schools for 5th–8th grade. I felt nervous because they put me and my sisters in different classes.

August 2014—Was also my first time having a White teacher. This was my first time being at a diverse school. The teacher was very nice and a good teacher. I'm sure I had As and Bs that year.

November 2015—I started playing basketball for my school. I felt happy because I was doing something I liked. I also had good grades for that year.

June 2016—I graduated from Henry R. Clissold Elementary School.

I was very happy and a little nervous to see what else was to happen in my life.

September 2016/2017—Freshman year of high school. I wasn't as nervous because I came in already having practiced with the basketball team, so I already knew some people and I had my sisters. I had good grades and the classes were pretty easy. I joined Student Ambassadors.

September 2017/2018—Sophomore year of high school. I was very happy—made a lot of new friends and still played on the basketball team. Second semester I passed the test to take dual enrollment classes at college. I joined the NHS (National Honors Society).

September 2018/2019—Junior year of high school I wasn't as happy. I had noticed some things going on in my life that needed to change. But I still played on the basketball team and NHS. I passed all my college classes and high school classes. I joined the Honors Society called Phi Theta Kappa.

September 2019/2020—Senior year of high school. I made some serious changes and am very happy about graduation. I also stayed on the basketball team and NHS for my last year of high school. I am on track to graduate with my high school diploma and an associate's degree in computer science.

The timeline is a quick way to see how the student views her world and what she values. One strategy to use with Morgan's timeline is to highlight major shifts in her life. Where on the timeline can we spot something different in her actions or thinking? For example, Morgan speaks of things in her life that needed to change during her junior year. At that point, her teacher can ask for more details to learn whether the student needs some adult support, if the student seems ready to share. The timeline can be tailored to major events, racial literacy, or pivotal points of growth. Teachers can use this short assignment to help students think about their own histories and the incidents that have shaped them into who they are.

Following are a timeline and an autobiographical narrative from another of Tina's students, Adaly, that show how important family is to her development. Examining these writings can be an entry point to help the student think about her role in society and how she navigates as a Latina woman. Reading these pieces, Tina begins to understand more about her students from their writing and then learns to instruct *with* them to develop their academic path.

Adaly's Timeline

May 14, 2002—I was born to Maria Nevarez and Javier Miranda at ages 23 and 26.

April 2003—My parents got divorced on April 2001 before I was born.

September 2007—I started school at Lionel Hampton Elementary School with my cousin.

2009—My mom met my stepdad and decided to move in together to start a life together.

April 2010—My first brother came into this world, named Erick. Born at 7 months.

June 2010—We moved out for the first time, we haven't stopped moving out since then.

April 2011—Second time my mom got pregnant my brother passed. Born at 6 months and his name was Axel.

January 30, 2013—My third and last brother, Daniel was born at 8 months.

April 2016—I was playing with scissors with one of my friends and my friend accidentally chopped off a chunk of meat off my right thumb. I ended up going to the ER and get stitched up. That was the last time

I played with scissors.

June 2016—I finally graduated from elementary school at Lionel Hampton School, I was happy to start my high school years.

September 10, 2016—I became an auntie of a beautiful baby girl named Zaia. She was the smallest baby.

September 2016—I started my first year of high school. It was pretty hard.

September 2019—I started my senior year of high school, feeling nervous but ready to get out and start something new.

February 3, 2019—My second blessing came to this world, another baby girl. Probably the last one, her name is Aeni.

March 2020—Currently on a quarantine and patiently waiting on graduation day and for more news. Staying at home is pretty frustrating and I feel like I'm getting sick of home.

Adaly's Autobiographical Narrative

I (Adaly) was the second child to my parents in May 2002, born four years later after my older sister was born. My parents divorced way before I was born; I didn't know that until I was older. I would see my dad a lot until a year later when my mom met my stepdad. Since that time, things had to change a lot. I started seeing my mom more but seeing my dad less. He couldn't come over anymore or spend holidays with us as a family anymore. I didn't like these new changes, but I had to get used to it. My mom eventually put my dad on child support and we could only spend time and see him every Sunday. We had to return home that same day.

A year later my mom got pregnant with my first baby brother; things got complicated and she gave birth at 7 months. After he was born and came home, we moved out for the first time. That's when my mom got pregnant again, it got complicated again, but this time he [brother] couldn't make it. Born at 6 months on April 26, 2011. That impacted all of us, especially my mom. She changed a lot after that, but we all tried being there for her. They decided to try again and my third brother came at 8 months. Our family was complete.

We see here that Adaly spends a lot of time thinking about family and how her family was constructed. Her history is important to her, and as readers of her story, we can hear both pride and concern for her mother and siblings, along with struggles of her own to accept changes she was not happy with. For a teacher, this would be an excellent opportunity to create conversation with the student around the complications of family in our lives, if the student seems ready to discuss that. Also, the teacher perhaps would connect her with writings by others, particularly Latina authors such as Elizabeth Acevedo, Erika Sànchez, and Claudia Hernandez, who talk about how they love family and navigate within their spaces.

In the next part of her writing, Adaly focuses more on herself and her own struggles as her family moves repeatedly, reflecting how the centering of "home" as a place of needed stability is key to her story. Adaly has clearly struggled, and while we teachers may not be trained psychologists, a student's bio can alert us that if a student's grades or attention falters, there may be serious reasons that call for us to offer support and a listening ear.

We moved out once again starting my freshman year. I was really nervous because I didn't know many people there. These years taught me so much about people and they passed by fast. From freshman year to senior year I can say I changed a lot, everyone changed good and bad ways. Then my sophomore year we moved out again, I was kind of happy because this time it was a house. We would move out to apartments until this time. We didn't last in that house either so we moved out one last time. Currently the house I'm at right now, they're planning on moving out again but by that time I probably won't be living with them anymore. Starting my junior year my life started getting a little challenging. So much started happening, I fell into depression. I isolated myself from everyone, including my family—I just couldn't speak up. . . It took me a very long time to get back up, but I'm doing so much better now. I do sometimes get it back, but I remember about all the good things in life, think about my nieces and that I need to make my parents proud.

The third part of Adaly's narrative is an exploration of herself as a Latina woman navigating academic spaces. She begins to think critically about her experiences and the challenges she faces as a person from Mexico who is trying to access the services needed to move forward, such as the FAFSA college financial aid application and job applications. Teachers can learn so much from exploring student narratives like this one, which provide windows into how we can direct them better to resources, supports, and opportunities. Here is how Adaly continues her narrative, focusing on her future.

My grades have been so much better than my previous years and I'm so proud of that. I just want to graduate. Even after everything that happened I'm glad it did, it opened my eyes and made me see things differently. Even as a Latina woman, it made things harder for me because not only some people look at you differently sometimes, but I was also born in Mexico. This made me realize things will be different than it is for other teenagers my age. It's hard getting a job, including applications and the FAFSA application was different for me as well. I know I have to work a little harder to get where I want to be and that's what I'll do. I just want people to know it's OK to fall because you'll always get back up, stronger and with bigger visions.

Considering all that students reveal in an autobiographical essay and timeline, Tina is able to use these tools as windows of opportunity to see the wholeness of her students. As students share stories, teachers can better understand how they can design and implement a responsive curriculum, as well as provide the adult support that is a major part of Critical Love. They can gauge instruction so that the students can see themselves in the curriculum and challenge practices that are inequitable. Tina can select texts and passages that speak to each student's interests. She can also provide model writing pieces that will encourage the student to take "writing chances" as the student explores different forms, modes, and expressions of writing for herself. When teachers know their students and connect them to authentic learning, they begin to lay the groundwork for students to learn to recognize, navigate, and interrupt inequities in this world. Using the essay and the timeline, teachers can notice when there is overlap and when there is not. The repetition represents a significant level of importance to the student.

For Adaly, the birth of her family members is pivotal. We learn as teachers that family relationships mean a great deal to this student. When we teach her, we can tie her familial ties and values to nurturing literacies. As effective teachers, we can use this knowledge to bridge learning for the student. When we design course learning segments for this student, for example, if the assignments can include family interviews or opportunities to involve members of the community, Adaly's personal connection to her learning would perhaps increase and thus engage her more and enhance the learning experience.

Connecting Urban Students of Color with Science—Christopher McDaniel

Teachers' learning about students happens not only in the English language arts classroom but in other content areas as well. How do we learn more about our students in other classrooms as we help them to think critically about some of the structural implications of race? Even when the initial focus is on a subject such as economics or water pollution, there is likely to be an underlying layer of racial inequity. Taking account of the culture of students of various backgrounds can involve not only understanding their learning styles and attitudes toward school but bridging from where they are in their lives to the content we want to help them learn—content that can speak to their daily experiences and that interrupts privilege, stereotypes, and generalizations. Building such bridges can be especially challenging in science classes, which can seem far distant from students' own worlds. Christopher McDaniel has developed highly crafted strategies to do so.

In my years of experience as an educator, I have witnessed many classrooms with students of Color in which the teacher has an excellent lesson plan and is excited about the lesson. However, only one group of students participates, and the rest refuse to engage. I have heard stories of students playing cards, playing games on their phone, and even FaceTiming other students at various schools. This can be disheartening and may cause some teachers to make incorrect generalizations about the population of students they are instructing. I believe that a well-planned system of engagement can enable a successful teacher to engage 95% or more of the students in each class. It can be a difficult task and requires an entire system of engagement that is inclusive of all students' ethical, cultural, and sociological beliefs. This can be especially difficult in a science classroom, where many students generally feel a disconnect and even a dislike for the content. In an effort to spark interest in science, I begin from day one to engage students by making a connection with them and drawing real-world connections between the world they live in and the science curriculum I am about to teach.

Using a Content-Focused Mixer to Learn from Student Interactions

On the first day of chemistry class, I use an activity familiar to many science teachers even before the COVID pandemic, called "the red plague lab." Students take two test tubes, one containing a clear unknown liquid many of the students believe to be water. The students pour half the contents of one test tube into an empty test tube. They cap the original test tube and use a dropper to mix the solutions in their second test tube with that of three different classmates. At the end, a pH indicator is added, and any students' test tubes that change color are deemed "contaminated." The students then are tasked with determining who started the contamination based on the color change in the test tubes. (If physical distancing is still necessary, teachers will need to be creative in modifying this activity.)

While they move around the classroom to compare their pH tests to see who is and is not a "carrier," the students get to know each other. But equally important for my engagement effort, I get to observe the social interactions between the students. It is essential to gain as much information as possible about the social structure of the class:

- Which students interact easily with others?

- Which students are more reluctant to engage with others?

- Do I see any social cliques?

- Do any of the students clearly show they do not get along with one another?

- Which students are easily engaged with the activity?

- Which students are reluctant to engage with the activity?

The more social information I can gather, the more it will help me to better engage my students in the future.

Connecting Students' Lives to the Subject Matter

The students who are hard to engage need to be identified as early as possible, and I need to get to learn their thinking. There are several methods that can be useful in trying to engage these students. An initial unit promptly introduces the topic of careers in science, aka "Money Talks." I always end the first day of class by telling my students, "Before I can teach you anything about science, I have to teach you about money." Some students will argue that they already know how to make money or that they're "already gettin' money." I tell them, "We'll see tomorrow." This challenges what the students think they know about money and makes them question from the beginning whether I have anything I can really teach them.

Every year I get the same question, and you may be asking it too: "How is this science?" I do this as a method of engaging students who place a value on money over education. I find that many of my students obsess about money even though they may not have a full understanding of what a working wage looks like. My students have many assumptions: they identify teachers, policemen, and public transit employees as the highest-paying positions in the neighborhood. Most of my students say $20 per hour is high pay and don't realize that with the right qualifications, they can earn much more. While there are many students who strive to learn, a lot say they do not value education because they can see the immediate money right in front of them in part-time jobs and side hustles. Many say that college is unaffordable. I have to immediately start attacking these schema in order to engage my students. The money unit, as you will see, helps them to think critically about who they are and how they are positioned.

Another part of the puzzle is that many of the students I want to engage with will not come to school on day one. If I can get the students who do show up excited enough about tomorrow's lesson about "money," the hope is that they will spread the word to the missing students to "come check it out." Further, the hope is that if they do not show up on day two, then once they find out what happened that day, they will show up on day three. Finally, I stand at the door at the end of class and look as many students in the eyes as I can and say, "Have a good day," and shake hands where appropriate. This lets me know who is "feeling me" and who's not. I make a mental note of any student who I sense has a problem with me so I can begin to look for a safe space to make a connection with that student. I try to spark any conversation I can with the students who I think or know from data have the potential to be frequently absent. This conversation is not geared toward attendance. It is to engage them with the lesson.

> Teaching for equity and interrupting bad practices require
> engaged students who trust and believe the adult in the
> classroom.

Christopher understands that to teach the lesson, teachers must first teach the students. And it is difficult to teach students whom you do not know, and who have not yet experienced the personal relevance of your subject matter for understanding and critiquing their world. Taking time to build relationships with students is essential. Teaching for equity and interrupting bad practices require engaged students who trust and believe the adult in the classroom. Christopher uses surprise and indirection to accomplish this engagement.

Day two. Generally, the students will spread the word that I "think" I know something about money and that I am going to teach them about it. My day-two activity is a webquest. I have the students use the internet to fill out the following form:

Job	Salary (Monthly)
Bills	**Monthly**
Rent	
Electricity	
Cable	
Cell phone	
Car note	
Insurance	
Groceries	
Disposable income	

I have the students identify a job that they can get with a high school diploma. If they already have a job, I let them use the salary from their real job. Most of the time, the students find jobs with an hourly salary listed. I have them calculate the monthly salary based on a 37.5-hour full-time workweek with an hour lunch. They then find an apartment, decide what bills they will incur, and how much they will pay for them. I give the students the leeway to decide for themselves how they will live, but try to guide them to a one-bedroom apartment with one income in the house. If they choose to live with someone else, that is fine. They can even choose not to get a car or cable television. When I first started teaching this lesson, all the students wanted cable, but now they all say they will buy a Fire TV Stick. The key is for the students to see how much disposable income they will have or lack at the end of the month with a job that only requires a high school diploma.

We then have a short conversation about the fact that they don't have kids factored into their budget. There may be students in the class who already have children, but most of the time they will not account for them in the activity or not mention they have them. Some students may be pregnant. This begins to make the conversation "real." We begin to talk about the cost of diapers and wipes. Many of the students are familiar with this and start to engage at a higher level. This lesson can easily take two days, which gives me another day to get students involved who miss the first two days or register late. By the end of this portion of the lesson, the students have a better concept of money and a better respect for the struggle many of their parents undertake in order to take care of them. We talk about how many of the students' parents are making these salaries and are raising multiple children. I tell them, "Go home and thank your parents." This sets the groundwork for me to play the "parent" card later in the semester if engagement starts to fall.

This is usually the point where students begin to question, "How is this science?" I ask them whether they have been collecting data. Did they analyze that data? Are they beginning to formulate ideas or questions based on that data? I tell them they have been doing research. I ask them whether they have been using credible websites. This revelation gets the kids excited because most of them have made no connection until now between what they are doing and science.

Once the class has finished the webquest and we have discussed how difficult it is to survive on the money they can make with just a high school diploma, I inform them that the next day I will show them jobs that pay three times as much. This is usually enough to get a buzz going. By now the students are

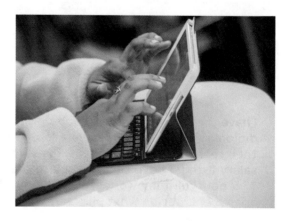

talking to their friends in my other classes about what we are doing. My first class is tipping my later classes off at lunchtime. This is hopefully going to pull in those last few students who are reluctant to show up to class, to give me a chance to teach them.

Christopher guides students to realize the value of science by using research methods and analysis of the economic realities of their lives as the tools. In his class, conversations about socioeconomics and neighborhood politics are precursors to the official course content and are needed to connect the students to it. He takes these opportunities to teach students how to research and gather data—and at the same time, he's scoping out who they are and how they relate to him and to one another, starting to build individual connections with students, using surprise and student gossip to draw in those who skipped the first days of school, and establishing that he knows and cares more about their lives than they might realize. How many of us as teachers go this far to make sure to help students connect our content to the realities and racial conditions of their lives, so that they can truly learn from and value what we teach?

Implications for All Our Teaching

Tina Curry invites students directly to explore their identities as readers, as writers, and as growing young people. Christopher McDaniel guides the students to discover an aspect of who they are through personal research that ultimately connects them with science. Although these educators' teaching strategies may appear very different, the students in both cases are discovering more about themselves. At the same time, the teachers are building connections with them, listening, observing, and learning about them, often through the lens of race, so that they can bring equity to their teaching. Here are some additional strategies that you can use to connect with your students:

- Virtual or actual home visits with students and their families
- Activities that involve the family or community and ask the student to reflect on the effort
- Family and community member interviews
- Photojournals of one day in the life of the student
- Vision boards about students' goals and hopes for the year

Learning about race and helping students see inequitable practices in their own lives can be a challenge, but oh, it is so worth the time and investment. Teachers can interrupt traditional practice by helping students to begin making sense of the world, whether it's by way of finding appreciation for their own language, learning processes, cultural practices, families, spaces for acceptance, or the relevance to their lives of academic subjects. These interruption practices break the status quo and enable teachers to see students for who they are and what gifts and talents they bring to the classroom.

Time Out to Talk

Tonya and Katy Discuss
Listening to Students

Transcribed and edited from a video call, June 28, 2020

Tonya: Yesterday I talked to Deon Arnold, who is fourteen, and Jordyn Hudson, who is seventeen [both of whom are featured in Chapter 6]. Both are African American high schoolers. Deon is in ninth grade and Jordyn in twelfth. They had some advice for teachers. Deon said he thought teachers needed to listen and figure out what kids—these are not my words—what kids could do, and support them. Jordyn talked about teachers being willing to collaborate and have conversations with children.

Jordyn and I talked about why teachers might be reluctant to have those conversations. I told her that I had just listened to a dissertation preproposal defense, and one of the points was that teachers are afraid to talk about race because they're afraid of how the conversation will go. It might not be an area they can control. They're not comfortable having the discussion themselves. Jordyn agreed and said that she's spent time talking to teachers, and she urged us to keep pushing them to have hard conversations, because if they don't, it doesn't help the students.

Katy: Wise words from a kid. Thinking about my colleagues when I was teaching high school kids, and of course my teacher candidates now: so many of them want control. They're afraid of things that are not something they can script.

Tonya: A dissertation candidate mentioned to me yesterday that parents don't want those kinds of conversations. They just want the subject and content, but when it comes to collaboration, social justice, hard topics like race, gender, sexual orientation, politics, that's not a place where school is to interject itself. Part of the problem, though, is that everything we talk about, those things are important. You might not understand the language to discuss these topics, but you cannot ignore them.

Katy: So how did we two come to realize the importance of listening to and learning about our students? The high school where I taught for sixteen of my twenty years is a school that, although it served primarily one community, had a great deal of socioeconomic diversity, from section 8 housing to close to million-dollar homes. Twenty-seven or thirty different home languages were spoken by my students. I got to a point where I felt, "I need to understand more. I don't understand them now. I see what's happening in their lives, but I don't understand how all of it fits into a larger societal context." Part of my impetus for pursuing a doctorate was that I wanted and needed to understand more about equity work.

Tonya: I've taught in rural, suburban, and urban schools. In Birmingham, when I first arrived in the urban school, I became not just a teacher but a student. It was the first time that I had seen a kid shot. A sixth grader ran into the school, into my arms. We called the ambulance. I remember red blood on her white kid's shoes. She wasn't the target—it was just crossfire. I began to want to know more about my kids and life, and how schooling could make a difference or illuminate their circumstances. But I wasn't ready as a teacher, so I stuck to the curriculum. However, after the basketball coach passed away unexpectedly at our school and the kids were devastated, I understood more about how schooling has to reflect the whole child. Thus began my journey of being a better teacher. The students often informed me, "Look, this is not gonna work. Let me tell you why." "Why is it not going to work?" "We don't understand how it fits. What does it mean?" They then visited my classroom during lunch or PE to give me additional "advice" to instruct them better. They just wanted to talk. They wanted me to listen.

Katy: My second teaching job was at a school in Cincinnati with a very diverse population. I think about one of my seniors who kept falling asleep in class. I have to admit I found it more than a little frustrating! I thought maybe his guidance counselor could give me some perspective, and I learned a lot! It turned out that the student had a two-year-old at home. He was the sole supporter for his mother, his baby, and the baby's mother. He came to school every day and then he went and worked a full-time job. I realized that if I was going to help this student, I needed to stop making assumptions about him—or any of my other students. I needed to have a better understanding of who my kids were as people, to listen to them and talk with them. It's not just about following the curriculum. Like you, I'm happy to be able to say my classroom was often a place that the kids came to hang out.

Tonya: While that's a good thing, there can be hurts that we need to help our students of Color to not just talk about but stand up to, so they interrupt and learn to not just let them pass. When I was about to move to my suburban school, I had a camp for both the kids I was leaving and the kids I was getting in the suburban space, and they shared. We went to the suburban school for a week. All the kids from the suburbs were then supposed to go to the urban school, so that the context would switch and they could learn about one another's environment. However, many suburban kids did not attend that week. Meanwhile, the students in the urban space had cleaned their school, had made bulletin boards. They didn't want their suburban friends to see their space as a deficit. They were let down when only a few of their suburban friends rode the bus to them.

Katy: That must have been a really difficult situation! What did you do?

Tonya: Well, the following week, back at the suburban school, we processed what was happening and asked one another some tough questions. "Why didn't you, my friends, want to come to my urban school?" was one the children asked of their suburban summer classmates. The conversations were tough but needed. I facilitated the dialogue between the students. My job as a teacher was to get the discussion started and then to listen to the hurt that emerged and to the healing statements that arose from the conversations. Hopefully some change in understanding took place where it needed to.

CHAPTER 4

Building Criticality for Students—
and Teachers

> Fear can easily become a barrier to exploring controversial topics in our classrooms, but should it stop us? It's imperative to discuss and explore issues so students feel empowered. . . . Approaching any controversial topic is challenging but structure helps and is necessary.
>
> —Gabriella Corales, high school American literature teacher

To become effective interrupters of racism, students and teachers need to know their community well, be able to access accurate information about racist conditions, learn to question and analyze those conditions, and then act to interrupt them. This process calls for openness on the part of both students and teachers to examine and rethink their attitudes about racial equity. It's worth repeating education professor Gholdy Muhammad's description of this stance as "criticality"—that is, not just a state of urgency but a more active process of critique, "the capacity to read, write, and think in ways of understanding power, privilege, social justice, and oppression, particularly for populations who have been historically marginalized in the world" (Muhammad 2020).

This questioning and analytical approach is essential for addressing racial inequities. It requires gaining awareness of the roles that racism plays in everyone's lives, and the discriminatory challenges that people of Color deal with. Students of Color are likely to be aware of challenges such as unfair discipline practices in their school, but some may be less knowledgeable about conditions such as the greater resources for schools in White neighborhoods or the concentration of pollution in their neighborhoods due to environmental injustice. As Christopher McDaniel explains shortly, some students haven't yet acquired the tools to fully understand and interrupt the inequities affecting their lives. White students may lack understanding of the destructiveness of racism or the ways they benefit from it. And all students may have preconceptions about peers whose race differs from theirs.

However, promoting criticality is not about blaming students for what they don't yet know. Rather, teachers who approach their work with criticality embrace and build on the knowledge their students do have about their own life situations. And they draw on the youthful passion, angst, curiosity, and energy that students can bring to the classroom. Our work is to reinforce these strengths, giving students tools, knowledge, and fortitude they can use to address the aspects of racism they choose to interrupt.

> Promoting criticality is not about blaming students for what
> they don't yet know. Rather, teachers who approach their
> work with criticality embrace and build on the knowledge
> their students do have about their own life situations.

There's much to learn for all of us as teachers as well. We can only help students develop their sense of efficacy and the dispositions to actively interrupt racism by getting to know their cultures and learning styles, and by encouraging their exercise of choice and decision-making in their learning. We need to listen to our students and be aware of how their approaches to learning may be quite different from our own and then support those approaches to ensure that they are indeed learning. And we especially need to promote equity by enabling students to question and examine issues deeply and independently. We educators, in other words, need to practice criticality ourselves. Yolanda Sealey-Ruiz's Racial Literacy Development framework helps us see the many layers of effort and understanding needed to support criticality:

- **Critical Love:** Many teachers feel deeply committed to their students, but Critical Love involves not just an attitude but specific efforts to strengthen students' abilities to critically analyze the conditions around them, and to support their particular learning needs.

- **Critical Humility, Critical Reflection, and Archaeology of Self:** Teachers must recognize how their students' backgrounds, knowledge, and concerns may differ from their own, and use this recognition to plan curriculum and inquiry projects that are relevant and effective. When we do this, students recognize our efforts and begin, themselves, to consider how their communication can connect with audiences they want to address—audiences in their communities who may have different perspectives than the students' own.

- **Historical Literacy:** This is knowledge not just about the past but about conditions and forces around us that have grown out of the past. This means critically analyzing the curriculum and reading materials handed down to us, with an eye for racial or other biases, and acting to revise them or even to work around them. In the science unit we are about to share, for example, Christopher McDaniel helps students to connect the science they are learning to the many forms of inequity—the long-standing poverty, poor housing construction, neglect of communities of Color, and biased governmental decision-making—that created the Flint, Michigan, drinking water health crisis and affect their own community as well.

- **Interruption:** Teachers can provide students with access to and practice with the tools not only to investigate issues deeply but then to use the knowledge and concern they have acquired to work for change around racial equity in their community.

So what does criticality about racism look like in the classroom? How do teachers pursue criticality themselves and then support and advance it with their students? It's not just about students having intense discussions about race. We see three types of learning that initiate criticality:

1. Gaining academic knowledge that enables students to analyze social issues affected by racism

2. Building analytical habits of mind in order to dig into racial issues more deeply

3. Reflecting on and critiquing their own ideas and perspectives

This work can look quite different from one classroom to the next, depending on the subject taught, the students' backgrounds, and particular teachers' styles and strategies.

Countless topics across the curriculum present opportunities to support students' criticality around race, and we can't possibly illustrate all of them. However, we can share several vivid examples. Christopher McDaniel explains how to give critical purpose to the learning of chemistry for his students of Color, whose neighborhoods are affected by the problem of unsafe drinking water. Vanessa Heller's affluent White and Asian sixth graders, meanwhile, have almost no conscious awareness of racism, even though they don't hesitate to use racially insulting language from the music they enjoy. So Vanessa seeks to guide them to transcend their very limited experience and begin to grasp the real problems with race in this country and with their privileged world that has allowed them both to benefit from those problems and to remain so seemingly oblivious. Both educators must themselves engage in the questioning and digging and reflecting that we call criticality, in order to understand how to help their students with it.

Discovering the Value of Content Knowledge for Criticality Around Race—Investigating the Problem of Lead in Drinking Water

Inquiring into racial inequity may seem easy enough in a social studies or English language arts classroom. But how do we do this for other content areas? Sure, there may be times when a teacher and class can pause from the regular curriculum to address a pressing issue that has arisen in the school or community, but we believe it is essential to incorporate racial criticality within the curriculum itself. Why? First, racism affects every aspect of American life and endeavor, so we must help students understand that. Second, developing criticality calls for knowledge and skills that are particular to each subject area.

Planning a project to build criticality requires a series of key steps. An educator will need to

- Understand the racial issues in the school and community.

- Consider the level of students' knowledge, about both racial inequities and the relevant subject matter.

- Identify a clear purpose—that is, specific goals and objectives: students' learning, the dispositions that the teacher aims for—both toward learning the content and toward addressing racial inequity. This includes advancing students' development of racial literacy, as Yolanda Sealey-Ruiz has outlined. We must be aware, however, that fresh and unanticipated realizations can emerge anywhere in the inquiry process, so we should allow space and time for them when they pop up.

- Identify required curriculum and content standards that the inquiry will address, to justify the inclusion of equity efforts for those who focus on curricular mandates.

- Determine information, questions, concepts, and skills to be introduced and explored.

- Plan the activities the students will experience.

- Create ways to challenge students to think critically about the issues presented by the material.

- Explore opportunities for meaningful student effort to use their new knowledge to act on the problem they have studied.

- Develop high-level assessment of students' learning.

Christopher McDaniel teaches in a neighborhood where many people, both students and adults, have not been given the opportunity to learn how scientific knowledge can address important inequities in their lives. So he welcomes his role as a teacher in helping his students discover the need and to engage in learning that will help them interrupt those inequities—and he designs inquiry units with this goal in mind. Clearly, in each subject area and with each student population, teachers will need to inquire with criticality themselves, to determine the specific connections between their subject matter and the racial issues that hover within it and are present in the surrounding community. Let's follow Christopher's use of the water crisis in Flint, Michigan (and Chicago and elsewhere), to promote students' racial criticality through science concepts.

> In each subject area and with each student population, teachers will need to inquire with criticality themselves, to determine the specific connections between their subject matter and the racial issues that hover within it and are present in the surrounding community.

CONSIDERING STUDENTS' LEVEL OF KNOWLEDGE AND THE PURPOSE FOR THE PROJECT

Over time, Christopher has made a point of learning about the conditions and mind-sets among his students and in the community where he has taught. He often walks around the neighborhood of the school at the end of the day, schmoozing with students he encounters. He regularly chats with students in the lunchroom as well, to inform his thinking about the students' awareness, and to learn about their interests. His understanding helps guide his teaching.

It can be difficult to engage students in a high school science class. Many of my students don't see any connection between their everyday lives and science... Establishing such a connection between the real world they live in and the science content I am teaching can make all the difference. I teach science in a predominantly Latinx community, and I try to infuse social and environmental justice into each of my courses. I provide my students with examples from their real world that show they need a basic understanding of the science to comprehend the things taking place around them every day. I want to give these students the tools they need to make thoughtful decisions about issues in their lives, particularly when scientific knowledge can help them understand those issues.

Christopher begins the inquiry with a bell-ringer jot to stir students' thinking about the underlying concept of environmental justice that will be explored in the unit, asking them to think about the meaning of each of the two words, *environmental* and *justice*. This prepares them to start considering the role chemistry may play in understanding a larger problem that impacts their lives. Then comes some provocative information.

At the beginning of every school year I show students in my chemistry classes an excerpt of the PBS *NOVA* special "Poisoned Water" [https://www.pbs.org/video/poisoned-water-jhhegn/], a documentary about the Flint water crisis, the vehicle I use to introduce my students to environmental racism. Initially, I only show two minutes of the video, but I show it twice, so the information can begin to sink in. Those first two minutes alone make clear that the crisis is connected with race, poverty, the loss of auto industry jobs, and the science of the lead poisoning that especially affects children. I ask them to take notes and write down any key terms or concepts they can pick up from the video.

Many of the students have very little information about what happened in Flint, but are at an age when they are beginning to question authority and starting to see the inequities present in different aspects of their lives. This immediately makes a connection for them. They see children their age and younger from neighborhoods similar to theirs being taken advantage of by people in power, and they learn how the children are dealing with life-threatening illness due to lead in the drinking water that came from the faucets in their own homes. Most of the students immediately engage with this video, and it becomes a topic of serious discussion. We do a quick think-pair-share about the video, and the students create discussion boards listing the things they think they need to learn to better understand the chemistry behind what happened in Flint.

CONNECTING TO REQUIRED CURRICULUM

Christopher never loses sight of his role as a science teacher. But it's not difficult to connect the science he is expected to teach with the social problems he knows the students will care deeply about. It is no surprise to Christopher that the items on the students' discussion boards match his list of content standards. As the students write and then examine their lists, they are hooked: they want to know the science so that they can get answers to their own questions. Then Christopher asks students to identify various resources around the room that they think will inform them about the topics on their lists, which in turn leads to Christopher's chemistry lessons. For example, when a student points to the periodic table on the wall, Christopher explains how it works, and helps students notice patterns among the various element groups and ways they can interact with one another. He points out that it's the bonding of lead with chlorine in the water that had previously formed a protective coating in the old lead pipes in Flint homes.

Most of the discussion boards include the same key terms, including *lead*, *water*, and *chlorine*. These are the terms the students find themselves wanting to learn more about. So I use their interest in understanding more about what happened in Flint to engage them in a unit on the concepts of periodicity and bonding, one of the units I need to teach. These properties give the students a basic understanding of the chemistry behind the Flint water crisis.

DIGGING DEEPER

Next, students read the news article "Brain-Damaging Lead Found in Tap Water in Hundreds of Homes Tested Across Chicago, Results Show," from the *Chicago Tribune* (Hawthorne and Reyes 2018). This not only raises awareness—spikes indignation, actually—but provides an occasion for a reading lesson in which Christopher helps students employ a variety of reading strategies to get the most from their effort and then to discuss it in small groups.

The students read and annotate this article in class. We then engage in a "domino reporter" activity in which students share how they felt with their discussion group and then summarize their group's conversations with the class. The students are outraged and imme-diately begin questioning the quality of water in their own neighbor-hood. They want to know whether their neighborhood was affected and how they can determine whether the water supply in their own homes is safe or not. I tell them about a Chicago Public Schools study on the lead levels in each of the water sources inside of every public school in Chicago (https://cps.edu/Pages/WaterQualityTesting.aspx). They can go online and look at the lead levels of each water fountain and sink in every school in the entire city.

Since the final project for the class is to research an environmental issue and create a poster about it, many of the students do compar-ison studies of lead levels in schools based on various socioeconomic factors such as race, ethnicity, income, and industrialization. In many of my classes, the students are interested in testing the quality of water in their homes and actually go home and discuss this issue with their parents. Since they have learned from the article that the city offers testing kits for Chicagoans to test their water, the students use our classroom computers to order testing kits for themselves.

To help students learn about more organized activist interrupters of environmen-tal racism, Christopher invites representatives from the Little Village Environmental Justice Organization (LVEJO) to speak to the class.

The LVEJO has effectively addressed environmental problems in Chicago's Mexican American neighborhood called Little Village (La Villita). Organization staffers visit the class and talk to students about the amount of pollution in the community created by the large industrial sites in the neighborhood. They show the students maps of Chicago that illustrate how most industrial areas are located in neighborhoods where African American and Latinx people live. For a lot of my students, this is their first time hearing about any type of environmental racism. It is also the first time they have heard of community organizations standing up and fighting for racial equity and equality and making a difference. This empowers a lot of students to action in this community. LVEJO has enlisted high school students to go out into the community and map industrial areas that are not being properly regulated by the City of Chicago. They have set up checkpoints in the community to count the number of diesel trucks in certain residential areas over time. This organization is essential to helping me engage my students so we can have real discussions about what science looks like in their community.

Finally, Christopher takes one more step to challenge students' criticality, posing a moral and financial question to push them beyond their indignation over the water problem to consider their own future roles in solving such problems.

Going further, I ask students to look deeper into the root of the problem with the water in Chicago by posing a challenging moral issue. They read that a lead service line links each home to the main water line located under the street. Changing this service line is necessary if an owner wants to reduce the lead level in the water entering the home. The cost of this replacement is incurred by the homeowner. The students often talk about graduating from college and coming back to the community and buying property. So I initiate a discussion about the duty of a person who owns a residential property in a neighborhood like theirs. I ask them whether, as a property owner, they would feel ethically, morally, or financially responsible for replacing that service line, even if their tenants were unaware of the problem with lead in the drinking water. It could possibly take years to recover the money spent to replace the line. They are asked to consider how they would treat their uninformed and unaware tenants, who could be some of the students they currently go to school with, or neighbors who currently live beside them. Will these more informed owners replace the service line for them? As you can imagine, some hot disagreement erupts on the question. This is just the kind of independent application of science knowledge to real-life concerns that I want my students to think about.

Christopher keeps the assessment process purposeful, requiring students to complete a final project and poster on an additional environmental problem, along with an in-depth exit slip as a wrap-up to help both teacher and students evaluate their learning. Equally important, as Christopher has described, he is able to directly observe students' thinking and actions to investigate the purity of the water in their own homes.

• • • • • •

At the end of this chapter, you'll find a guide to planning criticality lessons and projects like the one Christopher has shared.

News Reading to Build Students' Criticality Around Race

Christopher McDaniel's Flint water crisis unit is specifically designed to build the critical consciousness of students living in the neighborhood served by his school. Meanwhile, in locations with few families of Color, or in places where the destructive side of racist conditions isn't overtly visible, advancing criticality and racial literacy is equally important. Students there may be relatively unaware of the racial inequities that are actually benefiting them, but they can learn to interrupt stereotyping and racist behaviors often learned from parents and peers. Teaching in an affluent, majority White community, Vanessa Heller has taken steps to address this need, as she immerses her sixth graders in readings to raise their awareness and, she hopes, broaden their interruption of racial injustice.

> In locations with few families of Color, or in places where the destructive side of racist conditions isn't overtly visible, advancing criticality and racial literacy is equally important.

This endeavor reflects Sealey-Ruiz's RLD framework as Vanessa draws on her own caring for her students—her Critical Love—to interrupt their noncritical behavior. She depends on her Critical Humility, learning what the students do and do not understand rather than making assumptions about them. In the spirit of Archaeology of Self, she has reflected on how her own teaching had not previously addressed contemporary racial implications in her social studies content. She has decided to introduce students to the Historical Literacy around racism in order to spark their own efforts to interrupt harmful words and actions.

SETTING A PURPOSE AND CONNECTING TO CORE CURRICULUM

When we initiate discussion or inquiry about race with students, it's important to be clear about their stage in the RLD framework, their needs and backgrounds, and the connection of the activity to their core educational growth. Having observed her students' racist remarks, thoughtless insensitivity, and lack of real knowledge about racism, Vanessa has analyzed their needs and her objectives in the following way.

My students are primarily White, plus about a third of the student population is Asian American. Just about all of them come from fairly affluent families. As is often the case with ten- to twelve-year-olds, they speak without thinking. Physiologically their brains are still developing.

Along with the careless comments from my own students, we have been having issues with bullying at our site. In addition, I am working with several colleagues on our Social Emotional Learning committee to investigate the causes of student anxiety and to take action to alleviate these stressors. I decided to put all these opportunities together. We had to stop what we were doing—stop "covering the curriculum"—to problem-solve, because we were the problem. Not only were students simply not being "nice" because they were thoughtless, but their comments and actions were right out microaggressions.

I discovered that what they knew as "race" and what they knew as "racism" were not connected for them. The students did know something about how race can play out through power relationships through our study of ancient people who discriminated against each other, but they did not connect that to today—nor had I really made the connection clear for them. They were also unaware of general power relationships and how these power differentials lead to subjugation of groups that lack power. And on a classroom/social level, I noticed there was a disconnect between their stated idealism that racism is wrong and what they said and did in the classroom and other social contexts that smacked of racism and generally mean behaviors.

Along with this analysis of students' behaviors, Vanessa knew it was important to connect their growth as reflected in the RLD framework with the curriculum she is called on to teach. It mustn't be just an add-on, but instead should bring a racial equity lens to much of students' learning. Vanessa thought about this in the following way.

Through my curriculum, I have always tried to build students' awareness of themselves and others and to realize the impact of their actions. We start each year with identity webs, which we add to throughout the school year as we learn more about ourselves. Developing students' awareness of self and others has been a goal of mine for some years now, and it parallels our study of ancient history. But it was only this year while working to contribute to this book that I realized I needed to go beyond an examination of our own identities to look at institutionalized racism and how the use of power benefits one group to the disadvantage of others. Focusing on issues of race and bias allowed a study of identity to have a context, a place in time, and hopefully a personal connection.

LEARNING MORE ABOUT STUDENTS' THINKING AND LEVEL OF KNOWLEDGE

As Vanessa began planning this new project, she realized that she needed to uncover more explicitly what her students did and did not know, so planning and execution proceeded together. At each stage, she asked the students to reflect digitally or on paper, which provided her with more information about their thinking and guided the design of the next steps.

My just-in-time unit thus focused on who we are and how we treat each other, through lessons on identity, race, racism, and biases, along with my future plans to encourage and equip kids to interrupt racism. I set up for the lesson by reminding kids of our classroom norms—respect, active listening and participation, etc. My students know how to have a scholarly discussion using sentence stems for accountable talk, but I did have small signs on each table with the sentence stems to help them express themselves civilly and scholarly if they forgot.

A day or so before the lesson, I collected some information through an online survey that allowed *me* to build background knowledge, to take the "conceptual temperature" of students via a confidential survey. I had an inkling that my students needed a gentle "in" to our lesson, given my suspicions that I was about to launch into a lesson unlike one they had ever experienced. So I used the following questions:

1. Have you ever been bullied?
   If so, what happened?

2. Have you ever bullied someone?
   If so, what happened and why did you do it?

3. Have you ever been called a name or names before?
   If so, what names have you been called?

4. What kind of names do you hear other kids call each other?

5. Have you ever been made fun of because of your looks, religion, skin color, language, way of dressing, etc.? If so, please tell me about it.

6. Have you ever been teased about anything else? What was it and how did you feel about it?

I did not tell them why I wanted to ask them these questions, only that my intentions would be revealed soon enough . . . and my students do love a good cliffhanger.

Some of the responses: An Indian student commented that other kids made fun of Indian clothing and traditions during the recent school-wide Diwali celebration, while another Indian student complained that she was described as Muslim when the speakers should have said "Indian." One student reported a peer referred to her as a "Russian spy." Another reported that "Some of the kids used to pull the sides of their eyes back and look at me because I am Asian. They would make faces at me while they did it too." One child was called an "Asian slave." An Indian student was told in elementary school that "Indian food is fugging stupid" and shared that this teasing about his food continued here at middle school. Other students were belittled as if gender, sexual orientation, accent, or religion were pejoratives, or they experienced general bullying and name-calling. Few if any of my students claimed they experienced they had bullied anyone beyond annoying their siblings on occasion. It was interesting to me that I had such a whole-some, innocent class and that being mean was what *other* kids must do.

Using a Thought Jot, I then asked the following questions, to which they responded on sticky notes—no discussion was allowed, just quiet thought and response.

- What is discrimination?

- What is race?

- What is racism?

I had three pieces of chart paper on the whiteboard with the questions posted above each. As kids finished, they stuck their thoughts under each question. I collected the sticky notes after each class to reflect on later myself but also to streamline/focus my selection of articles they were going to read.

I was eager to see what my students already knew about these hot topics. Well, they didn't know much. Definitions of race ranged from skin color, country of origin, one's culture, gender, or even one's species (homo sapiens, one child replied). There was clear confusion between race and culture. A few students mentioned identity and referred to race as a "classification system" based on shared characteristics. Generally though, I could tell that "race" was a necessary term to define.

The replies for racism and discrimination were closer to the mark. The kids were pretty clear that discrimination involves various forms of exclusion and judgment and that racism is treating others injuriously because of their race (though the kids were unclear on what race actually is). It was also clear that they knew racism and discrimination hold negative connotations.

LAUNCHING THE INQUIRY

Vanessa used the responses she collected and the understanding she had gained about the level of their awareness to plan and guide the students' inquiry into racial inequity.

With this knowledge, I had to find articles that introduced these terms in a way the kids could understand (since they had incorrect background knowledge or none at all), and the reading material had to align with what I was teaching—since I had literally stopped our social studies unit to sneak this project in. I found Newsela to be an excellent starter source in that they have a variety of articles on race and racism, and the topics do indeed relate to the unequal treatment of others we learned about in early civilizations. And because I had students at a variety of reading levels, the ability to choose the same text at different readabilities worked very well for our needs. I found one article that introduced the idea of race and systemic racism, and decided that I would read this article with the whole group first before breaking into smaller groups for a read-around. I wanted to make sure I eased my students into this—and I wasn't sure where I was headed either—so I was easing myself into this awareness of racism, too.

Day 1. Whole Group:
"Definition of Systemic Racism in Sociology"
(ThoughtCo.com, adapted by Newsela)

Station 1. "How unintentional but insidious bias can be the most harmful" (*PBS NewsHour*, adapted by Newsela) 	Station 2. "Don't jump to conclusions about race being based on just DNA" (Associated Press, adapted by Newsela) 	Station 3. "Kids exposed to racism have higher risk of depression and sickness" (*Washington Post*, adapted by Newsela)
Station 4. "Study shows racial segregation, child poverty rising in United States" (Associated Press, adapted by Newsela) 	Station 5. "Rich whites and poor students of color more and more separated in schools" (*Washington Post*, adapted by Newsela) 	Station 6. "Ending School Segregation in the U.S." (USHistory.org, adapted by Newsela)

Articles used for whole-class and small-group readings

Day 2. Whole Group:
"More White Americans Believe Racism Is a Big Problem, Report Says" (Associated Press, adapted by Newsela)

Station 1. "U.S. education officials to gather info on discrimination against Muslims" (*Washington Post*, adapted by Newsela)	Station 2. "Girls as young as 6 believe men are smarter than women, study shows" (Associated Press, adapted by Newsela)	Station 3. "A History of anti-Semitism" (*Encyclopaedia Britannica*, adapted by Newsela)
Station 4. "'Asian-American' is a broad term that unites some and divides others" (*Washington Post*, adapted by Newsela)	Station 5. "How racism was first officially started in 15th-century Spain" (*Atlas Obscura*, adapted by Newsela)	Station 6. "Do teachers treat children differently based on their color? Study says yes" (*The Guardian*, adapted by Newsela)

Articles used for whole-class and small-group readings

Once we all read the first article, students discussed with each other and then on sticky notes, responding to the following prompts:

- What did you already know?

- What surprised you?

- What do you wonder?

- What do you agree/disagree with?

We did a quick share out for those who felt comfortable. This brought the "tough" topic into the space, and thankfully the kids welcomed it as a topic for discussion and examination. I was pleasantly surprised that they were instantly interested in the topic and most were eager to talk about it.

Students then read the designated article at their table and discussed it. Once done, they responded on stickies first, then shared out to their group. I also had one student from each group share a bit about their group's article and the conversation they had about that topic. I collected and organized these sticky notes and then groups rotated for the next article, and so on through the whole set.

Their responses told me they didn't have the words to even speak about racism meaningfully. My students were indeed racially illiterate, and in trying to figure out my next steps, I realized I was racially illiterate as well. Like my students, I first needed the words to talk about racism before I even attempted to interrupt it. Thus, we prepared a glossary for ourselves.

COMPLETING THE UNIT AND EVALUATING THE OUTCOMES

Though the students were now engaged in the reading and discussion activity about race, their uninformed comments told Vanessa that she needed to add another step. This would both deepen students' thinking and further inform her about whether they realized the problematic implications of what they were learning.

To wrap up the read-around, I used Google Question, so students could respond and have a running conversation. They replied online to the following prompts:

What are your takeaways from our readings and discussions?

How can you, as a student living in the United States, accept your own responsibility to take better care of one another?

Here are some students' thoughts.

> A takeaway from our discussion is that there are so many different forms of racism in the world. Often we do not even realize what we are saying is hurtful. A way we can take better care of each other is by making sure what we are going to say or do isn't racist or plain out hurtful before we do it. Run it through your brain first. [Student 1]

> It hurts to see that POC are treated differently than people who are white and that we are not as represented in things like news. The topic that got me the most was micro-aggression. . . because as a person of Color born and brought up in the US, I always got the question "Where are you from," and my answer would be the US, but since I look differently in the clouded judgment that all Americans are white, I would get the question "No, where are you FROM." Although I know they weren't trying to hurt my feelings, I still got hurt by it. [Student 2]

> I learned so many things that I didn't know about racism. I learned that you can get physically ill from getting bullied because of your race. I am very upset about this. I can't change other main big things, like, you cannot be racist. But I can do small things like warn someone when they are saying something unintentional but offending. [Student 3]

> The big thing that I learned was that words hurt. My friend Alberto looks like he is . . . white, but he is actually Latino. As his friend, this [hearing racist comments] hurts my feelings and offends me when this happens so I can only imagine what this

does to him. I know people don't mean to say these things but they do. I feel like I could make the world more equal by sharing my thoughts on social platforms and the news so I can make a change in this world for the good. [Student 4]

I think from the discussions I had from my seat partners I learned that there are real problems in the world besides my drama. That we need to make a change, and it is up to us to make a change. We are the face of the future. As a child in the U.S. I feel like I have a responsibility to take care of one another, to treat everyone equally. This taught me there are REAL problems. [Student 5]

It was clear from their responses through the reading of the six articles that students were becoming more aware that racism exists today. There seemed to be many who were surprised that schools are still segregated even though the law says this is illegal, that the stress of racism can make a person physically ill, and that people of Color are paid less than Whites. The consensus was that students would now think before they speak—mainly to avoid microaggressions—and that being "nice" is within their realm of control. While I was disappointed that students' overall solution to racism seemed to be solved by "niceness," I do realize that these were introductory steps.

Students were interested in microaggressions and vowed to work hard to not make them. Several students of Color shared experiences of microaggressions—particularly when peers ask them where they are "from." Their peers of Color nodded along in understanding and their White peers nodded with realization that what they *mean* may or may not match what they *say*, but the *impact* of their words is real. Indeed, addressing our needs for the right words to speak about racism was now combined with our need to identify microaggressions and how to prevent them.

A Guide for Planning Projects to Promote Criticality on Issues of Race

You can see from Christopher's and Vanessa's units that it takes some planning to initiate students' criticality and help them move from there to actions to interrupt racial inequities.

The following guide will be helpful in creating critical antiracist inquiries in your classroom.

Preparing for the Project

- List racial equity concerns you are aware of in the community and/or school.

- Do some background research to learn of any additional racial concerns that may not have initially made your list, and add them to it. These may include broader issues beyond the school such as housing, food deserts, and infrastructure problems in the school's neighborhood.

- Review and record your own present knowledge of students' awareness and/or concerns about race. Consider that students may be dealing with pressures they do not always wish to discuss openly in class or with you.

- Design and conduct a preassessment of students' awareness and/or concerns about racial equity. This may be a bell-ringer with several key questions, or it may require an in-depth inquiry, such as interviewing students of varying backgrounds. Be sure to ask about students' strengths and their ideas for learning about race, as well as areas about which they may have less knowledge.

- On the basis of the information gathered, identify an issue to explore that is most relevant to advancing their development of racial literacy. While you may begin to figure this out yourself, students are likely to have valuable perspectives beyond your own to help you with this decision.

- Reflect on your own assumptions, beliefs, biases, wonderings, and experiences (or lack of them) related to the issue and to students' lived experience, to ensure that your approach scaffolds students' learning and does not limit it.

Plans for Conducting the Project

- Identify specific learning objectives for the project, related to the racial equity issue you have chosen for the students to explore.

- Plan assessment(s) that will indicate what students have learned and done in the course of the project. Be sure to include ways of observing student learning that may go beyond or differ from what is anticipated by your objectives. Include plans to observe any actions students take to communicate about or interrupt racial inequity.

- Choose resources (readings, videos, online material, information from experts, student testimony, etc.) to be used to provide students with reliable information and perspectives for the inquiry.

- Plan strategies to support students' processes for interpreting the information and issues and to challenge their thinking to go deep and get beyond superficial conclusions. Consider how you can give students the space and support to deal with information that may make them uncomfortable or that may even be painful.

- Identify strategies for respectful discussion that are supportive of students, particularly those who could be harmed by misunderstandings. Plan for how misunderstandings or disagreements can be repaired rather than merely suppressed, so that you are prepared in case they do take place. If this work is new to you, you may wish to consult professional materials on guiding challenging discussions.

- Determine what actions or further inquiries can come next.

Postproject Reflection

- Note adjustments, if any, that you found you needed to make to your plans.

- List activities that you found to work well.

- Plan any changes or adjustments to activities needed when you use this project in the future.

- Document evidence of students' learning that you observed. Be sure to include not only the extent to which students achieved your planned learning objectives but also discoveries and understandings you may not have anticipated. Include information that indicates how students' development of racial literacy may have advanced. And of course make note of any actions that students take to communicate about and interrupt inequity.

To Conclude

Christopher's and Vanessa's lessons are just two examples of the many that can be introduced in classrooms to awaken and support students' critical examination of racism and its oppressive impact in our schools and communities. There are so many opportunities to guide students to exercise criticality throughout the curriculum to more deeply understand and critique the content they encounter—the stories, the history, the art and music, the contributors to and uses of science and math. In fact, the work is not always pretty—great innovators of Color have often been omitted from history. Fortunately, more and more educators are pursuing antiracism through creative and powerful classroom lessons, activities, and materials. We hope that our two examples will inspire you to seek these out and create your own, responding to the specific needs, cultures, interests, and levels of Racial Literacy Development of your students. In Appendix 2 we provide data on racial inequities throughout the education system that you can use to help students critically examine how deeply racism permeates the school world of which they are a part. Then you can move to the next step: helping students claim their voices to interrupt racism, as we illustrate in Chapter 5.

Time Out to Talk

Steve's Frustrations

Transcribed and edited from a video call, June 30, 2020

Steve: Tonya, I know we're supposed to plan the schedule for sending more chapters to Bill Varner today, but do you mind if I just sound off for a few minutes first? I'm feeling very frustrated and really angry, and being stuck in the house thanks to the COVID epidemic, I can't even do anything about it. I feel like I'm going crazy.

Tonya: Sure, Steve, what's bothering you?

Steve: There's just so much that's so terrible and so discouraging that's going on, in education and out in the world, and I don't even know what to do with my anger. Just this morning, in *Education Week* online, a new research study revealed that 70 percent of White educators say the experience of people of Color in history textbooks is either fairly well or well represented. Even lots of people of Color think so, too. How can that be?! When events like the Tulsa massacre or the Birmingham march or the existence of Black literary societies in the nineteenth century or dozens of other positive or hateful developments—when they are invisible? How could they think that? And this is what we're hoping to change!

Then today's *New York Times* reported that there have been not just five or six "I can't breathe" deaths at the hands of police in recent years but at least seventy. Seventy! Police training has even taught—wrongly, of course—that if a person says, "I can't breathe," they are using breath, so the cops believe they are lying. One police station even had a sign on the wall saying, "If they say they can't breathe, they are breathing." Or some cops just don't care. One was recorded responding to the cry from a man in a choke hold, "So! Who gives a——!" When does this ever stop? And what can *we* do—I feel like our book will be just a drop in the ocean.

That choke-hold information just felt like the final straw for me. I was reading all this at breakfast, and I was so angry. My wife is now making our bagels herself, and they are wonderful, but I couldn't even taste the bagel I was eating.

Tonya: I hear how frustrated you are, Steve, and I don't blame you. I know it's hard.

Steve: I won't stop working on the book. In fact, it's one of the only things that seems constructive right now, and helps me calm down. But Tonya, you are always so even-tempered—in fact, your words weren't even that strong in the one passage that I questioned, in Chapter 2 of our book. I am so sorry I ever even complained about that, considering how angry we should all be feeling right now.

Tonya: To me, my words are strong, and they are among many others I have spoken and written for several decades. A lot of people are just waking up. You know, this is a long struggle, and it's been going on for a long time. I have known this. More people are finally aware of it now. Maybe the best we can do is prepare the next generation to continue the work and do a better job of advocating for what's right. We do as much as we can—that's all we can do. And we have to just keep on working on it. We've been protesting and making statements for many years and being active. But I come home and I'm still African American. I still have to live it. I can't leave it.

Steve: Yes, well there's my privilege, being White. I can come home and be angry and not directly feel the impact.

Tonya: Yes. So there are times to turn over the tables. There's a season for everything. And now is a time to be really vocal and more active. But it's not that we haven't been active. We just haven't been heard.

Three days later:

Steve: OK, Tonya, it's time for me to stop my complaining. Every great (as well as the unrecognized) activist has also been an optimist. Without that, change could never have happened. The writing guru Peter Elbow talked about the believing game and the doubting game, in *Writing Without Teachers*. And with students I've always adopted the believing game. So now it's time for me to get back to it. We see positive changes even among ourselves as we are writing this book. And the present moment, with so much demonstration by people of all colors, offers some possibilities to achieve real antiracist policies, even if it won't all be perfect. This book is exactly what I need to be doing, what we need to be doing together.

CHAPTER 5

Promoting Student Voice and Independence

> Our lives begin to end the day we become silent about things that matter.
>
> —Martin Luther King

As Gholdy Muhammad (2020) and Detra Price-Dennis and Yolanda Sealey-Ruiz (2021) explain, criticality and racial literacy are active processes, so helping our students *use* their knowledge and skills to *act* to interrupt inequity is the end goal. How then do we create classroom conditions in which our students can find and claim their own voices, enabling them to engage in acts of interruption inside and outside schools?

- How then do we create classroom conditions in which our students can find and claim their own voices, enabling them to engage in acts of interruption inside and outside schools?

On a literal level, "voice" starts with having or developing the confidence and skills to speak up, in class and elsewhere. The expectation that students participate actively through discussion and collaboration is a staple in America's learning standards, and very quiet students are often misjudged to be less knowledgeable and less able than their more vocal peers—a judgment that needs interruption. What do we do when we recognize that the voices of some students are literally louder than those of others? How do we make sure our quiet students are heard, while respecting cultural practices and individual inclinations that have led them to be silent or nearly silent in our classrooms? How do we ensure that our own classroom practices have not contributed to their silence? Simultaneously, as we seek to amplify the voices of our quiet students, how do we ensure that our more outspoken ones are not silenced in the process?

Claiming one's voice goes beyond the literal act of speaking, however. As documented in Shirley Brice Heath's (1983) groundbreaking study of home and school discourse patterns more than thirty-five years ago, "school language" mirrors that of the dominant culture, a condition that continues to this day. As a result, although the discursive norms of US classrooms may be comfortable and familiar to some students—particularly White students of economic means—these norms may be quite unfamiliar to others. We know that young people enter our classrooms carrying the cultural practices and individual characteristics that their upbringing has provided them. As a result, knowledge of different groups' common cultural practices offers a starting point for helping students navigate the translanguaging they may need for academic success. There's extreme danger, though, in overgeneralizing: learning about common cultural practices can slide quickly into stereotyping, especially in regard to racially and ethnically linked characteristics. We must look at our students as individuals, making note of their unique identities, to support them in claiming their unique voices.

Another danger we face is that despite the grand language of standards documents, what "counts" as speaking up in many if not most US classrooms—and especially in those populated by children of Color— is prescribed in ways that reward compliance over creativity, reproduction over originality, and the search for single "right" answers over consideration of multiple perspectives (McNeil 2000; Love 2020). If we are going to cease our complicity in reinforcing racial, cultural, and linguistic inequities, we must interrupt that status quo. Although pushing against these inequities may not be easy, schools must build the brave spaces (Arao and Clemens 2013) where young people's voices are lifted up and celebrated, so that when our students leave our classrooms, they can take their classroom lessons out into the world to interrupt the inequities there.

In this chapter, we share insights into some of the ways two of our colleagues, Adelfio Garcia and Shonterrius Lawson-Fountain, grew to help their students access their own voices. Although Yolanda Sealey-Ruiz hadn't yet laid out her RLD framework when Adelfio and Shonterrius started their careers, you'll see from their stories that these two educators began—and continue—their work from a place of Critical Love. Both have engaged with each layer of Sealey-Ruiz's framework, to ensure that they and their students are equipped to interrupt injustices around them.

Adelfio is himself a soft-spoken individual, one who, to this day, holds back from sharing his thoughts until they are clearly formed in his mind. As a Chicago Public Schools teacher and principal, Adelfio developed a great facility in identifying the needs of his silent students and providing support for their voices. His reflections on the ways his own school experiences informed his interactions with young people can encourage all of us in our own Archaeology of Self. Shonterrius also reflects on the ways her personal history has informed her teaching. She provides examples of next steps, describing how she built on her knowledge of her students to help them activate their voices in creative and effective forms. We close the chapter with reflections shared by Jaeden Henderson, a young man who has taken the lessons learned under Shonterrius's guidance to raise his voice in his community and beyond.

How Your Experiences Can Sensitize You to Students' Attitudes About Their Voice

Your own history may be similar to or very different from that of your students, but either way, you can use it to think about their needs. Here's how Adelfio reflects on his.

Looking back at my humble beginnings and my educator's life, I certainly can say that as a child I was rarely alone. My siblings and I had many social and academic interactions that were at times both exhausting and rewarding. However, most interactions at school were in "soft voice," almost whispering or making no sound at all.

I grew up in Mexico during the time when all students sat in rows facing the front of the classroom; the teacher lectured and assigned pages to complete. Our job as students was to pay full attention to instruction and complete all the assigned work individually. Elementary, high school, and some college courses there and here in the United States were no different from that type of instruction style to which I was accustomed. We were trained well in silencing our voices, keeping our wonders and comments silent. Few students dared to ask questions, voice their comments, or even raise their hand to ask permission to use the bathroom. I was, like the rest of my classmates, to have little time to interact with my teachers or students in the classroom.

Adelfio's experiences helped attune him to the quiet students in his own Chicago-area classrooms, especially those who speak Spanish as their first language, as he does. His life experiences as a bilingual, bicultural individual who came to the United States as an adult gave him insight to support his Latinx students as they navigated cultural contradictions in their schooling.

It is my experience that Mexican mothers, like mine, expect children to behave in class, be quiet, and limit conversations with other children during class to the minimum. Once I became aware that the upbringing of my Mexican students was the same as mine, I saw it as my professional responsibility to make my Latinx students aware of the agentive power of talk, especially in American classrooms.

Here's how Adelfio explains his process of observing some of his students to better understand how voice worked for them.

Sylvia, Juan, and Maria always sat quietly in the back row of my classroom. They mostly smiled and softly talked (if they talked) while class discussions were in full swing. Most of their gestures and body language indicated listening, agreement, or disagreement with comments their classmates made during instructional discussions in the classroom, but their verbal contributions to daily conversations were very limited, their voices hardly ever heard, and sometimes they whispered even when asked directly to express their thinking in class.

It would be easy to perceive these quiet students to be less capable than students of different cultural and linguistic backgrounds, but with these three and others like them, I often saw that there was a rampant conversation going on inside them. Facial expressions, a lifted eyebrow, a glint in an eye, or a simple smile hinted that something was bubbling in those students' minds.

Planning Culturally Sustaining Strategies to Support Student Voice

Supporting student voice in culturally responsive, culturally sustaining ways may involve multiple approaches, as Adelfio found. He recognized that he needed to develop a repertoire of strategies to capitalize on those subtle signals of engagement and to support his quiet students, particularly his English language learners. One strategy is to provide students with opportunities to rehearse their thinking before being expected to speak to the class, and to ensure that such rehearsal can include conversation in their native language.

Speaking is the most challenging act for English language learners, especially for those who recently arrived to this country at an older age. Speaking requires a person to quickly organize thoughts, make meaningful points, choose the right words, and speak with recognizable pronunciation. In my own life as well as in my teaching experience—and well documented in research—English language learners open up to speaking in English in *social* situations long before they are willing to share their thinking in *academic* English. Because learning standards require students to participate in class discussions, group projects, collaborative work, pair-share activities, and the like, we need to give students time to rehearse their speaking abilities in English. Or, we can encourage them to use their native language when negotiating meaning with class peers.

Early in his career, Adelfio found that he needed to interrupt the dominant instructional practices in the middle school where he taught, for these practices were not serving his bilingual students well and were not making use of their social language skills. "Traditional" cooperative learning as implemented in Adelfio's school called for students to be grouped heterogeneously, with language learners mixed in with native English speakers for the purpose of developing their language proficiency.

At first, I purposely mixed my English language learners in groups where they were supposed to collaborate and participate with native English speakers, as my administrators expected me to do. These efforts were not successful: the linguistic interactions were minimal. Still, many of my English language learners managed to turn in written assignments with great opinions, arguments, and research-based knowledge. To get them to speak, though, I ventured on putting my quiet students in their own groups, where they did begin to collaborate, express their thinking, and voice their comments. I realized that I had to trust myself to interrupt the dominant view of cooperative learning. I had to trust my students—and to communicate that unconditional *confianza*—trust—to them. Finally, these efforts paid off as my quiet students grew the confidence to claim their voice.

Adelfio scaffolded his students' participation in cooperative learning groups by first having them work together with others with similar language backgrounds. This step helped these students build confidence and competence to speak out in a variety of ways, in and out of the classroom. However, ultimately, the goal is for students to be able to work together across language backgrounds; flexibility in the ways we approach cooperative groupings can support students at every stage of development.

Of course, there is often more than one situation to address, and more than one step to take to make space for all voices. Adelfio found that in addition to the challenge of getting his quieter students to begin speaking up, he needed to help his vocal students listen more. In his first-year classroom, Adelfio perceived that some of his students "showed their excitement through their voice level, often calling out responses freely," which went against the norms of the school. Adelfio's initial inference was that these behaviors likely had cultural foundations, so he rejected labeling them as misbehaviors requiring punishment. Still, he admits that he felt ill-equipped to meet the needs of all the different students in his classroom.

Developing Cultural Competence: Yours and Your Students'

Adelfio found himself wrestling with what many refer to as cultural competence—his own and that of his students. Scholar Django Paris (2012) synthesizes Gloria Ladson-Billings's ideas on this concept, articulated in 1994: "By 'cultural competence,' Ladson-Billings was speaking of supporting students in maintaining their community and heritage ways with language and other cultural practices in the process of gaining access to dominant ones" (94). Adelfio's own upbringing had provided him confidence and competence in working with his Latinx students, and his pedagogical training in the United States had provided him with strategies known to be supportive for White students. Nonetheless, he felt poorly prepared to support his Black students, especially those whose discourse patterns did not mirror his experiences or the school's expected norms. He did not yet know enough about the "community and heritage ways" some of his students brought to the classroom to discern their individual needs. Critical Love made him unwilling to characterize students based on pervasive stereotypes, yet he didn't know what to do to support the styles of voice of all the different groups of students in his classroom.

My pedagogical formation had left me unaware and unprepared. My mentor teacher and other teachers in the building noticed my struggles but offered few ideas on how to handle the different levels of outspokenness among my students, and what ideas they did share reflected the traditional (White) cultural view that students who speak "out of turn" should be punished. Their fruitless suggestions and my limited experience prompted me to seek assistance in other places.

An African American student named Ty helped me decide to seek that assistance from his family. Ty was a highly active student whose voice resonated through the entire classroom during classroom discussions. One day I happened to overhear him tell a friend, "Well, I don't play when my momma says, 'Get on it!'" I realized that Ty's momma's phrase was much more direct than anything I'd said to him. My indirect ways of trying to get Ty to lower his voice and focus on work—using phrases like, "You are showing disrespect to students in your group"—were not effective. At this point, I realized that Ty's momma might help me with him. I was the one that needed to build confidence in addressing parents, in understanding the power parents and families bring to education, and in overcoming my own insecurities in reaching out for help.

My first parent/teacher meeting afforded the opportunity to speak with Ty's momma. Her main suggestion was to draw upon the power of speaking to him using tone, words and phrases, and body language to make my expectations direct and explicit. I took a deep breath and asked her about the phrase Ty had said that she uses, and asked whether it might be one I could use, too. I made sure to be clear that in no way was I trying to sound like, act like, or mimic someone I'm not, an African American person. She confirmed and granted me permission to use the phrase as needed. I even put it on a paper strip that I would just show to Ty privately if he was dominating the airspace. Sure enough, that helped Ty to focus. When I began weaving into my teaching and my own Latinx style other phrases, mannerisms, and tones that family members at the parent/teacher meeting had offered to me, I found that all my students began to take turns, allow others to voice their opinions and ideas, and have more democratic discussions during instructional time. Learning from the parents and families whose cultural and racial backgrounds were different from mine expanded my horizons and made it more possible for me to ensure equal airtime to each student in respectful ways, to see that no quiet voice went unheard, no louder voice was silenced, and all students were recognized as the individuals they are.

Critical Humility led Adelfio to reach out to Ty's mother at the parent/teacher meeting. She helped him develop a greater understanding of her child as an individual. Of course, it can be easy for a teacher to overgeneralize groups of students who share the same ethnic or racial characteristics, particularly if that teacher has had little previous experience with those groups. As teachers, writers, and learners, we must avoid making assumptions that don't apply; doing so can be hurtful to our students. Although you may perceive particular cultural patterns, these may or may not reflect the individual students in your classrooms, who have their own ways of being in the world. The strategy Adelfio took with Ty worked for Ty, but would certainly not be effective for every child.

Learning from Student Voice

Turning to another thoughtful teacher's need for cultural competence, we now hear from Shonterrius Lawson-Fountain, who found herself challenged to develop her own knowledge in order to lift up her students' voices. Unlike Adelfio, Shonterrius was hired in a school where the majority of students shared her racial identity. However, she quickly found that this did not guarantee that she and they shared cultural norms and expectations, and at first she prejudged them, as she knew their family life did not match hers.

At the start of my career, I faced my own cultural iceberg. In our household, being excellent everywhere—academic and social settings— were nonnegotiables. We knew who we were as Black girls because of how it was instilled in us. We were proud. We were resilient. We were fierce. So, of course, I took those expectations into my first classroom, not realizing that everyone did not have the same experiences I did growing up. I still expected excellence, but my students and I had to work together to define excellence and work to achieve it—to build their identity and self-image. I quickly learned to be less judgmental in this process. Many of my students, for example, only had access to books with majority White characters who lived experiences to which my students could never relate. I also learned to see students not as little automatons walking in straight lines and doing as they were told but as little people who would one day become adults. I realized, just like an iceberg, the surface of my students is only a small portion of who they really are. There is so much depth to every student.

Like most other first-year teachers, Shonterrius faced many challenges.

My first year of teaching, in the fall of 2005, was also almost my last year. I was 21 years old, very young. Some of the students, middle schoolers, were bigger than me, and they could tell I was afraid of them. But I went back to school and went back to school—every day. I never gave up. All I did was community-building activities for about the first two weeks. I learned early on, I really learned, that I had to make sure that I found out who my students were. That's when I realized the importance of the statement, "you can't teach them if you didn't get to know them."

It is clear that Shonterrius drew upon Critical Humility to consider how she needed to address her own biases in order to serve her students. Engaging in Critical Reflection, Shonterrius realized that she needed to listen carefully to the young people in her charge. Three keys informed her practice, then and to this day:

- Ensuring that her students saw themselves represented in the texts and materials used in her language arts classroom

- Connecting the prescribed curriculum to the textual forms that her students seemed to love best: poetry and music

- Focusing on building relationships, which undergirds everything she does

"Getting Lit with Fountain"—the nickname my students gave to my class—began when I decided to dismantle my own biases and assumptions about teaching urban, underserved students. How can we expect students to envision promise, birth their gifts, talents, and understanding of knowledge, if all they are ever shown are inadequate, stereotypical, baffling images of themselves?

Powerful Literature Is Part of the Equation for Supporting Voice

Promoting student voice involves much more than just inviting students to speak out. Everything we bring into the classroom can help us do the work.

Shonterrius quickly realized that promoting student voice involves much more than just inviting students to speak out. Everything we bring into the classroom can help us do the work. Shonterrius explains how she learned to use literature for this purpose.

I started on this journey embodying the change I wished to see in instructional practices. Coming in as a new teacher, budding with bright ideas and visions of students who thirst for knowledge, I walked into a group of seventh graders and immediately—and mistakenly—thought, after listening to them, that they would despise reading. However, it wasn't that they despised reading itself: these students hungered for stories that gave at least a snapshot, a representation, of their reality. Looking at all of the books in my almost nonexistent classroom library and our school library, I knew I had to introduce my students to authors to whom they could relate. My students did not know Sharon Flake even existed. I can distinctly remember the first time I placed a copy of *The Skin I'm In* (2000) in the hands of my book club students. As we read aloud, they listened on the edge of their seats, almost salivating for more.

In class I ditched the textbook and started novel units beginning with *Esperanza Rising* (Pam Muñoz Ryan, 2000) and *The Cay* (Theodore Taylor, 1969). These books, both of which were written by and feature main characters who are people of Color, told relatable stories. The students were taken aback at the thought of characters who faced identity issues in a world where they were born with strikes against them, just as the students themselves did. It was these first students who helped me realize that before I could ever begin to help them understand language, literacy, or anything academic, I had to address their needs according to Maslow's hierarchy. . . I had to dare to be different and ensure my students felt like they were valued, had a voice, and a place to just be their authentic selves.

I've recently read *Tough Talk, Tough Texts: Teaching English to Change the World*, by Cindy O'Donnell-Allen (2011). She proposes a similar idea that justifies why it is necessary for us as educators to counter oppressive narratives and ensure students have access to culturally relevant, diverse literacy instruction that is representative of their lived experiences. As Jimmy Santiago Baca writes in his foreword to the book,

> Rather than limiting students with cumbersome carbon-copy texts linked to standardized tests, *Tough Talk, Tough Texts* insists that we offer students books that are not simply large, bulky Hallmark cards but that instead challenge them to consider

difficult issues, push them to think deeply and grow. Rather than train the mind to tolerate social poisons such as racism, inequity, sexism, and purposeless violence, why not help students learn to understand them and respond by means of civil, intelligent discourse? It's no use pretending these poisons don't exist. . . We must not only teach tolerance for opposing points of view, but also help students develop the moral and intellectual fortitude to face down and transcend inequity. (O'Donnell-Allen 2011, ix)

Bringing Voice to Life Through Students' Love of Music

Once students are supported and engaged, teachers can help them bring authority to their voice. Teachers have developed many powerful activities to help students do this. We'll focus on using music and poetry, two of the most effective media for activating that power with young people. While Shonterrius realized early on that she needed to add culturally responsive texts to her bookshelves, she also understood that her students love music, so she began integrating music into her classroom routines and curriculum. Drawing upon what she'd read about the calming effects of baroque music, she began playing classical music as her students entered her room each day.

Music was always calming for me, and it was also a safe space. So I played classical music—and the kids hated it at first. But there was one little boy who said, 'I kind of like this!' and he was calm.

Shonterrius shared with the students that she herself loves classical music, but she also wanted the students to be able to share music that they love, too. So she began using song lyrics to teach key analytical and literary skills—and to spark her students' recognition of the power of their voice. She began developing a unit she calls "Music Is Poetry; Give Me the Beat!" This unit begins with analysis of popular songs for their messages, their style, and their connections to the students' lives; it moves the students through inquiry into the narratives conveyed in the songs; and culminates with the students' presenting original works of their own. Over the years, the unit has grown and evolved, but right from the beginning, Shonterrius knew this unit would be one that, as she says, "defines me as a teacher."

The first song we ever analyzed in my seventh-grade class was "One Mic," by Nas (2001). I asked the students what they would do if given a one in a million chance to hold the coveted mic. I realized my students had a lot to say. Yet many of the students were baffled from the beginning because they were not used to hearing music in the class, especially rap. Honestly speaking, they were hesitant because no one had ever asked them to express their thoughts on their community, much less in school. Many of the students wanted to talk about why they had to ride public transportation because they were too far from the school bus routes. The lunchroom menu was a hot topic because they could not understand how the adults were served "good" food—hot meals—while they were eating what they called "cold crap." I too felt their frustration as the teacher. However, at this point they also realized the representations they saw in the media, in music, and even in literature were not true depictions of how they perceived themselves and their community. This group of seventh graders learned how to interject their voice and break down misconceptions in order to seek truth—becoming interrupters—by first acknowledging how their perspectives had been shaped by experiences and the lack of accurate representation of their situations. Then they wrote their own truths.

The goal for the "Music Is Poetry" unit was and is twofold. First, I want students to understand the power of playing with language using figurative language, allusions, connotations, creating movement with poetic elements, and so on. Secondly, I think it is most important for students to understand that they must represent the best version of themselves. It makes me think of the Dr. Seuss quote, "There is no one alive who is youer than you." They do not have to accept or confine their identity to the labels prescribed by society. It is OK for them to own their truth—experiences, culture, dialect, feelings, traditions, etc. As teachers, we can perpetuate oppressive ideals and practices or interrupt them. I choose to interrupt by any means necessary.

Through the close reading of the lyrics and poetry and peeling back the layers of an artist's motivation, the students began to see how an author's stance impacts craft and structure and meaning. Through analyzing the artists' writing, students started to see how their own experiences, cultures, beliefs, and self-perceptions influenced how they navigate the world. They also learned why music is transcendent as they shaped their own voice through authentic writing, rooted in research and coupled with the composition of music and/or poetry.

Steps in the "Music Is Poetry; Give Me the Beat!" Unit

Writing is a bridge to opportunity, and what better way to get students writing authentically than through the use of music, poetry, and art—all of which transcend time. In the classroom, this unit if done in full can take about a month, but through it, the teacher can tackle all of the literacy and argumentative writing standards. The rich authentic student discourse birthed through each activity helps students learn the power of rhetoric and how it assists in conveying meaning, expression, and thought.

Getting Started

Before instruction begins, I look at my standards, the texts I have available, and other resources to align themes and develop my learning targets and create the assignment. I also look at student inventories I have administered to get an idea of their hot topics—trending ideas and concepts they really want to talk and write about. This step is essential because for the final project, students must choose a social justice issue and explode it through their original poem, song, or spoken word presentation.

I begin by stirring students' emotions with a mirrors activity. I give students an opportunity to look in a mirror and I ask them what they see. Based on trust I've built up with the students over time, I ask them some probing questions to help them peel back the layers of their identity. This is done individually either in a secluded corner or just outside the classroom door. While I am doing this, the rest of the students are writing in response to the following prompt: "When your life is over, what will people say about you? What did you value? What contributions did you make in this world? If you cannot provide evidence, what is preventing you from being your true, authentic self?"

Next, we close-read Gil Scott-Heron's "The Revolution Will Not Be Televised." After a first read with students annotating, we watch the filmed version that includes images (https://www.youtube.com/watch?v=BS3QOtbW4m0) and annotate using an observation protocol. This particular poem really gets them thinking about connections to their present situations and leads to rich student discussion about who will speak for them; it is the perfect segue into discussing what social justice is and represents. Next, each student does a brain-dump on a sheet of paper listing everything that is not right with the world from their perspective. We then identify patterns in the themes, issues, and concepts in Scott-Heron's verses and identify personal connections to their lived experiences. Now, we can develop a collaborative list to help them each focus on a global or local issue that affects their reality physically, mentally, or financially.

Building a Playlist

I now share music and poetry from a playlist I have built from classic and contemporary rhythm and blues, country, and pop music, and spoken word pieces. I choose pieces that I predict will spark debate, conversation, introspection, and action. For example, songs like Lalah Hathaway's "Little Ghetto Boy" (2015), India Arie's, "I Am Not My Hair" (2005), Common and Andra Day's "Stand Up for Something" (2017), Common's "Black America Again" (2016), Marvin Gaye's, "Mercy, Mercy Me" (1971), and Tim McGraw's "Humble and Kind" (2016) are usually on my playlist. I intentionally select poems and songs with implicit and explicit messages that may be biased and can be discussed from multiple perspectives by comparing the artists' biographies and motivations, the lyrics, topics, themes, concepts, and ideas.

Every song and poem is annotated during the first read for connections, concepts, and statements students want to challenge and change. We also look at the impact of diction, the author's purpose, tone, and writing style with emphasis on how they use rhetoric. Students analyze and evaluate the pieces to learn the authors' use of rhetorical devices of ethos, logos, and pathos plus poetic elements to spark change. The commentary in the students' annotations guides their collaborative conversations and helps them focus on the potential impact of the issue, concept, or idea portrayed through the stanzas and lyrics. How do the ideas critique or support social norms that isolate, diminish, and make Black and Brown people and others who are not born with privilege—or as my students say, "us!"—invisible?

By the end of week one, we do an activity assessing students' value systems, using a controversial piece of visual art. I display a picture of a family over a casket with dollar amounts for how much everything costs, but with "priceless" written over the casket. Students reflect on why they think the artist chose to depict death this way, and it forces them to think about what is most important to them: What do they really need versus what do they simply want? Is how they define themselves based on what they want people to perceive or a true indication of their character and identity?

By this point in our studies, students are beginning to notice patterns and the impact that repetition, symbols, and description have on how a message is conveyed. They also have begun to narrow in on an idea of what social justice issue they want to highlight, so they are ready to start researching their issue to determine its importance, how it is represented in mainstream media, and what message they want to convey about its impact. I teach specific argumentation moves they will need for an essay which must accompany their original song, poem, or spoken word presentation.

Writing Their Truth

When they have completed some research, students are ready to begin writing their truth. I turn them loose to write their songs. Once they have written their lyrics they have to select a beat. Layering the beats takes about 3–5 days, depending on access to technology and students' ability to play with music and produce. They cannot choose a random beat that sounds good, but must really think about how it couples with their words, mood, and tone. The words are what's most important; the music is the backdrop and cannot detract from the meaning they are trying to convey. Some students use Garage Band and literally create their own tracks, while others opt to use free downloadable beats from YouTube.

The results of original songs and spoken word pieces are authentic artifacts of learning. Students are able to construct defensible, debatable, and nuanced claims about issues that matter to them. They learn how to use effective moves in their arguments, and ultimately realize that they do not have to conform to others' perception of who they are and will become. They write about issues that are related to the change they seek in society, issues of diversity, race, acceptance, and local problems like inadequate housing and access to sidewalks.

Over the years that I have taught this unit, not one student has refused to complete this assignment. It honors their voice and requires them to consider the impact of choice and human behavior on the world. My students are able to experience firsthand the challenges and benefits of using social media and pop culture as a platform for advocacy. Not every student shares openly on the stage, but even the lyrics and poems students have submitted for me to read have been powerful, compelling me to reflect on my role in promoting equity, access, and acceptance.

The Impact of This Work to Support Student Voice

Ultimately, we want our students to carry the work forward, and we know that they can: just think of the student-organized rallies for gun control following the 2018 school shootings in Parkland, Florida; Malala Yousafzai's activism for educational rights; and the many rallies and protests organized by young people in response to the death of George Floyd. Still, as classroom teachers, we are not always privy to what our students do and become after they leave us, so it can be inspiring to hear from a student who has taken the work that he began under Shonterrius's instruction to raise his voice for positive change.

Jaeden Henderson, now seventeen years old, attended a summer writing camp sponsored by the Red Mountain Writing Project, and participated in Shonterrius's camp version of the "Music Is Poetry; Give Me the Beat!" unit. According to Shonterrius, "Jaeden was always a thinker." At the age of fourteen, Jaeden composed and performed for his campmates a blues song he titled "Stealing My Shine." In Jaeden's words:

I have always been a loud person. I knew my loudness was different and so my writing has helped me evolve my loudness into a channel to say what silent people may not ever get to say, all through my songwriting and my music. If someone would have told me, over the years, that what I learned by writing essays and reading poems and stories would have a direct effect on my ability to write my own music, I would have accused them of lying, but while attending the RMWP Music Week Camp, I found my voice in writing through song. I learned how to turn a five-paragraph essay into a four-minute song that had a catchy beat, smooth feeling, and powerful words. I'll never forget how I felt when I wrote the song "Stealing My Shine," which was a song about how people have what I labeled as "User-Spirits," and they will use you for their own benefits. And as a society, this is how most people behave, as well.

Writing is so much more than a pencil and piece of paper. It helped me grow in my voice and my ability to be heard. The fact that I can use a pen and pencil and mic to stand up for myself and be heard is mind-blowing. My writing is more powerful than just my speaking. It is a precious skill to take words and make them have meaning; the music, the beat is an added bonus. Through camp, I gained confidence in writing and understanding how through a pencil, pen, paper, and keyboard I could effect change. I learned to use my songs as a way to campaign. Through songs, I can make you think just as much as if I was standing in front of you giving you a sixty-minute lecture where you have to take notes. In three or four minutes you know what I am saying to you, and you can act on it. Think about it. Change. It is more than just music.

I want to make people think. We all bring unique gifts and talents to the table. There's no competition. In this song, I was really trying to portray that no matter who you are, my gift is not a stepping stool for your fame to be catapulted. We all should work together to give people meaningful and genuine expressions of ourselves. Stealing the shine of others is a hindrance to your shine. When people come to understand this they will be more apt to esteem others better than self.

What I loved was that writing camp was not just so much, "We are going to write an essay today." There was not so much of the normal "Write to this prompt" type of teaching. My learning how to use literary skills and let my voice shine through while telling a concise story has allowed me to have complete ownership in my musical production process.

The thing with writing is you have to be willing to go outside the space that gives you the most comfort because it will push you to go to lengths never even thought of in order to get the point/message across. We all know the struggles that Blacks have received for centuries, as have many other races. As a young Black man, I always have a target on my back. Doesn't matter if I'm one of the most successful entrepreneurs in the world, there is still a target on my back. Society has set it up this way. Our race and the perception of our race are still corrupted as in the days of slavery. We are still suffering from what has happened oh so long ago, but I do believe that a shift is coming. The days are becoming more revealing in showing us that this race battle has no meaning, it never was meant to be a war. We were all created as one, not as Black, White, or anything else. As a writer I have learned how to be unfiltered, to understand that perspective, and to share it in my music; we are one.

Listening to Jaeden's passionate statements, we realize that it is essential for us to draw upon every available resource to empower our students to claim and raise their voices, as Jaeden does. As Adelfio and Shonterrius show, that means paying close attention to every subtle clue students offer of their engagement with our instruction, welcoming the assistance of the students' families in guiding our practice, selecting materials and strategies that resonate with students' lived experiences, and—most important—building trusting relationships with our students so that the courageous work of interrupting inequity can begin in our classrooms.

> As Adelfio and Shonterrius show, that means paying close attention to every subtle clue the students offer of their engagement with the instruction being provided, welcoming the assistance of the students' families in guiding our practice, selecting materials and strategies that resonate with students' lived experiences, and—most important—building trusting relationships with our students so that the courageous work of interrupting inequity can begin in our classrooms.

Steps for a Unit to Raise Student Voice Through Poetry and Music

1. **Activate students' reflection on their values and issues.** Shonterrius uses a "Who do you see in the mirror?" activity, along with asking students to write in response to these questions: "When your life is over, what will people say about you? What did you value? What contributions did you make in this world?"

2. **Analyze lyrics of a pop song on social change.** Engage the students in examining written lyrics as well as viewing a video performance of the selected song. Shonterrius uses "The Revolution Will Not Be Televised," but you may decide to use another that raises issues of race, based on the cultural makeup of your student body.

3. **List issues and concerns in students' lives and their community.** Start by asking the students to create individual lists and then work in pairs or small groups to look for common themes as well as issues they may not have thought of.

4. **Analyze and discuss a collection of song lyrics that present a variety of viewpoints on hot issues.** You may create your own playlist based on the context of your classroom. Engage students in analysis of both written lyrics and performance videos, focusing on rhetorical strategies as well as social and racial issues.

5. **Revisit students' thinking about the issues and their own identities.** Shonterrius uses a visual image of a casket to spark her students' thinking. This leads directly to each student choosing an issue to research individually.

6. **Write about the issue in two genres: song lyrics and an argument essay.** Shonterrius uses this step to teach argumentation strategies.

7. **Set the lyrics to beat rhythms.** These rhythms can be found online, or students may create their own. There will inevitably be students in your classroom who know how to do this and can help others as needed.

8. **Perform the songs.** Obviously, all this work can culminate in a performance event for all students who want to share their work. As Shonterrius has noted, not one of her students has ever failed to complete this project.

Time Out to Talk

Continuing to Learn

Transcribed from a video conversation Dec. 2, 2020

Steve: Tonya, there have been a number of times when I've said something that you corrected me on, or pointed out limitations to my thinking. I would realize the problem right away, and wonder to myself, *How come I didn't get that on my own?*

Tonya: It is a growth process, this equity work.

Steve: For example, in talking about my autobiography, I stated that one of my privileges growing up was that I lived in a neighborhood that was White and safe and that it was a "good" neighborhood. You called me on that because it implied that neighborhoods with people of Color were not good neighborhoods. You recast the idea, pointing out that the actual privilege my family had was that they could *choose* where to live, while there were others who didn't get such choices. When I think about it now, I can see that it's like a little piece of racism still there in my head that I wasn't aware of.

Katy: Yes, Steve, you and I have stated that we still have a lot to learn, and that was one example of what our process sometimes involved.

Steve: As I reflect back on those moments when I would say something and you would stop me: now, you're always gracious and make it easy to take, but I wondered how you felt when I said something like that. Somebody else could take it as a microaggression. I didn't think you felt that way, but you did point out the problem.

Tonya: I didn't feel attacked by your statement. I thought it was from a deficit perspective, but because we have a relationship, I didn't feel as though you meant harm. I thought about it as an opportunity to dialogue. But if a person does not have a relationship with somebody and conversation points seem insensitive, someone could be offended by what was said. Relationships matter in this work. And people enter it at all stages of experience and development. I think we should be open and honest about where we are situated in it and be truthful as we enter into the conversations.

Katy: Another time that you spoke up for a more equitable approach was when we were reviewing the research topics on racial bias in appendix 2. The data is so unrelentingly grim, revealing how racism shows itself in every aspect of educational endeavor. Steve, you had put that material together, and the titles of the sections were all worded negatively. I remember one section was titled something like, "Exclusion from Opportunities for Advanced Learning." Tonya, you proposed changing it, and it became "Ensuring Opportunities for Advanced Learning." And Steve, you then added several pages on the achievements and resilience of people of Color, and you even included an excerpt from the autobiography of our contributor Shonterrius [Lawson-Fountain], paying tribute to the Black teachers and family members of her youth.

Tonya: The challenge is to appreciate resilience amid the difficulties, without suggesting that everything is OK or letting people off the hook about the need for equity.

Steve: It looks like seeing the racial condition clearly and putting it clearly is something I'll be continuing to work on.

CHAPTER 6

Creating Interrupters

> The teacher's role is not merely to help kids fit into an
> unfair system, but rather to give them the skills, the
> knowledge and the dispositions to change the inequity.
>
> —Gloria Ladson-Billings

Talking about race is challenging. It's personal, private, and public all at once. Developing racial literacy and applying it in truth in our lives is hard work. And we are now in a time that has placed race front and center, forcing us to have much-needed, long-overdue conversations about racial equity. Many of us are discussing racial equity and examining our own biases, causing interruption in how we look at and understand race. But let's be clear. The hard work is not pretty, convenient, or short lived. Bettina L. Love (2020) talks about how difficult this work can be: "Understanding how racism works and understanding how White privilege functions within our society does not bring us any closer to justice, but it's only a start" (51).

In this book, we have talked about racial literacy self-awareness for ourselves as teachers, with colleagues, and with students. We've described ways to support students' racial criticality and voice. But as Sealy-Ruiz's RLD framework tells us, we must now bring this work into the action of interrupting inequitable practices. We'll share the stories of two activist teachers, Tina Curry and Vanessa Heller, advancing awareness and interruption with fellow teachers. We'll look at how two students, Deon and Jordyn, model the activism that's possible for young people. And finally we come back to outline some ways we can help students in our classrooms find the same kind of courage and ability shown by Deon and Jordyn to interrupt inequities.

> We are now in a time that has placed race front and center,
> forcing us to have much-needed, long-overdue conversations
> about racial equity.

One-on-One Trust-Building Discussions

One first step to move this work toward active interruption is to act to develop trust with one person at a time. Although we have proposed doing this through shared autobiographies, we want to revisit building trust in school and out-of-school spaces using another very particular strategy.

Maybe you are preparing to bring up some issues around race with fellow teachers in your school or with a community stakeholder. Perhaps there were incidents that reflected bias, or you believe that some students are turned off to learning because they don't see how the lessons relate to their lives. If you were to bring this issue up in a meeting, you are pretty sure (knowing your colleagues and community stakeholders) who among them will be receptive and who will be unwilling to consider any changes, who might grow defensive, and who might try to throw a wrench into your whole effort. How might you prepare the way so that the discussion is more likely to be fruitful, rather than just a butting of heads?

One place to turn to is the world of community organizing. Organizers are often faced with the task of bringing disparate people on board for a particular effort by building wide support for it, winning over the opposition, or at least quieting the doubters. Their favorite tool for this work is what they like to call the "one-on-one relational meeting," a strategy developed years ago by activist and founder of the Industrial Areas Foundation, Saul Alinsky. The approach is to hold a discussion with just one person at a time to learn about their interests and underlying values, and to share your own. It is *not* an occasion to gain support for a particular point of view or project. That can come later, if such a step proves to be appropriate. The object is to begin building some trust by listening to and respecting each other and by having the two of you exchange knowledge about yourselves. This is not about just chatting or becoming best buddies—it's informal, but purposeful.

In other words, before diving into a fraught discussion that might easily crash and burn, you can prepare the ground a bit. Such preparation is not about coddling people. It's about acknowledging that in any exchange there is always more than one level of communication occurring at once: the surface content plus an underlying motive—or a perceived motive. And it's not a bad idea to establish as clean an understanding as possible about that underlying motive. We've seen teachers with wonderful instructional ideas whose motives are questioned by a colleague who charges, "You're just trying to advance your own career and get on the good side of the principal!" That may just be sheer resistance, of course. But it also reveals a lack of trust.

Another reason to hold one-on-ones is that to build trust, it is safer for both parties to engage in challenging conversation when no one else is involved. There's less need to save face when others aren't observing. And even if the discussion goes badly, at least it wasn't witnessed by the whole faculty. Like any tool or strategy, however, one-on-ones may not always be appropriate. Perhaps the resistant person you want to reach simply won't agree to talk or seems to believe that you are being manipulative. Or an incident may have blown up suddenly, leading to an immediate meeting that leaves no time to lay groundwork. Schools, just like other organizations of humans, are complicated places!

If you are going to try one-on-ones, what might the start of one look like? Here are some steps you can take to use this approach:

- Begin by explaining that you want to get to know the person better since the two of you have to work together on various projects at the school.

- Then ask a simple question: "So if you don't mind my asking, I'd like to know how you got into teaching?"

- After your partner has shared some personal history, offer a bit of your own. For example, Steve might say, "In college, I never thought about becoming a teacher. I started off in engineering, got bored, changed to physics, but ultimately it just didn't work for me. I felt kind of lost until a girl I wanted to date told me I'd be a good English teacher, and for some reason that I'll never understand, I believed her. The dating thing never worked out, though . . ."

- Then would come such questions as, "What are some things especially important to you in your teaching?" along with follow-up questions when significant facts or ideas come up.

Often it's surprising how much you may actually have in common with the other person, along with your contrasts and different, fascinating backgrounds. About a half hour is plenty for the whole thing.

Whom might you invite to join in a one-on-one? It's good to start with a trusted friend, if possible, to try out the process. People are always surprised at how much they learn that they didn't actually know about their partner, even when they've worked together for years. A practice conversation with a friend can also enable you to anticipate objections when a real issue does come up with someone else. Holding a one-on-one with the school curmudgeon might seem daunting, and it might take some explanation as to why you want to talk. Still, this might prove to be the most productive discussion of all. You're not likely to become best friends, but some respect and understanding might make a difference.

Creating a Teacher Equity Group at Your School

To make the world better for our students, we have to find ways to have open and honest conversations about creating spaces and curriculums that allow students to develop as learners. This can be a challenge, but it's important to work through the frustrations and resistance to reach some success, as Tina Curry found in her effort to develop a similar space for teachers in a Chicago school. She was determined to get coworkers to create more equitable learning processes for their students. This is Tina's narrative about her journey to create challenging but needed learning spaces for teachers so that they could develop and share their own racial literacy. There are lessons in her experience that we can all learn from.

Tina's Journey to Create Equity Spaces

After three years as a teacher and instructional coach at a Chicago school, I began grappling with questions about how my life's work made a difference. I reviewed the attendance, discipline, and grade data for the school as a whole. Data were eye opening. I found that Black boys were being suspended and disciplined at disproportionately higher rates than their Latinx peers; and special needs students, who were mostly Black students and who were already at an academic disadvantage, were experiencing even more gaps in learning. Permeating throughout the building was a quiet but accepted, deeply rooted belief on the part of White teachers expecting Black students to fail. Now, this is not something that the White teachers would say overtly, but when White teachers made comments that reflected acceptance of poor grades and lacked energy to discuss next steps for success with Black children, then the underlying belief was clear. I was devastated by all of the complacency and the lackadaisical attitudes when it came to addressing Black scholars' achievement.

I was determined to do my part to transform education in my school for the next generation of Black students. That is when I got the idea to start an equity book club for teachers. In early March 2019, I sent the following message to teachers:

Become the change we need to see in the world. Take the first step in having impact by joining our equity book club, which will examine books that share ideas on how to transform learning for our students. Our goal is to bring together people who love to read and who want to build a community focused on discovering, discussing, and celebrating the non-fiction literature aimed at reshaping education. To help us on the journey to being transformed by what we teach and how we teach, we will be reading progressive texts.

We started the book club with just seven teachers, and in two weeks that number went down to five due to attrition such as school duties and time commitments. We met every other Wednesday after school to discuss our first text. This book club created space for us to engage in developmental experiences where we reflected and tried new approaches. In essence we were trying to pay back an educational debt. Our work was no longer just about the theoretical framework but how we were using it. We came to the revelation that when we messed up, we harmed students' learning and development as scholars. We all began to change the way we did school so that students benefited more. The group remained small but committed.

Tina started the book club looking at articles and books. Seemingly, this was a logical way to begin a professional development series, but as we shall see, engaging in racial equity work in groups can require a different approach, one that is unlike the traditional adult learning space that usually begins with reading and examining texts first.

> I then knew that I could not be afraid to continue this work, and so I grew bold in my actions. Instead of starting with the reading of the text, I asked my colleagues to engage in "heart" work first.

Hoping the next school year would yield more positive results, I disappointedly learned that the inequities and disparities were just as apparent and just as visible the following year. I was enraged by the oppression in my school and all the places it was hiding. I decided to have another book club, this time with Cornelius Minor's book, *We Got This: Equity, Access, and the Quest to Be Who Our Students Need Us to Be.* I had the opportunity to serve as a conference panelist to discuss a keynote address given by Minor. When I told him about the work I was implementing and the resistance I was up against, he said to me, "To kill a revolution, all you have to do is keep the participants too afraid to innovate." I was inspired by him to do and to act more boldly. I then knew that I could not be afraid to continue this work. Instead of starting with the reading of the text, I asked my colleagues to engage in "heart" work first. I designed a schoolwide equity initiative, involving every teacher team and any team whose work directly or indirectly impacted the life of young people, challenging each team to create an equity goal around this question: "What is one aspect of our school that you would like to address so that our students can be included, represented, and heard, which will lead to their success?" I wrote every teacher the following message:

My goal is to encourage everyone in our school to begin and continue conversations about race and equity and to affirm the inherent value of all people. In full transparency, my role here is not to make sure you do not get upset, or to make you comfortable or even to make you feel safe. My role as the facilitator is to create an open and non-adversarial environment that sets the conditions for you to engage in brave and courageous conversations about race and equity. You may be someone who has been wanting to discuss race and equity but you don't know how. Please join me on Wednesdays from 9:15 am to 10:00 am [a common planning time set up when instruction was online during the pandemic] for race and equity conversations grounded in empathy.

Tina had started her initial-year book club focusing on the texts first, but she did not experience the gains that she hoped she would see for students. As the facilitator, she realized that she needed to refocus her efforts. The reality is that equity effort requires self-work, something that traditional, content-oriented professional development does not always involve. So she continued her efforts, encouraging teachers to participate in courageous conversations around race and equity, as we described in Chapter 2. As you will see, this "new space" still did not appeal to everyone initially.

The letter was received well by the teachers of Color. When many of the White teachers, however, did not participate, I wrote to my colleagues again.

I want to caution you that my message may ruffle a few feathers, but it is rooted in my deep hurt and disappointment around the lack of participation from some colleagues in our weekly race and equity conversations. To my White colleagues, I genuinely miss your participation in the race and equity conversations. During this challenging time, taking on the challenge of equity work may be too much to handle. But I do know that we are stronger when we work together in all things. Would you please consider joining us for these conversations? Your perspective and your insights are needed. Our united school needs you.

After this direct appeal to my White colleagues, several White teachers joined the equity group. Having participation from all races was important to this antiracism conversation because I realized that White teachers could continue to have conversations in places that

I was not invited. If change was ever going to happen in this school, all races needed to participate. I started this time, and had the most success when I allowed myself to be vulnerable, sharing my own story about being a Black woman who experienced racism in Chicago and how real and personal it was for me. I talked about the feelings of rejection and dismissal I had often experienced when talking with White colleagues because my stories were different and therefore received as unimportant. We then followed my narrative with an article or book chapter to discuss, weaving in pieces of our own experiences as teachers and individuals. The conversations became more powerful and life altering when White colleagues united with colleagues of Color and learned to hold space for disagreement and even disharmony. I don't want you to think these conversations were without anger, blame, rejection, and pain. We continued to have difficult conversations filled with tensions. But when members of the group started to share pieces of their own narratives, slowly and deliberately, walls of trust started to build. It was then in the group that the culture and climate started to shift.

Tina's new approach to conducting equity discussions opened space for colleagues to hear, feel, share, and learn. Her vulnerability opened opportunities for others to share their own experiences with and thoughts about race. Setting the norms and boundaries, creating a brave space, and participating as the facilitator are important in establishing an effective equity circle. One of the participants wrote Tina:

This work is influencing me because I have started having more conversations around race outside of this meeting. I feel more confident in confronting someone when I hear them say something about race that I don't agree with—including my family members and loved ones. I've learned that my silence is harmful. I've also started reading more works on my own.

Tina's experience has shown that several elements are needed for an equity circle to work. If you are creating your own group, Tina explains how she learned that you will need to find particular strengths within yourself:

1. Be resilient. Bring your whole self to the conversation each week to foster an inclusive environment where multiple perspectives are welcomed. We must respect all backgrounds and value differ-

ent opinions, beliefs, and experience that we each bring to this work. And even when we hear something that we do not agree with, we still return to the group to learn.

2. Be courageous. We confront approaches that have been absent from our practice. We take risks to do the self-work that is necessary for change. We walk the walk and become more comfortable with the uncomfortable. We give ourselves permission to courageously lead and participate in these conversations. We disagree without being disagreeable and challenge thoughts and ideas without demonizing each other.

3. Be committed despite the inevitable struggle. Everyone's journey will not be the same, but everyone committed to the work must take the equity journey if we have any hope of more favorable outcomes for our students. We must face the reality that we have a society and people that are "fraught with racial bias and privilege" [Gorski 2019], and we all must self-excavate.

4. Be a learner, because it matters. It is critical for us to teach, share, and connect with the intent of being transparent and accountable. We realize that we do not stand alone in this work. In *We Got This: Equity, Access, and the Quest to Be Who Our Students Need Us to Be*, Cornelius Minor [2019] says there are three stages in the business of equity work: self-work, systemic awareness, and active change making. Because this work has to be addressed with a sense of urgency, it can be tempting to go straight to the active change making. To get to the point where every child has a chance to access an equitable education, though, we must spend some time learning and digging, which is what race and equity conversations are all about.

5. Be relentless in your pursuit of your own critical awareness and activity. Equity work is challenging because it is difficult, disruptive, uncomfortable, and requires people to change their behavior and practices. It necessitates a paradigm shift. Moreover, when it is done effectively, it forces people to face unsettling truths about themselves, their assumptions, their experiences, their interactions, their privilege, and the inequities, disparities, obstacles, and disadvantages they intentionally or unintentionally create for others.

6. Be willing to give up something. Perhaps the most difficult aspect of equity work for those who benefit from racial inequity is the realization that they will have to give up some privileges they hold dear in order to empower those who have been victimized by systemic and institutional inequalities to receive the equity they have been previously denied. This may include friendships

with those who do not share an antiracist stance. It may be a
curriculum decision that needs to be rejected.

Ultimately, you must have the openness and integrity to admit that there are racial
inequities in your school that you have the power to end right now. We challenge you
to identify one to begin to address, create a plan to tackle the inequity, put your plan
into action, and create the deliberate, thoughtful space needed to engage in honest,
respectful, productive, and constructive conversations to make the change.

Interrupting for Equity Beyond Your School

Changes can take place from within our schools, but we can also lead and participate
in changes outside our own sites. One way to do this within the education world is to
bring together teachers from a variety of schools. Vanessa Heller created a new space
to make a difference, reaching a wider audience beyond the school walls and providing
for more teacher diversity. Her experience shows us what interruption can look like,
with both successes and missteps.

Vanessa teaches at an affluent school in southern California where the student body
is nearly 60 percent White, 25 percent Asian American, 10 percent Latinx, and 1 percent
Black. Vanessa realized, though, that her privileged students and colleagues needed to
be a part of the important equity conversations just as much as students and teachers
at other places. She wanted to talk about teaching interruption for racial equity with
her creative-minded, progressive colleagues without the formality and restrictions of
school. As she was working on contributing to this book, she wanted to effect change,
so she developed the Teaching for Equity (TfE) group. She begins her story by describing how she entered this work.

Vanessa's Discoveries as a Facilitator of Teachers for Equity

Through self-study, my work with this book's authors, and the events
of 2020, including the murders of Ahmaud Arbery, Breonna Taylor, and
George Floyd, the shooting of Jacob Blake, the focus on #BlackLives-
Matter, and the political climate in response to the unrest, there was
no way I could remain complacent. But I also had to consider what
I could do to take action that was within my realm of influence, so
that I could possibly make an impact to interrupt for equity. I began
compiling resources [see Appendix 3] gathered from my own self-
study, social justice social media groups, and other contributions from

colleagues. I also decided to gather friends together in an informal group to talk about the issues to see if we could develop antiracist practices and perhaps even influence some policy.

I talked with a few friends I thought might be interested in this, and they wanted to talk, to have difficult conversations. Before I knew it, I had more than twenty folks, in state and out of state, who joined the group. I am working to increase the diversity of the group—right now the group consists primarily of White teachers, but there are also a few members of Color, as well as White teachers with children of Color and spouses of Color.

So my starting this Teaching for Equity group does raise the question: What right does a White middle-aged suburbanite woman—a Becky, Karen, or Amy—have in starting a group like this? But my reasoning then, as it is now, is that as a White female teacher, people like me make up the majority of the teaching workforce (about 80%). Particularly, it is essential when I teach in my White suburban area because we must do this work of interrupting with all teachers and all students. I work with educators who want to do better by all kids and need a place to start or continue their equity work. If I can provide that forum by simply offering a time, place, and agenda, I was and am willing to get it done.

We are working on creating a safe space for each other and for our students. As a facilitator of Teaching for Equity (TfE), I am keenly aware that I am just beginning to have these conversations with myself. As a privileged White woman leading an equity group to combat antiracist practices and policies, I must seek to understand my own place in this system. My challenge is to work on facilitating and listening. I am impulsive and direct, bossy by nature, and the more nervous I get, the more I talk. Silence is noise when I am uncomfortable. My tendencies can hinder progress at times, and if this group is going to succeed, I will need to learn to listen more, speak less, and hear silence as "thinking" time. I have some self-excavating—as Sealey-Ruiz calls it, Archaeology of Self—work that I still have to do, now more than ever.

Our First Attempt

Let me tell you about the first meeting. I kept telling everyone that this was a safe space, everyone should share openly, and all ideas were welcome, but I did not ever get quiet for others to share. And then I had us engage in an activity that I was sure was a great idea. I asked the teachers to talk about our families.

Many teachers I know start the school year with getting-to-know-you activities that ask students to write or draw about themselves (family, hobbies, favorite things, etc.). In *Being the Change* by Sara Ahmed [2018] and in *This Book Is Anti-Racist* by Tiffany M. Jewell [2020], both authors describe identity activities along similar lines, but have children add characteristics of gender, ability, race, ethnicity, etc. My idea was to model an in-class activity with TfE: we were all adults and had buy-in just by being in the group, so what could possibly go wrong with this activity?

I listed categories members could write about (see figure 6.1), passed out paper, pencil, etc. I was excited because this activity had been successful with students. Mind you, half the teachers in the group were in my backyard in person and half were on a virtual platform. I had a hard time fielding questions from online members and couldn't really see their facial expressions, talk to everyone, write, etc. I also had everyone create an identity web, but I did not do my own because I was the administrator.

So I missed the facial expression of frustration and hurt of a web-based participant who is White. I missed the comment that she wrote about her adopted son who is Black. And while several of the White participants talked about generational family bonds dating way back, she said her son doesn't know his ancestry because he is adopted. In addition, because he is Black, he was most likely historically separated from his ancestors by the slave trade in America. Then she further shared her frustration that her son is asked to do ancestry projects year after year in school, an emotionally draining event each time. Rightfully, she had tears in her eyes, and at the same time, she was angry.

Figure 6.1. Vanessa's Identity Chart

I felt like a failure. My "inclusive" activity had hurt my friend. I alienated a participant, literally doing the opposite of what I intended to do for an "inclusive" assignment. I tried to recover by addressing the issue with the group, trying to keep it academic, asking follow-up questions, such as, "What do we do when kids don't know some information?" and "I have had adopted students before—some knew they were adopted and some didn't—but I had not asked kids to add such personal information as their race and religion. What do we do when students don't have access to certain information about themselves?" These questions were partially well received by the teachers in the group, for which I was thankful, but the truth is, the group lost its energy as a result of my shortsighted exercise and the truthful, passionate response of my friend.

Vanessa's Lessons Learned

I learned a lot from leading this group. The first lesson learned from our first TfE meeting was that even with the best of intentions, we can unintentionally inflict pain on our friends, colleagues, and students. I overlooked the possibility that my actions could be hurtful—not thinking from the perspective of a student or adult who may not have the requested knowledge and if she did, she may not want to revisit it publicly. This lesson hurt my heart, but it is just one example of how much I have to learn. We were able to talk about this idea in the group and in the subsequent meeting. I also called my friend to apologize, and we had a really good talk about her frustrations on behalf of her son.

The second lesson I learned from the very first meeting was that even though I assured everyone that we had a safe space to share openly, I myself wasn't willing to share openly. A few of us shared what we wrote on our identity webs, and then I spoke up—but deliberately left out information about my own family because I still have unresolved issues with the way I grew up. Even though I am an adult sharing with other adults whom I feel comfortable with, I did not feel comfortable with myself enough to share. What a hypocrite. This must be how some of our students feel, also, when we ask them to share and be open with the entire class. For the next meeting, I opened up the session with our need to examine unintentional harm, and the need to model transparency and openness. I did indeed share about my unconventional childhood, briefly but honestly. I was relieved with the support I received from colleagues.

Third, I learned that silence is peace, not loud, unbearable noise. When we have uncomfortable conversations, it is perfectly fine to let the silence surround us as we process. Eventually, someone will speak and share, and if not, we can move on to another thought or point. When we talk, we feel like we are in control—control of the conversation, steering the direction of thoughts; thus the converse: when we do not talk or others do not contribute, we feel out of control. As a result, to gain control, we begin to speak—using fillers and sharing stories that take the emphasis away from the important point on the table. Sometimes it is quite essential to be quietly out of control.

Fourth, I continue to learn as I facilitate this group. When I started contributing to this book, I was on the first virtual meeting with my fellow authors—talking, sharing, giving my perspective, letting everyone know the work that I was doing with students in my classes. I was then confronted by a Black teacher-writer who essentially challenged me to listen and not overlook the contributions of others—namely his—to the conversation. He stated that he felt that I had dismissed his point; maybe I'd overlooked it or did not consider it to be as important as my own. It is possible I was thinking about what I was going to say rather than listening to what he was saying. But that was an eye-opening moment for me. Had I really done to him all of the things I asked my students not to do? Had I just brushed past a colleague's contribution, a Black male, which silenced him for part of the conversation?

Thank goodness he confronted me and challenged me to evaluate my stance and how I walk this space, although it was a tough pill to swallow. And I continue to struggle with my privilege and Whiteness. I imagine I still overlook others, but I am more intentional about my own purposeful interruption practices—more thoughtful, more reflective, and less focused on me and my privilege as a colleague and teacher, and more willing to learn about my own biases.

Mistakes while doing this work will happen. But as a White person, I realize that I cannot hold on to my privilege if I am going to move the fight for equity forward. I have to give up airspace. I have to give up power. I have to listen and let others be experts. I have to be uncomfortable, and I am working every day to be better at this work, and it's tough. So, we have a lot to learn, but I have hope and a willingness to confront my own privilege. Our students require us to be the teachers they need.

Vanessa continues to grow in this work, as we all do, and creates opportunities to expand her thinking, despite the challenges. Bettina L. Love (2020) tells us just how difficult this is:

Being an abolitionist means you are ready to lose something, you are ready to let go of your privilege, you are ready to be in solidarity with dark people by recognizing your Whiteness in dark spaces, recognizing how it can take up space if unchecked, using your Whiteness in White spaces to advocate for and with dark people. And you understand that your White privilege allows you to take risks that dark people cannot take in the fight for educational justice. (159)

What We Can Learn from Two Students Interrupting for Equity

As teachers, we must do this racial literacy development work for ourselves first, next for our students, and then take it out into our educational context to interrupt for change. But often our young people don't wait for us. They go ahead and take action themselves, and it is we teachers who must learn from them and play catch-up. We offer two stories to inspire us and show the possibilities for our own and students' interruptions for equity, knowing that there are more and more such stories emerging across this country.

Deon, a middle school student who is an interrupter in his community, shows us what we can encourage and support with our students—and in fact what we can often learn from them. Deon developed the group Solutions to promote conflict resolution among his peers. Deon became interested in making a difference in the lives of others at an early age, before he attended school. When he watched Marvel movies and super-heroes, he saw that they were doing good and fighting evil. They were bringing hope to people and filling them with joy. Deon asked himself, "Can I do that one day? Can I bring that sort of peace, hope, and joy that the Marvel heroes brought?" He didn't know how to do it, though, because he didn't have the knowledge or foundation at that time. As he grew older, that fire that he had to make a difference, the passion to do more, continued to emerge within him.

As an elementary-age child, he would sit with his mom, Javonti, watching the news, and they would discuss the many stories featured on television locally. He would ask questions about the various acts of violence, such as shooting and fighting, that would occur. His mom would reply, "People get angry. They don't know how to talk and work things out. Instead, they let their emotions get the best of them, and eventually it leads to something that gets out of control." Deon listened to her talk about the need for conflict resolution to keep problems from becoming larger issues. Looking back, Deon states, "My mom molded it in me. She molded me to know how to resolve conflicts and the process of doing it. She was my teacher. She put it out there for me to find it and she widened my viewpoint." Deon and his mom discussed the grave need for conflict resolution

in the community. Deon's mom died when he was in fifth grade, but Deon continues to shape their shared dream into reality. His grandmother continues to nurture Deon's desire to see change in the world through conflict resolution.

Deon has always taken every opportunity to learn more about community activism. At a town hall meeting, Deon, then a middle school student, had the perfect opportunity to ignite what his mom had taught him. Sitting in a large crowd of adults, Deon stood boldly and asked the city mayor a poignant question: "We have a lot of violence in our city. What can kids do to help with conflict resolution in today's society in our city?" Everybody clapped loudly for Deon in support of his desire to make a difference. The mayor soon afterward named him the "Kid Mayor for the Day," giving Deon an opportunity to shadow the mayor and gain insight into the workings of the city. This inspired Deon to hold on to his desire to create a program to resolve conflict. Deon says, "I knew I had to create a team to help with this because it always takes a team to make change. I didn't want to get people that I didn't know and didn't trust. I wanted people who could come up with solutions and stay to the end—ones that were loyal to the cause."

Acting on this need, Deon formed a team of nine friends from his church to help him with his vision. They formed a bond together to work and make change. Deon explained that they met and conducted their own relationship-building exercises at the beginning of the process to get to know each other as a team. Drawing on a variety of free sources they researched on the internet, they created a four-week summer training series for themselves to learn how to resolve conflict, which focused on four core values: communication, decision-making, peer management, and community love. With the help of parental advisors, the training was successful for the ten middle schoolers.

During the school year, the group, Solutions, conducts conflict resolution workshops for preteens and teens. The team writes skits based on real issues they have seen or experienced in school, at home, or in the community. Depending on the needs of the group they are teaching, the team enacts a relevant, rehearsed skit that includes all the core values. One skit that is popular, for example, demonstrates a conflict at a locker between two teens who spread gossip. After the students act out the scene, the leaders stop and ask the attendees how they would handle that situation. The leaders provide space for all types of responses, even some that may not work. Sometimes the group starts with peers who are more combative, but after giving these students a chance to talk through it, they invite the participants to come up with more plausible solutions that are better than being physical and combative. Deon is used to initial "bad solutions," so he continues to ask, "What is your additional input so we can create a better solution?" He has a few steps that he likes to give to teens.

- First we take deep breaths.

- Then draw something for five minutes.

- We take a drink of water and collect our thoughts.

- We think about what's going to happen, we imagine, if we do the wrong thing, what will the consequences be?

- We think about what if we choose another option, what will the consequences be?

- We think about another option, too, if we need it, and consider the consequences.

- Then we think about the best solution so we won't get hurt and nobody else will.

To further his work, Deon presented his Solutions work to a foundation board this year, and the team won $500 to continue making a difference with teens in the city.

Deon's teachers did not know initially that he possessed this passion or the skills to create, maintain, develop, and manage a group of teens who desired to make a difference in the community. It was his community who supported him in this work—from public speaking and speech writing to organizational management and financial literacy. Deon offers advice to teachers for kids like him:

Don't put off your students. Listen and communicate with them on a basic level so you won't tear them down. Keep their hope alive. Give them experience of what will happen in life. Listen to their views and try to help them with it. Talk with them on a basic level. Help them become encouraged and motivated. Stand behind them. Don't just let family and friends be the only ones behind them. Push them forward to be the best person that they can be because of the simple fact that "your generation didn't do it, so let us, this next generation, accomplish it."

So ask yourself: What talents and passions exist in your students that have not shown themselves in your classroom? And if a young person like Deon can do this, what actions can you, as a competent adult, take to interrupt conditions that undermine students' learning? Hidden within your students may be interests you do not even know about that could be helpful to you, as the teacher, and to the students, just like Deon. There is really no reason that teachers cannot step up to create and support interrupter practices with students. And if the kids can get out to act for equity in the community, we can too.

Jordyn's Social Justice Journey

Nurturing students' racial literacy requires commitment and tenacity on the part of both students and their teachers. Students who are interrupters can experience resistance, too, so it's essential for us as teachers to support them in the activism that we are encouraging. Jordyn, a seventeen-year-old activist, is another young person endeavoring on her own. She is an example we can learn from, both for our own teaching and as an example of courageous interruption in the face of adults' resistance. She tells her story about growing up in the South and the role that history has played in her own awareness and development. You will see that Jordyn has strong convictions and is grounded in her community.

My parents have always taught me that it is important to understand my history. They've always taught me that I am a little Black girl coming from Birmingham, Alabama, the birthplace of the Civil Rights Movement, so therefore it is imperative for me to understand all the work that young people have done in my backyard. It really instilled in me a love of Birmingham history and civil rights history. I've marched on the Edmund Pettus Bridge in Selma, Alabama, several times during the anniversaries of Bloody Sunday.

I also participated in the Children's Crusade in 2016 and sat in the 16th Street Baptist Church with Martin Luther King III and the Foot Soldiers of the Civil Rights Movement. Also, because Thomas Blanton died recently, I remember going to the Alabama Parole Board to hand-deliver letters to fight against his release, because he was one of the KKK members who bombed the 16th Street Baptist Church and killed the four little girls. It was clear to me that children have historically played an active role in the Civil Rights Movement. The children's work, their dedication and their energy, really did shape the culture of

that time period, and I feel that it's important for me and other like-minded teens to get engaged and to shape the culture in our communities so that racial bias and inequities are eliminated from our society.

When I personally experienced racial bias and inequity at my school, my history motivated me to actively participate in what I want people to become. I came to my school in about eighth grade, but going to a predominantly White institution, I'm one of few African Americans in my grade and in the whole school. With that said, I have to take on the burden of sometimes being the spokesperson for the African American community, which is hard. It's a huge responsibility at such a young age to be able to articulate everything so clearly and poetically to children, and sometimes to have to educate your teachers. There's been a lot of different moments where I've had to teach my teachers. I've had to teach students concepts of microaggressions, derogatory slang that they've used to me and other students, and just really having to imperatively school them on terms and their racial bias at such a young age. Now it feels normal, but when I was in eighth grade it was definitely tiring to have to continue to explain that to them.

Last year, as a junior, culturally it was challenging for me at my school. Academically, I did fine, but it was hard to have to keep up that energy and explain to everyone what was going on about diverse issues. With that said, I tried to bring to my school a diversity and inclusion initiative last year, because I thought it was needed. As a member of the student governing body, I had the opportunity to create a major event that would impact my school. Naturally, I created an initiative to help my teachers, administrators, and classmates because many students at my school faced issues around racial bias and racism. The administration did not necessarily want to implement the diversity initiative last year because there were a lot of changes going on in the school, but now because of the current events that are going on in our society with racial bias and inequity, the administration is more interested. That was definitely a struggle for me last year—being heard and feeling that I was represented as a Black female and having to be that person to represent my race at my school. That was hard.

When Jordyn talks about the toll it takes on her to have to explain bias, Blackness, and antiracism to adults and other classmates, she raises important questions about how we as teachers need to stand behind her. One way to address this so we can better support students like Jordyn is for educators to get to know the students, through authentic conversations and student bios, as described in Chapter 3.

Last year, I gave my presentation to my then head of school, supported by two teachers who were helping to chair my initiative. I've always been very active in student government and my community. Last year, even though I couldn't get a diversity initiative going, I was the Commissioner of Citizenship. In this role, I was in charge of a big community service day where you bring students to different community service organizations and they volunteer or you do community service on site at the school. It was a huge day. I planned it over the months and over the summer with my peers who helped me plan. We worked hard getting speakers and booking organizations for our students to go work with. When I was finished giving my presentation, my head of school had a couple of questions to ask me afterwards. He asked me questions to do with the different initiatives I was bringing. We finished with that, but then he asked me, "Why are all the speakers that you bring in African American? Why are they Black?" That was a hard-hitting question because I was bringing in great speakers to the school. I brought in an outstanding news anchor, I brought the district attorney, just to name a few. I worked hard to organize a quality program. In the past, I never felt represented through other speakers in previous years, so I thought it would be an eye-opening opportunity to bring in really wonderful African Americans who were doing powerful things in our community. For him to ask me why all of the speakers were Black broke my heart. He never would have said anything if all the speakers were White. I think now he understands what he said was wrong and how he said it was wrong, but it truly did break my heart in that moment. But several conversations took place for him to understand why his comments were biased and racist.

I created a digital platform, Shape the Culture, and hosted a rally in 2020, devoted to young people fighting inequity, inequality, and racism. It was called "Be the Change Unity Rally." I thought it was important for young people to be able to voice their concerns when it came to racism in our country right now, and that's what we did. We brought in many youth speakers to speak about what they thought was going on and what they wanted to see change, and I think it inspired many students and young people and their parents, as well as teachers who came, to realize that they are the voices of change. I thought that it went really well.

My favorite quote of all time is from Barack Obama. He says, "Change will not come if we wait for some other person or some other time. We are the ones we were waiting for. We are the change that we seek." We had a Civil Rights foot soldier who came and spoke to us at the rally. It's up to us and our generation to be the change. She talked about when she was a Foot Soldier and how they were able to make a difference. When we were at the Unity Rally, many of my friends who talked to me afterwards understood that we look at the kids who marched in the streets of Birmingham in the 1960s, and they were courageous and changed our country at such a pivotal time, but right now we're at another pivotal time with racism and inequity and injustice, and we must act on it. It's our time to come forward and fight and change. The biggest lesson was, we come from Birmingham, we take that pride, but it's now up to us to "take the torch" and to come up to the stage and fight.

My "Shape the Culture" digital platform features all the uplifting and wonderful initiatives that young people across the country are implementing. To name a few, I have an interview coming out with a filmmaker from Atlanta who's seventeen. He's doing amazing things there. Also, I am meeting with a Birmingham native who's about to graduate from Howard and has his own lifestyle brand. I am talking with another young woman who lives in Columbus, Georgia, who just started her own nonprofit on teens' voter advocacy and understanding the importance of their vote. What's next is making sure that the platform evolves into a movement that must be able to change things through public policy. We started this with the rally to fight racism, inequity, and inequality, but obviously, there's more work to do, and it continues. To continue this work, I have advice for teachers that I hope will help them help us.

Jordyn's Advice for Teachers Who Are Creating Interrupters

I think that academics are critically important. I think the challenge has to do with connecting students to the learning. We've read literature like Ta-Nehisi Coates, and it was important for us to be able to have dialogue with each other to tackle issues such as racism, inequity, and injustice. It's hard reading those types of books by yourself, especially if you don't go through the struggle. I think about dealing with racism through what I hear students say in class. It's important for students to have that conversation with students who go to the same school as them and may not look like them, because they're not going to go through the same struggles. They're not always going to understand, but it's important for them to be able to see what the students go through and hear what they have to go through as well. I think conversations, dialogue, seeing how other students feel represented is important. Also, we must continue pushing our teachers to have those hard conversations. I've had to do it at my school with my diversity and inclusion initiative. Pressing my teachers, emailing them constantly, just to make sure that the work continues, that this issue gets talked about and that it doesn't get pushed under the rug.

Teachers and Students as Active Interrupters

What can we begin now to understand about teachers becoming interrupters? The teachers who are creating opportunities for colleagues to grow and develop are important parts of the effort to move this work forward in the school and in informal communities. Both Tina and Vanessa have continued to engage coworkers, despite their first efforts, which were not as successful as they had wanted. There is no way that we will get this right all the time. That is why building relationships is so important: when you fail, a group that understands you will give you more grace as you develop into your own interrupter.

Meanwhile, we must not leave students like Deon and Jordyn to forge ahead without us. By creating their respective groups, Solutions and Shape the Culture, the teens are interrupting practices and bringing their voices to spaces that can make a difference. In both instances, though, we see that teachers and schools were not that involved in support of the students' work. The school did not know about Deon's group, and in Jordyn's case, the administration did not initially appreciate her contribution. We need to not only support them but learn from them and be inspired by their example to take action ourselves.

As teachers and students learn to be interrupters in schools and in out-of-school spaces, it is important that their two worlds come together. As you learn more about yourself and your own biases, and as you grow, you will learn more about the genius of your students. You can then see the possibilities in what students bring to school—their gifts, passions, talents, and wants for themselves. The two worlds must not exist each in isolation. We can integrate interruption practices into the curriculum so that our students understand how the world and school intersect. We are preparing them not just for personal success but for immediate connection to who they are in the world and to their agency in the fight for equity. Jordyn leaves us with this advice to teachers.

Teach the whole person. Public service and civic engagement really lay the true foundation for future service. Find ways to get your students out of the classroom, and do something that connects your lesson. Do something that [allows you and your students] to give back to the community together.

Jordyn has issued a challenge. We have worked, talked, and written with teachers who have created new spaces, uncomfortable spaces, for change to take place. Tina, Christopher, Shonterrius, Brandon, Adelfio, Vanessa, and we three authors don't always get it right, but we seek to create new equity spaces that allow us and others to challenge our thinking and actions. This work is messy. And we have seen students work for change—Jaeden, Deon, and Jordyn, who represent so many more bold students we teach—who know that interrupting is the only way to create change. We can support the students in our classrooms to do exactly the kind of active, out-in-the-world interruption of racial inequity that these students have carried out. Deon and Jordyn drew encouragement from their parents, and we must serve the same role for the young people in our care.

By nature, people cling to their habits and their power. Only when we interrupt those practices will change occur, but mind you, it will not be easy. Racial inequities abound around us, and until we are willing to see them, confront them, and continue to interrupt them, we must face the reality that we are a part of the problem and that we are contributing to unfair treatment of Black and Brown peoples. Jordyn's challenge is for all of us to do something greater than ourselves, bigger than our usual disconnected practices, more concerted and impactful, for racial equity.

Back to the Classroom: Creating Your Own Teacher Interruption Plans

In this chapter, we've seen teachers and students who have learned to interrupt beyond the classroom, using their voices to make a difference. Still, Deon and Jordyn call on us to bring interruption practices into our classrooms through writing, reading, discussing, and creating our own projects in school. Our first responsibility, after all, is to our own students, helping them develop not only self-awareness, criticality, and voice but readiness to act and interrupt for equity. That is the goal in Yolanda Sealy-Ruiz's RLD framework.

The work of creating and implementing plans to teach students to interrupt practices begins with first understanding some of the common challenges that we face when thinking about standing up for something meaningful. Once we recognize that there are practices that need interrupting, the second step is to think about actions that need to be taken. We suggest starting with five "interruption alerts" that you can introduce to students to use in their own reading, writing, discussing, and thinking when racial issues emerge.

Interruption Alerts

- **A Time to Report and Speak Up.** A moment in reading or discussion when you notice that the character or the person involved should call attention to inequity.

- **Letting It Go.** Noticing when something is problematic and deciding whether the character or person should have let the issue remain unattended or not.

- **When Silence Is Compliance.** In a reading or discussion, noticing when the character or the person does not participate or avoids the issue.

- **Giving Voice to Others.** Seeking opportunities to ensure that multiple perspectives are heard or noticing when other perspectives are missing.

- **Part of the Problem or Part of the Solution.** Considering the role that the person or character is playing in the text or situation.

Activities to Enact One or More of These Interruption Alerts

1. **Talk Back to the Literature.** All year long, as the class reads books and articles, students can use sticky notes that indicate one of the five interruption alerts. When there is a place in a book or an article that the student believes the character or person should enact one of the interruption alerts, they can mark it in the book. This will allow students to think about how people make decisions to interrupt practices and why these actions occur. For example, in *The Watsons Go to Birmingham*, racial tension exists in several places in the text. Joetta, the youngest Watson, receives a White doll from a White neighbor, which is confusing to the young Black girl who does not look like the toy she received. A student may read that part of the chapter and use the When Silence Is Compliance interruption alert to indicate that the mother's quiet acceptance of the gift was complying with a social norm that was harmful to her daughter. But another student may decide to use the Letting It Go interruption alert, citing that the time period in which the author was writing did not allow for Black and Brown persons to reject a gift from a White person without retribution. Both of these interruption alerts could lead to insightful discussion.

2. **Write to the Interruption Alert.** Teachers can use the interruption phrases as writing prompts to ask students to reflect on their

own decision-making processes or those of others. The products of such writing could connect with instruction in specific writing genres such as memoir and biography, with social-emotional learning lessons, or with study of nonfiction articles across the content areas. Building on the use of sticky notes and class discussion, teachers can ask students to critically analyze specific issues presented in the content being studied, and to share their analyses in writing. For example, in a science class that is studying cell mutation, the teacher might share an article about Henrietta Lacks and the unsolicited contributions her life has provided to understanding the biology of cancer. The students can select an interruption alert to write an argument essay or speech about what should have been done or what can still be done today for a more equitable action.

3. **Practice and Role Play.** You can encourage students to apply the interruption alerts in their daily lives. Role-playing scenarios in which students encounter bias, microaggressions, or inequities can help them develop strategies for speaking up in constructive ways. Practicing the language to use when encountering a difficult, hurtful situation can provide young people—and adults!—the courage to speak in ways that can be heard.

4. **Create to Act.** Teachers can support projects in any subject that will enable students to use one or more of the interruption alerts to think more critically about a stance and then create a plan of action. For example, in history, students may study the origin of Thanksgiving. A few students may choose the interruption stem "Giving Voice to Others" as a way to hear the perspective of Native Americans and create a blog with different perspectives about the holiday. Or students could plan an alternative celebration to take place in the classroom or the whole school. Or the class could create alternative celebratory yard signs, such as ones that honor Indigenous people. Or students could seek to connect with Indigenous people in their community or state and learn their views—that is, actually listening to the voice of others.

Overcoming Resistance—A Final Thought

Some teachers worry that their activities to support students' inequity interruption efforts might meet with resistance from administrators or parents who do not recognize the value in this work. We suggest that the best way to deal with this is to involve fellow educators, students, families, and even community members to create equity initiatives and policies, so that no one is acting alone or without support. Educator and author Sonja Cherry-Paul (2021) describes how she took the next step and developed a racial equity committee at her school to create proposals and policies for the school and district to build real commitment to equity. That way, there's clear justification and support for lessons that help students learn how to become active and constructive interrupters, thus supporting the broader growth of equity throughout the school and community.

> The question now is this: What will you do differently, more intentionally, more actively, more boldly, to interrupt racial inequity practices systematically on a daily basis?

The question now is this: What will you do differently, more intentionally, more actively, more boldly, to interrupt racial inequity practices systematically on a daily basis? Sure, we can talk to like-minded friends and teach an additional piece of Black literature or mention an additional scientist of Color, but that will not make the change that will interrupt practices. Actually, by substituting surface change for real systemic change, such actions will make matters worse and maintain the status quo. No more business as usual. In literature classes, for instance, instead of just telling students about a Black author, we need to work with them to read the work, discuss the context, critically analyze the privileges of the time and who had them, and challenge students to evaluate how those privileges impacted the writing at the time. Then take it to another level—ask whether those privileges still exist for some people but not for others. Then ask the question: So what are we going to do about this? And then work with your students to create and implement an interruption plan. Work with other teachers to design and enact interruption plans. We challenge you to be bold. You may never have been asked before to do racial equity work in your entire life. Our hope is that we have given you ideas and examples of how you can move to everyday action to challenge systemic racial inequities. Every day is an opportunity to interrupt.

EPILOGUE

The collective writing of this book has taken us on a profound journey. In true National Writing Project style, we have spent over two years together, walking the talk of the ideas and processes and suggestions described here. We started with writing our own autobiographies, and we have considered the ways that race has played a role in our lives and shaped our identities, engaged in meaningful one-on-one conversations with each other, reflected on our practices, researched to gather more information, and reflected some more. We have talked and talked and talked, and we have written and written and written. There has been much pain around us. But working together has helped us get through the pain, take care of one another, take action for students now and for the future, and find moments of joy. The work of interruption is bigger and more import-ant than any one of us.

All of us who have contributed to this book hope that something in our words helps you become an interrupter. We've had our share of doubts and struggles as we've worked to set our thoughts to paper and live the ideals we espouse. We challenge each of you as we challenge ourselves to ask the hard questions, engage in the hard conver-sations, and embrace the hard work that can lead to greater equity. May the words of the late civil rights leader Congressman John Lewis provide all of us with the courage and perseverance to keep going, to interrupt inequities when we see them, and to get into some "good trouble."

> Do not get lost in a sea of despair. Be hopeful, be optimistic. Our struggle is not the struggle of a day, a week, a month, or a year, it is the struggle of a lifetime. Never, ever be afraid to make some noise and get in good trouble, necessary trouble.
>
> —Rep. John Lewis, 1940–2020, in a Tweet from June 27, 2018

APPENDIX 1

Equity Warriors Past and Present

Although many of you know well the work of the writers and thinkers who advocated and worked for racial equity before us, we still need to remind ourselves of them and their work. Little that we have to say is new. The ideas, analyses, stories, arguments, and bravery of our forerunners and contemporaries are the building blocks for the ideas we share now.

How far back shall we reach? Gholdy Muhammad (2020) traces the educational programs of the nineteenth-century Black literary societies across the country, whose leaders emphasized "cognition (reading and writing skills) as well as social and cultural practices (*learning about identity and equity*)" [emphasis ours] (32). Much as we try, we know that we cannot name everyone who has influenced us, and for that we apologize. Nonetheless, we have been influenced by the equity efforts championed by such key figures as the following.

Trailblazers in the Profession

- Gloria Anzaldúa (1942–2004), noted scholar and author of *Borderlands/LaFrontera: The New Mestiza*, was a guiding force in the Chicano and Chicana movement.

- Mary McLeod Bethune (1875–1955) founded a school for girls that became Bethune Cookman College, was active in leading the National Association of Colored Women, and served multiple US presidents.

- Charlotte Brooks (1918–1998) served as president of the National Council of Teachers of English in 1977 and edited *Tapping Potential: English and Language Arts for the Black Learner*, 1985.

- Anna Julia Cooper (1858–1964) advocated for the equal education of women and for a focus on college preparation for all African American students, along with her broader civil rights activism.

- Vivian I. Davis (19?? –2017) served as president of the National Council of Teachers of English Commission on College Composition and Communication and was the winner of NCTE's Distinguished Service award in 1994.

- W.E.B. Du Bois (1868–1963) was a giant in advancing thought around race. His concept of "double-consciousness" has been invaluable for understanding the educational needs of students of Color. However, his elitism about education and leadership is not something we endorse.

- Marjorie Farmer (1922–2012) served as president of the National Council of Teachers of English in 1978, received an NCTE Distinguished Service award in 1981, and promoted the involvement of teachers of Color in the organization. She cowrote a progressive textbook on composition.

- Paulo Freire (1921–1997), noted author of *Pedagogy of the Oppressed*, articulated the core philosophy of students creating their own curriculum relevant to their condition and their needs.

- Asa Hilliard (1933–2007), scholar of African cultures and education, analyzed Black students' "achievement gap" as an educational service gap, in *Young, Gifted and Black*.

- Vivian Paley (1929–2019) explored multiculturalism in the classroom, examining her experience as a White teacher of children of Color, and ways she could best support and promote a racially diverse classroom.

- Inez Beverly Prosser (1895–1934) studied the psychology of Black students in integrated schools. Her life and brilliance were unfortunately cut short by an auto accident.

- Darwin Turner (1931–1991), poet, literary critic of African American literature, and longtime chair of the University of Iowa's Afro-American Studies Department, argued for the need to include a Black critical view of American literature.

- Carter Woodson (1875–1950), historian of American Black experience, is best known for his demand for better and more enabling education for children of Color, in *The Mis-Education of the Negro*.

Contemporary Advocates Who Continue to Teach Us

- Sara K. Ahmed is the author of *Being the Change: Lessons and Strategies to Teach Social Comprehension* and coauthor of *Upstanders: How to Engage Middle School Hearts and Minds with Inquiry.* She provides professional development internationally, and has served on the Teacher Leadership Team for Facing History and Ourselves.

- Michael W. Apple is a critical scholar, activist, and curriculum theorist whose work examines intersections between education, culture, and power. His *Ideology and Curriculum* and *Official Knowledge: Democratic Education in a Conservative Age* have each been cited as being among the most influential books on education.

- April Baker-Bell is the award-winning author of *Linguistic Justice: Black Language, Literacy, Identity, and Pedagogy*, a text that proposes a pedagogical approach to counter the marginalization of Black English—and the young people who speak it—in the classroom.

- Arnetha Ball founded an early education center for students from diverse backgrounds. Her research focuses on preparation of teachers to make a difference in the educational lives of poor, underachieving, and historically marginalized students. She served as a president of the American Educational Research Association.

- Cherry Banks, known for her expertise in multicultural education and the importance of teacher self-knowledge, cowrote many books on multicultural education with James Banks.

- James Banks, often called the father of multicultural education, wrote *An Introduction to Multicultural Education* and many related works on the topic.

- Eurydice Bauer is the John E. Swearingen Chair of Education and Professor in the Department of Instruction and Teacher Education at the University of South Carolina. Bauer's research examines the sociocultural contexts in which literacy takes place and the various roles of the participants, combining ethnography of communication with ethnographic case study research.

- Rudine Sims Bishop, author of *Shadow and Substance: Afro-American Experience in Contemporary Children's Fiction*, and considered the mother of multicultural education, promoted literature as a tool for children's self-affirmation. She coined the concept of "windows, mirrors, and sliding doors."

- Maneka Brooks focuses her work on improving literacy instruction to meet the needs of bilingual and bidialectical young people.

- Ayanna Brown researches discussions of race, contemporary African American studies, and discourse analysis. Dr. Brown was the 2013–2014 Chair of the National Council of Teachers of English Assembly for Research.

- Gerald Campano is associate professor and chair of the Reading/ Writing/Literacy Division at University of Pennsylvania's Graduate School of Education. He has received the David H. Russell Award for Distinguished Research in the Teaching of English from the National Council of Teachers of English for his book *Immigrant Students and Literacy: Reading, Writing, and Remembering*.

- Sonja Cherry-Paul is Director of Diversity and Equity at the Teachers College Reading and Writing Project, and is cofounder of the Institute for Racial Equity in Literacy. She is the coauthor of four books, including *Critical Literacy: Unlocking Contemporary Fiction*.

- Jamal Cooks has been a leader in the National Council of Teachers of English. He currently serves as dean of language arts at Chabot College in Hayward, California, where, among other things, he administers the RISE Program, which supports formerly incarcerated students attending Chabot College.

- Lisa Delpit is the author of *Other People's Children: Cultural Conflict in the Classroom* and other writings that stress serving the needs of students of Color and undoing the power dynamics of White supremacy.

- Tricia Ebarvia is a cofounder of #DisruptTexts and serves on the advisory board of the Pennsylvania Writing and Literature Project. As a high school teacher and department chair, she champions antibias approaches to instruction.

- Elyse Eidman-Aadahl is the executive director of the National Writing Project, where her leadership has brought together educators from diverse contexts and backgrounds to think about and develop equitable literacy practices in today's digital world.

- Christopher Emdin's work includes a focus on youth empowerment, particularly in relation to science education. He is the author of *Urban Science Education for the Hip-Hop Generation* and *For White Folks Who Teach in the Hood . . . and the Rest of Y'all, Too.*

- Patricia Enciso is professor of teaching and learning administration in the College of Education and Human Ecology at The Ohio State University. She is author of numerous articles including "Borders, Home, Spirituality, and Language: Sociopolitical Themes in Latino/a Children's Literature 1990–2015" in *The Américas Award Honoring Latino/a Children's and Young Adult Literature of the Américas.*

- Michelle Fine has focused her research on social justice issues and inequity in the education system. Among many books she has written and edited, *Off White: Essays on Race, Power and Resistance* analyzes White privilege and how it is embedded in American society.

- Tracey Flores chairs the Latinx Caucus of the National Council of Teachers of English and is founding cochair of the Commission on Family and Community Literacies of English Language Arts Teacher Educators.

- Antero Garcia researches the ways that technology and gaming influence young people's literacy learning and identity development. *Doing Youth Participatory Action Research: Transforming Inquiry with Researchers, Educators, and Students*, cowritten with Nicole Mirra and Ernest Morrell, is just one of his publications focusing on the power of young people's voices.

- Geneva Gay is the author of *Culturally Responsive Teaching* and is an advocate for multicultural education.

- Lorena Escoto Germán chairs the Committee Against Racism and Bias in the Teaching of English for the National Council of Teachers of English and is a cofounder of #DisruptTexts and of Multicultural Classroom Consulting.

- Kris Gutiérrez researches and has published widely on the educational needs of students from nondominant communities and English language learners. She served as president of the American Educational Research Association in 2011.

- Marcelle Haddix focuses her work on the schooling experiences of students of Color and the importance of centering Blackness in educational practices and spaces. Her book *Cultivating Racial and Linguistic Diversity in Literacy Teacher Education: Teachers Like Me*, was awarded the 2018 Outstanding Book Award from the American Association of Colleges for Teacher Education.

- Zaretta Hammond is the author of *Culturally Responsive Teaching and the Brain*. A former English teacher, she continues to center literacy, equity, and classroom practice in her research and activism.

- Shaun Harper's research focuses primarily on racial and gender equity and inclusion in educational, corporate, social, and organizational contexts. He also studies Black and Latino male student success in high schools and in higher education, college student engagement, and intercollegiate athletics, and has served as the 2020 president of the American Educational Research Association.

- Violet Harris is the editor of *Teaching Multicultural Literature in Grades K–8* and the author of many articles addressing multicultural education and the needs of students of Color.

- Shirley Brice Heath, researcher and author of the classic study, *Ways with Words*, revealed differences in language use across various cultures that led to success or mismatches for students in school.

- bell hooks, writer, educator, activist, has written more than thirty books, including the famed *Ain't I a Woman? Black Women and Feminism, Teaching to Transgress: Education as the Practice of Freedom,* and *Teaching Community: A Pedagogy of Hope.* She promotes an education that advocates for freedom but also community building.

- Betina Hsieh focuses much of her work on the ways that teachers' personal identities impact their professional identities, particularly among Asian American educators.

- Matthew Kay is the author of *Not Light, but Fire: How to Lead Meaningful Race Conversations in the Classroom* and a founding teacher at Philadelphia's Science Leadership Academy.

- Ibram X. Kendi is the National Book Award–winning author of the books *Stamped from the Beginning: The Definitive History of Racist Ideas in America* and *How to Be an Antiracist*, among others. A leading scholar of antiracism, Kendi was named one of *TIME* magazine's 100 most influential people in the world in 2020.

- Valerie Kinloch's scholarship on literacy, language, culture, and community engagement of youth and adults has produced numerous books and articles on race and literacy, including the critically acclaimed *Harlem on Our Minds: Place, Race, and the Literacies of Urban Youth*. She is 2021–2022 president of the National Council of Teachers of English.

- Carmen Kynard focuses her work on race, AfroDigital/African American cultures and languages, Black feminisms, and schools as political sites. She is the author of many publications on race, gender, language, and critical digital literacies, and currently serves as editor of the *Journal of Rhetoric, Politics, & Culture*.

- Gloria Ladson-Billings, known for groundbreaking work on Culturally Relevant Pedagogy and critical race theory, is the author of the widely read *The Dreamkeepers: Successful Teachers of African American Children*.

- Carol Lee, retired professor of learning studies and African American studies, founded four African-centered schools and cowrote three books on education, including *The Role of Culture in Academic Literacies: Conducting Our Blooming in the Midst of the Whirlwind*.

- Curtis Linton is noted as an authority on educational equity and racism. With Glenn Singleton, he cowrote *Courageous Conversations About Race*. He is the CEO of Curious School.

- Robert Livingston is the author of *The Conversation: How Seeking and Speaking the Truth About Racism Can Radically Transform Individuals and Organizations*. His research focuses on equity and social justice.

- Bettina L. Love is the founder of the Abolitionist Teaching Network and author of the books *We Want to Do More Than Survive: Abolitionist Teaching and the Pursuit of Educational Freedom* and *Hip Hop's Li'l Sistas Speak: Negotiating Hip Hop Identities and Politics in the New South*.

- Alfredo Luján is the 2020–2021 president of the National Council of Teachers of English. Alfredo is dean of students and teacher of English and study skills at Monte del Sol Charter School in Santa Fe, New Mexico.

- Danny Martinez is 2023 Chair of the National Council of Teachers of English Assembly for Research, and winner of the NCTE Janet Emig Award for Exemplary Scholarship.

- Richard Milner is 2022 president of the American Educational Research Association, has created an opportunity gap framework, and has written several books, including *Rac(e)ing to Class: Confronting Poverty and Race in Schools and Classrooms*.

- Cornelius Minor focuses his work on connecting schools and communities around equitable, sustainable practices. He is the author of *We Got This: Equity, Access, and the Quest to Be Who Our Students Need Us to Be*; with his wife, Kass Minor, he has established a movement known as the Minor Collective.

- Nicole Mirra's book *Educating for Empathy: Literacy Learning and Civic Engagement* exemplifies her quest to bring together literacy education and youth civic action in order to develop more equitable and just schools and societies.

- Luis Moll introduced the concept of "funds of knowledge" that students bring to the classroom, and conducts research on the connections among culture, psychology, and education for Latinx children in the United States.

- Renee Moreno has served in leadership roles on committees and caucuses of the National Council of Teachers of English. She is a mentor for the esteemed NCTE Cultivating New Voices (CNV) program. She is currently working on a book project with artist and professor Carlos Frésquez entitled *They Want Us to March but We Want to Paint: Chicano Artists in Denver (1968–1972)* on the Chicano arts movement in the city.

- Ernest Morrell is a past president of the National Council of Teachers of English and now serves as the director of NCTE's James R. Squire Office for Policy Research in the English Language Arts. His scholarship in the fields of literacy, critical pedagogy, postcolonial studies, and popular culture and education across the African Diaspora has earned international recognition.

- Gholdy Muhammad, a former middle school language arts, reading, and social studies teacher, is the author of *Cultivating Genius: An Equity Framework for Culturally and Historically Responsive Literacy*. She is professor of education at the University of Illinois Chicago.

- Sonia Nieto, in *Affirming Diversity: The Sociopolitical Context of Multicultural Education* (and many other books), has critiqued the failure of American education to equitably serve students of Color and advanced multicultural approaches as a means to address this need.

- Pedro Noguera is a sociologist, writer, and editor of numerous books on racial equity in education. He has focused on the challenges for students of Color, especially Black males, and the ways in which schools are influenced by social and economic conditions.

- Cindy O'Donnell-Allen teaches courses in literacy pedagogy and research at Colorado State University, where she directs the CSU Writing Project and the English Education program. Her current work focuses on the ways in which youth and educators can use critical multiliteracies as instruments for identity development, meaning construction, and social action in order to achieve a more just and peaceful world.

- Ijeoma Oluo is a self-described "writer, speaker and internet yeller." The author of *So You Want to Talk About Race* and *Mediocre: The Dangerous Legacy of White Male America*, she was named to the 2020 TIME100 Next list.

- Django Paris is the James A. and Cherry A. Banks Professor of Multicultural Education at the University of Washington. His work with H. Samy Alim on culturally sustaining pedagogies has moved the conversation forward around student-centered teaching.

- Kim Parker is a cofounder of #DisruptTexts and the editor of the *Journal of Adolescent & Adult Literacy*'s column "Students and Teachers: Inquiring Together." Through her work, she seeks to support the success of young people of Color and help them and others see their brilliance and promise.

- Theresa Perry is professor of Africana studies and education at Simmons College. She is coauthor of *Young, Gifted and Black*, and coeditor of *The Real Ebonics Debate*, among other books; is faculty director of the Simmons College/Beacon Press Race, Education and Democracy Lecture and Book Series; and is coeditor of *The Real Ebonics Debate*.

- Detra Price-Dennis is the founding director of #JustLit and focuses her scholarship on ways to identify and amplify equity-oriented pedagogies in K–8 classrooms. Her recent book, with Yolanda Sealey-Ruiz, is *Advancing Racial Literacies in Teacher Education: Activism for Equity in Digital Spaces*.

- Timothy San Pedro, at The Ohio State University, has authored *Protecting the Promise: Indigenous Education Between Mothers and Their Children*. His scholarship focuses on the link between motivation, engagement, and identity construction to curricula and pedagogical practices that relate to Indigenous histories, perspectives, and literacies.

- Yolanda Sealey-Ruiz developed the Racial Literacy Development framework to help educational communities increase their understanding in the service of enacting more equitable school experiences for Black and Latinx students.

- Glenn Singleton founded the Pacific Educational Group, a consulting firm whose focus is on forging racial equity. There he developed a protocol called "Courageous Conversation" to help facilitate interracial dialogue. He is coauthor of *Courageous Conversations About Race*.

- Allison Skerrett is Louise Spence Griffeth Fellow for Excellence and Director of the Urban Teacher Program at the University of Texas, Austin.

- Geneva Smitherman is the founder of the Michigan State University African-American and African Studies Department and author of many books celebrating the beauty of Black English.

- Claude Steele is known for work on stereotype threat and its application to the academic performance of students of Color, described in *Whistling Vivaldi: How Stereotypes Affect Us and What We Can Do* and in *Young, Gifted and Black*.

- Alfred Tatum, Provost and Executive Vice President for Academic Affairs, Metropolitan State University of Denver, is a leading scholar of African American boys' literacy development and an activist for antiracist instruction in English language arts.

- Beverly Tatum is the author of the classic *Why Are All the Black Kids Sitting Together in the Cafeteria? And Other Conversations About Race*, as well as *Assimilation Blues: Black Families in a White Community* and *Can We Talk About Race? And Other Conversations in an Era of School Resegregation*. She also served as president of Spelman College.

- Ebony Thomas is associate professor in the Division of Literacy, Culture, and International Education at the University of Pennsylvania Graduate School of Education and author of *The Dark Fantastic: Race and the Imagination from Harry Potter to the Hunger Games*.

- Julia Torres is a cofounder of #DisruptTexts. As a teacher and activist committed to education as a practice of freedom, her practice is grounded in the work of empowering teachers and students to use language arts education to fuel resistance and positive social transformation.

- Joe Truss is a former middle school principal and creator of the Culturally Responsive Leadership program that provides training in antiracist school leadership.

APPENDIX 2

The Prevalence of Racism in
American Education

The inquiry activities outlined in Chapter 4 and the student voice strategies in Chapter 5 involve students not just expressing opinions or beliefs but also crafting well-reasoned and well-informed arguments. This calls on students (and indeed all of us as educators and citizens) to learn about both the deep structural inequities that press on people of Color and the strengths they draw on. Here we outline a sampling of the data and reports that show both of these two sides of the racial condition as it manifests in the world of education. These materials serve as a starting place for engaging students and colleagues in the work of becoming interrupters described throughout this book.

Because people of Color deal with racism, we must first emphasize the courage and resilience, the strengths and joys, the rich cultures and creativity that have been engendered in spite of the forces of White supremacy. Nothing could be more illustrative than teacher-writer Shonterrius Lawson-Fountain's memories of the culture and learning passed on to her by her beloved Black teachers.

I have the fondest memories of the strong-minded, classy Black women who dared not apologize for their sheer intellect, beauty, and self-expression, who disrupted education in positive ways through their methods and particularly through the texts we read. Our [text-book] readings were always paired with counter texts. I remember reading about slavery in my history book and Mrs. Watkins telling us to rewrite our history text with truth. We researched counter narratives. . . We had to learn to appreciate the contributions African Americans made to society, whether they were highlighted as phenomenal feats or revolutionary acts. From Mrs. Levy I learned to never accept absolutes, but explore deeper and alternative solutions to problems. Mrs. Anderson and Mrs. Bates helped us see the world beyond Black and White and learn to appreciate every perfect imperfection in our character, as it was in our individual uniqueness that we harnessed our strengths. Mrs. James taught us to justify our claims with evidence, and never to apologize for the truth. Mrs. Betts taught us to project our voice, and position ourselves with confidence in writing and speaking. . . She truly honored our voices and made an effort to understand who we were as little intellectuals. She would say, "You are not students, you are legends in the making." Other helpful teachers were Ms. Stringer, Ms. Reynolds, Ms. Boykins, Ms. Washington, Ms. Gaitor, Ms. McClure, and Ms. Dabney. But above all has been the influence and support from my parents, Samuel and Janice Lawson.

Tracing the centuries of Black and Brown cultures that lie behind Shonterrius's experience demands not just a book but entire libraries of books. One resource is the John Hope Franklin Series in African American History and Culture (forty-three books published by the University of North Carolina Press). Princeton African American Studies professor Imani Perry recommends *Creating Black Americans: African American History and Its Meanings, 1619 to the Present* by Nell Irvin Painter (2006) as "a compelling narrative history." To learn about the Black literary societies that flourished across America in the nineteenth century as one striking example of the growth of Black culture, read Gholdy Muhammad's *Cultivating Genius* (2020). For exploring the extensive literature on Latinx cultures in the United States, an in-depth resource locator is available: Michigan State University's (n.d.) *MSU Libraries Research Guide*. For Indigenous American cultures, the online guide "Native American Resources: Sites for Online Research" (Danowitz and Videon 2010) catalogues a wide range of resources.

Public and professional achievement is part of Black and Brown people's resiliency as well, though we must remember that while the rise of such leaders can be strongly symbolic and offers role models and voices for change, their achievements don't in themselves alter the broader structural racism affecting the lives of people of Color.

How Racism Rolls in the World of Education

The problems outlined here are exceedingly troubling, but facing up to them should not be seen as a rejection of American society. Rather, understanding them is a caring expression of Critical Love; such understanding provides the knowledge needed to bring the country closer to its ideals. As we study these materials, we need to remember that the racist conditions they describe also enable the continued privileges, whether acknowledged or not, that benefit White people yet reduce the quality of our entire society.

BIAS IN DISCIPLINE

Black boys in school are 23 percent overrepresented in the total number of students suspended (US Government Accountability Office 2018). In schools that permit corporal punishment, Black boys are twice as likely as White boys to be struck by an educator (16 percent vs. 9 percent) (Gershoff and Font 2016; Southern Poverty Law Center, 2019). Considering how punishment, suspension, and expulsion can disrupt a child's education and resulting future, it's no surprise that this pattern leads to Black males' greater involvement in the school-to-prison pipeline (Bacher-Hicks, Billings, and Deming 2019; US Commission on Civil Rights 2019; Sparks and Klein 2018).

In schools that use corporal punishment, Black girls are three times as likely to be hit as White girls (6 percent vs. 2 percent) (Gershoff and Font 2016). Nationally, Black girls are suspended more than five times as often White girls, and Black girls are 2.7 times more likely to be referred to the juvenile justice system than their White peers (Georgetown Law 2019). The issues for the girls, however, are especially connected with adultification, as described in a recent study:

> Adults view Black girls as less innocent and more adult-like than their white peers, devoid of any individualized context. In other words, adultification bias is not an evaluation of maturity based on observation of an individual girl's behavior, but instead is a presumption—a typology applied generally to Black girls. (Blake and Epstein 2019, 1)

Black women and girls, however, have plenty of suggestions for solutions to this problem:

> When asked for suggestions to help overcome adultification bias against black girls, focus group participants said they hoped that the awareness raised by the Center's [Georgetown Law Center on Poverty and Inequality] research would lead to meaningful action to decrease this bias, and emphasized that targeted training for teachers and other authority figures would be most effective in helping them overcome their biases.

> "I feel like, as teenagers, we still need to be protected . . . we still should be cared for and taught wrong or right. And it doesn't matter if we're like black or whatever," said one study participant (age group 13–17). (Georgetown Law 2019)

Discipline bias is especially harsh for students of Color who also have disabilities. Nationally, at least 73 percent of youth with emotional disabilities who drop out of school are arrested within five years of leaving. As reported in 2014 and 2015, Black students constituted 15 percent of all students with disabilities, but were 40 percent of people with disabilities in correctional facilities (US Commission on Civil Rights 2019; US Government Accountability Office 2018).

This bias extends even to the youngest schoolchildren. While Blacks make up just 18 percent of children in preschool, they represent nearly half of preschool children suspended (Gilliam, Maupin, Reyes, Accavitti, and Shic 2016). Of course, suspensions result in children's missing school, so they advance to successive grades lacking skills they were previously denied the opportunity to learn (Anderson 2015).

In case someone wants to argue that students of Color cause more trouble, research shows that Black students do not misbehave more than White students (Skiba and Williams 2014). Rather, the perceptions themselves are biased. As the NAACP Legal

Defense and Educational Fund (2017) noted, "Bias can lead service providers, as well as police officers, to treat identical individuals differently depending upon the perceived race, religion, or ethnicity of the individual" (11). In fact, school resource officers in urban schools see students as out of control and a threat, whereas officers in Whiter, more affluent schools seek to protect students from outside dangers (Curran et al. 2019).

An Example of Positive Change

Restorative justice as an approach to discipline has grown in school districts around the country, and has been especially supported in California. As one report summarizes,

> [Restorative justice] focuses less on punishment and more on righting wrongs and building healthy relationships within the school. It usually involves convening circles in classrooms or other school milieus that focus either on establishing bonds among students or addressing conflicts. (Washburn 2019)

The Restorative Justice program in the Oakland, California, school district has been in place for over a decade and has served as a model followed by numerous districts across the country. Schools across Oakland have reduced the suspension rate of African American students by over 5.2 percent, surpassing the average 3.4 percent decrease that would be necessary to eliminate disproportionality in a brief number of years (Chan 2018). And overall, between the 2011–12 and 2017–18 school years, suspensions dropped in Oakland Unified School District by 48 percent, according to state data (Washburn 2019).

Implementation of restorative justice can be challenging because it is expensive and requires a cultural shift in focus from punishment to student learning for both teachers and students. Oakland's Restorative Justice staff includes a director, four coordinators, and about two dozen restorative justice facilitators in various schools. Facing budget cuts in 2019, the district board at first voted to eliminate the program. It was so popular, however, that community advocacy forced a reversal, and the City of Oakland even committed over $600,000 to fund it for the year.

ENSURING OPPORTUNITIES FOR ADVANCED LEARNING

Starting with preschool, children of Color have less access to enriched education programs than White children (Renzulli 2019; Patrick, Socol, and Morgan 2020; Ujifusa 2019). Multiple studies also confirm that, in the early grades, Black and Brown children are underrepresented in "gifted and talented" programs (Renzulli 2019; Aldrich 2019).

In high schools, Black students are often discouraged from taking Advanced Placement courses because school administrators mistakenly fear they will fail and hurt the school's record and reputation (Murphy and Silverole 2019). Thus, fewer high schoolers of Color sign up for college-level cocredit courses. Statistics show that 27 percent of Black students and 30 percent of Latinx students enroll in dual-credit work, whereas 38 percent of White and Asian students earn early college credit this way (National Center for Education Statistics 2019). This extends to STEM classes, where girls of Color are particularly underrepresented (Pack 2019).

These phenomena are compounded by the fact that many Black and Brown children attend urban schools that have fewer resources for offering advanced or special-interest classes. In fact, even in regular algebra classes, students in schools with a predominantly Black population are taught less content than students in White neighborhoods (Morton and Riegle-Crumb 2020). Even physical infrastructure makes a significant difference in children's learning. Though too little research focuses on this, teachers frequently observe that students in underfunded schools are justifiably angry about the condition of their building. In one striking account, Brian Schultz's *Spectacular Things Happen Along the Way* (2008) traces a fifth-grade class growing at first angry and then highly energized to get their crumbling school building rehabbed. The letters and photos the students sent to the district were so well written that administrators accused the teacher of composing them—until the press and political activist Ralph Nader got hold of the story. The project clearly demonstrated the abilities and commitment that students of Color (or any students, for that matter) can generate when they engage in rich learning activities that connect with their interests.

Examples of Positive Change

Several school districts, including Memphis, Tennessee (Kebede 2020), and Aurora, Colorado (Lauterbach 2019), have dropped standardized tests as entry requirements for gifted programs and are making the programs themselves more supportive. Another large but unnamed district shifted its process for identifying advanced-program students from an easily biased informal referral to screening all students, with a test score cutoff appropriately adjusted. This produced a 130 percent increase in Latinx students identified and an 80 percent increase for Black students, though the program was later discontinued due to cost—and the bias reemerged (Ferguson 2016).

RECRUITMENT AND SUPPORT FOR TEACHERS OF COLOR

A teacher in a focus group expressed her frustrations in her work:

> I feel like the curriculum and the way we continue to educate our students is not changing, and as a result, teachers of color feel trapped in a system. As an individual of color, I often feel as if I am not always able to make the changes I want as I am forced to operate within a system that seems unwilling to change. Furthermore, I also feel policed as an individual of color. I have to appease the dominant culture in regards to the way I communicate with my students, the way I dress, the assignments I choose to implement in the classroom. (Gewertz 2019)

Racism creates many challenges for teachers of Color (Ginsberg and Budd 2017):

- Teachers of Color tend to work in schools with fewer resources and less support to help the students.

- They are often mistakenly viewed by White peers as school disciplinarians instead of intellectual leaders.

- They feel frustrated by their inability to change school discipline and tracking policies that are unfair to students of Color.

- Pressure to comply with national and state standards and testing mandates can inhibit teachers of Color from using culturally relevant/responsive pedagogy.

- They fear negative evaluations from supervisors, and speaking out on racial issues can get them labeled as "troublemakers," silencing their voices and preventing bonding even with other teachers of Color.

- White mentors assigned to assist teachers of Color are often uncomfortable discussing race and inequality, leaving teachers of Color all the more alone.

- Feelings of isolation leave many teachers of Color questioning whether the teaching profession is personally and professionally sustainable for them.

Teachers of Color face additional pressures as well. As reported in *Education Week*:

> Teachers . . . describe workplaces where their hairstyles or wardrobe choices are unwelcome, or where they're not allowed to customize their instruction so it's culturally relevant for their students. They discuss meetings where their ideas are rejected, only to be embraced [later] when they come from a White colleague. (Gewertz 2019)

Finally, there are the constant microaggressions that teachers and other Black and Brown professionals experience, often daily (Brown 2019). Although we know many teachers of Color who are thriving and inspiring their students, these conditions often make it more difficult to serve their students well.

We know that students of Color benefit academically from having at least one teacher who looks like them (Gershenson et al. 2018; *Educational Leadership* 2019); and in fact, all students ought to have the opportunity to learn from teachers of various races. As Gloria Ladson-Billings has pointed out, "There is something that may be even more important than Black students having Black teachers and that is White students having Black teachers! It is important for White students to encounter Black people who are knowledgeable. . . What opportunities do White students have to see and experience Black competence?" (quoted in Ferlazzo 2015). Yet since 40 percent of US schools do not even have teachers of Color on staff, many students, whatever their color, never get to benefit from that experience (Lowe 2018).

Michigan provides an example of both the need and the solution: 18 percent of students in the state are African American, but only 6 percent of teachers are Black. More than half of Michigan school districts have no African American teachers at all. For the Latinx population, the disparity is even greater: Latinx students make up 8 percent of students, but barely 1 percent of Michigan teachers. In Detroit, however, active recruitment by the school district and the teachers' union resulted in attaining a healthy 67 percent teachers of Color in the district (Wisely 2019).

Across the country, the lack of Latinx teachers is not much different from what Michigan has experienced (Meckler and Rabinowitz 2019). Latinx students need role models and teachers who can connect with their interests and learning styles (Mitchell 2019; Geiger 2018).

Examples of Positive Change

Not surprisingly, having a Black principal increases the hiring of Black teachers by 5 to 7 percent. Black teachers stay in their roles longer in schools led by Black principals—reducing Black teacher mobility by 2 to 5 percent (Superville 2019), and their work experience is more positive (Hazard 2019). Increased support from administrators and fellow teachers has been shown to reduce the rate of teachers of Color leaving a school (Bednar and Gicheva 2017). Nevertheless, the number of Black principals is low, and studies show that it's more difficult for Black candidates to land a promotion than it is for White candidates (Bailes and Guthery 2020).

Some educators of Color have initiated support groups around the country to help one another deal with the particular pressures of the job. One example is the Compton

(California) Male Teachers of Color Network. Over a three-year period, the group has brought together teachers and administrators for bimonthly meetings. One valuable outcome is that teacher members have begun taking greater leadership roles in their schools (Arundel 2021).

DEVELOPING WHITE TEACHERS' EQUITY SKILLS

White teachers in front of students of Color often have not acquired strategies or the mindset for supporting the different learning needs of the students. The pressure to address standards and prepare for standardized tests can squeeze out the time for this. And White educators may be unaware of the microaggressions, unconscious bias, or other obstacles that their students experience. White teachers, as research shows, have on average the same level of racial bias as the general population; 70 percent showed such bias (Starck et al. 2020). More overtly, many White teachers still believe it is appropriate, even necessary, to "not see race," though experts have long pointed out that this prevents teachers from recognizing students' identities, learning needs, and strengths. Blogger Larry Ferlazzo's (2020) five-part series of posts on how to deal with teachers' claim that they don't see race presents analyses and proposed interruptions by twenty-eight education experts on this widespread problem.

The widely read *White Fragility: Why It's So Hard for White People to Talk About Racism* by Robin DiAngelo explores both the defensiveness many White people feel and the way their silence helps ensure the continuation of racism and White privilege. DiAngelo explains that American individualism leads people to view considerations of race as matters of personal blame rather than as results of the systemic racist conditions in which we are all immersed. Expecting such blame leads defensive White teachers to avoid the conversation altogether. As Utah 2014 Teacher of the Year Allison Riddle (2018) explains:

> Making connections with students involves recognizing their unique characteristics, and this includes recognizing race when it is relevant to a student's academic and social needs. For White teachers, however, the fear of looking racist can swallow up an objective viewpoint, and a well-meaning teacher may actually miss out on significant opportunities to help students of color succeed. Averting conversations about a student's race perpetuates an atmosphere of ambivalence and may discourage other teachers from digging deep to solve learning problems for students of color.

Examples of Positive Change

Some school districts have initiated programs to advance teachers' equity efforts. The Boston Public Schools' Office of Opportunity Gaps has conducted "cultural proficiency" seminars weekly among faculty across that city. As related in 2019 in the *Hechinger Report*, "Teachers describe these 45-minute sessions as candid and, more often than not, uncomfortable. But they say the discussions are helping them to become better educators within a system in which predominantly white staff teach in schools with significant numbers of black and Latino students" (Diallo 2019). Other districts, too, are initiating "implicit bias and equity" training to critically examine teachers' own experiences, in order to address unacknowledged biases. These programs are often far too limited, though, and expect too much from brief training sessions, or impose bureaucratically mandated participation that can engender resistance instead of engagement (Schwartz 2019; Payne 2008). School principal Joe Truss (2019), who led a more in-depth multi-year equity process in his school, described it this way:

> Racial-equity work is like trying to defuse a bomb and cutting the wrong wire. It can result in white rage, broken relationships, grievances, and further harm to oppressed students. I saw this personally at VVMS [Visitacion Valley Middle School in San Francisco], as situations got awkward, uncomfortable, and uncertain. This pushed some folks to identify who they could be safe with, be it for comfort or growth. But this messy middle is precisely when we need to stay curious, be vulnerable, and innovative. Racial-equity leaders must be both intentional and responsive when doing this anti-racist work.

DISTRICT-LEVEL STRUCTURAL INEQUITIES

The conditions we've described so far add up to create district-level inequities in many school systems. In addition, though, are deeper structural problems, such as school-district boundaries drawn to ensure demographic segregation that results in inequitable resources. For example, the Waterbury, Connecticut, school district is touched by eight other districts, each Whiter, more affluent, and receiving more dollars than does Waterbury. The neighboring Wolcott School District, where 87 percent of students are White, spends $2,000 more per student than Waterbury, which is 82 percent non-White (Harris 2019). Another example is Lower Merion High School in the Philadelphia suburbs, which is 60 percent Whiter than the Philadelphia district and spends nearly $10,000 more per pupil (Harris 2019; Mezzacappa 2019).

Across the country, nearly one thousand school-district boundaries separate communities where students are significantly more White and wealthy from communities where students are significantly more Black and Latinx and less wealthy. Although this might seem a small number compared to the country's 13,500 districts, almost nine million students in America—one in five public schoolchildren—live virtually across the street from a significantly Whiter and richer school district (EdBuild 2019). State and federal contributions do not do the job of correcting the economic imbalance. Further, resegregation by redrawing school boundaries continues unabated, particularly in areas where Whiter neighborhoods border those of people of Color, regardless of whether the latter are rich or poor (Samuels 2019). Further complicating the picture, resistance to access for students of Color can take place within a district as well as across district boundaries. New York City, for instance, has tried in vain to reform the policies and testing that resulted in enrollment of only 7 Black students out of a freshman class of 895 at NYC's most selective high school (Strauss 2019).

An overriding process that sustains district-level inequity in many locations is the cycle in which segregated neighborhoods are viewed negatively, feeding stereotypes that lead people of means to resist living there. As well, politicians oppose funding changes that could improve the area's schools (Edsall 2019; Quillian 2017). So as property values drop, tax revenue is reduced, which in turn undermines education and other community resources, which further puts off people with higher incomes. And the vicious cycle continues (Massey 2016). Thus it's no surprise that many Black and Brown students do not receive equitable resources or educational opportunities, in spite of many White people's asserted belief in racial equality—and so the inequality continues.

Nevertheless, along with the circumstances we've outlined, there are locations with high property values populated primarily by people of Color, with schools and communities successfully serving people of Color (Mannie 2017; Kimmons 2012). There are many neighborhoods enriched by Black and Brown cultures that are deeply treasured by the residents. The point is that no matter where people live, their children deserve equitable resources.

Examples of Positive Change

Although some lawsuits have been successful at gaining more equitable resources for communities, advocacy groups can be more effective at attaining this objective by working to change the political climate in a community or state (Martin et al. 2018). Thus, in 2018 and 2019, a movement of teacher protests lead to substantial increases in school funding in Arizona, North Carolina, Oklahoma, and West Virginia, four of the twelve states that had cut school "formula" funding most deeply over the last decade (Leachman and Figueroa 2019). And because state funding represents 47 percent of total funds for schools, it turns out that state legislatures are a good focus for such advocacy.

STUDENTS' FRAME OF MIND

Contemporary trends in the mental state of youth of Color go in both positive and negative directions. On the positive side, nationwide demonstrations, not only against biased policing but addressing the many ways racism has challenged Black and Brown lives, have activated students of Color to advocate for equity in their education. Recently, for example, a field trip to the National Museum of African American History and Culture in Washington led students from a Denver high school to demand better inclusion of Black history in their school and district history curriculum (Chang and Mehta 2020). Similar advocacy has occurred in numerous other communities (Lockhart 2019; Palochko 2020). Online journals such as *Education Week* have interviewed students about the racial challenges in their schools and the changes they seek (Gewertz, Schwartz, and Will 2020).

Yet there are troubling patterns as well.

A study sponsored by the Emergency Task Force on Black Youth Suicide and Mental Health on behalf of the Congressional Black Caucus (CBC) found this:

> For black youth between the ages 10 and 19, suicide is the second-leading cause of death. In 2017, 3,000 black youths in this age group died by suicide. The study also noted that "the suicide death rate among black youth has been found to be increasing faster than any other racial/ethnic group." (Clay 2020)

The inequities that we've outlined throughout this appendix surely affect the mental state of students of Color. While there are plenty of highly successful students among this group, repeated racist experiences increase rates of depression and depress grades (Kowalski 2020; Gewertz 2020). The COVID-19 epidemic made this worse, leading to further increased anxiety for students of Color, compared to White students (Prothero 2020b). At the same time, students of Color have less access to mental health services (Prothero 2020a), and they seek these services less often than their White counterparts (Klisz-Hulbert 2020).

Examples of Positive Change

A report from the federal Substance Abuse and Mental Health Services Administration (SAMHSA, n.d.) outlines comprehensive mental health programs that have been instituted in several school districts. These programs are focused on behavior much more than on issues such as depression, however. One that appears more focused on psychological health is the School-Based Mental Health Services Program of the Behavioral Health Services agency, Little Rock, Arkansas.

Because of the dearth of research, programs, and resources for addressing depression in youth, we include here the recommendations provided in the 2020 report to the Emergency Task Force on Black Youth Suicide and Mental Health on behalf of the Congressional Black Caucus (Coleman et al. 2020, 8):

1. Establish online and regional training academies for school-based personnel and mental health providers on how to recognize signs of depression, suicidal behaviors and other mental health problems.

2. Fund the development of a model curriculum for administrators, teachers, other school personnel, parents and community-based organizations and around mental health and suicide, leveraging the expertise of the Working Group of the Taskforce. Such a curriculum would include training in anti-bias, anti-oppressive and gender equity practices.

3. Develop culturally-effective guidelines for national suicide and mental health hotlines and organizations relating to Black youth, leveraging the expertise of the Working Group of the Taskforce.

4. Identify and promote best and promising practices for increasing the pipeline of social workers and other mental health providers to address the dearth of school-based personnel who can address the mental health needs of Black students, with the goal of placing a proportionate number of social workers and other mental health providers in each school relative to the student body population.

5. Develop a certification program for medical personnel, clinicians, school personnel and others who interact with Black youth in an educational or healthcare setting, to ensure they are trained to address the mental health needs of Black youth.

6. Develop a screening tool for use by providers across healthcare professionals and institutions relating to suicidal thoughts, ideation and self-harm, as well as a protocol on how to treat and connect Black youth to care.

7. Identify and implement highly universalized models, such as Mental Health First Aid and Zero Suicide.

This report (Coleman et al. 2020) includes many relevant resources as well.

In Conclusion

Additional aspects of racism affecting children's schooling include bias in policing, violence and activities of gangs, and challenges in health care. Each of these is a problem to be studied in depth itself, so we cannot give them the attention they deserve in this book. However, judging just from the conditions we've outlined, it's clear that Black and Brown students face challenges. Yet it's also inspiring that a large number succeed, and all have potential and voices that need to be heard.

APPENDIX 3

Online Resources

Curated by Vanessa Heller, the following is a collection of resources on race and racism, as well as teaching ideas and lessons.

General Resources

Becoming a More Equitable Educator: Mindsets and Practices

MIT Open Learning Library five-unit course (fee based) on equity teaching practices.

Black Lives Matter at School

A national coalition organizing for racial justice in education.

Building Racial Justice and Equity

Articles from *ASCD Express* e-newsletter and *Educational Leadership* magazine.

Clear the Air

Educators promoting equity discussions for fellow educators; founded by Val Brown.

Courageous Conversations

Courses and events, including online discussions, promoting productive conversations on race; founded by author Glenn Singleton.

Culturally Responsive Leadership

School principal Joe Truss provides articles, workshops, and a blog on antiracist education.

Culturally Responsive Teaching Network

The Disproportionality Technical Assistance Network (of the Wisconsin Department of Public Instruction); materials on culturally responsive education.

Education for Peace and Social Justice

Antibias and antiracist education materials from the American Montessori Society.

Embrace Race (see especially its action guides)

Articles, webinars, action guides, and book lists for guiding children to develop positive attitudes and think critically about race.

Facing History & Ourselves (see especially Fostering Civil Discourse) Originally focused on holocaust education, but expanded to address broader equity issues. 	**JumpStartPD** Online community for creating and improving professional development on equity in teaching and schools. 	**Leading Equity Center** (see especially the guide provided) Website of Sheldon Eakins, equity speaker and trainer.
Mikva Challenge Organizes student social action groups in schools, in Chicago, Southern California, and Washington, DC. 	**National Council for Community and Education Partnerships** (connected with Gear Up) National association dedicated to supporting underserved students as they pursue postsecondary education. 	**One Circle Foundation** Programs, guides, and workshops promoting equitable school culture.
Racial Equity Tools and Glossary Large collection of tools and strategies (2,500) for learning, planning, and acting for racial equity. 	**Showing Up for Racial Justice (SURJ)** National network of groups and individuals working to undermine White supremacy and work for racial justice. Includes resources. 	**Talking About Race** Guide to discussions on race by the Smithsonian National Museum of African American History and Culture.

Teaching Tolerance (now renamed *Learning for Justice*) Extensive resources, including articles and lessons on equity and other social justice issues. 	*The 1619 Project* Curriculum Pulitzer Center's *The 1619 Project* began with a special issue of the *New York Times Magazine*; reframes US history based on the arrival of initial enslaved Africans. 	

Teaching Resources

Anti-Racism Resources Compiled by Sarah Sophie Flicker and Alyssa Klein in May 2020; geared toward White parents. 	**Black Students Matter: Resources for Antiracist Teaching and Instruction** Resources and leveled articles on race and equity, provided by Newsela (free and paid versions available). 	**Building Equitable Learning Environments (BELE) Library** The Equitable Learning Library helps educators, parents, and policymakers find resources and recommendations for creating more equitable and empowering learning environments.

Common Beliefs Survey: Teaching Racially and Ethnically Diverse Students	**First Book Marketplace**	**Scaffolded Antiracism Resources (Google Doc)**
Survey to probe teachers' common beliefs about racially and ethnically diverse students; created by Greater Good in Education.	PreK–8 equity education books and materials.	Resources to support progression of antiracist awareness for White people, assembled by Anna Stamborski, Nikki Zimmermann, and Bailie Gregory.
Solve in Time Gamified problem-based learning activity on racial equity, based on design thinking; created by Dee Lanier.	**Building Communities for Justice—Webquest** Webquest materials for a grades 6–9 social justice unit created by Paige Gonzales (Ocean View School District, California).	

Book Lists

40+ Books for AntiRacist Teachers	**50 Books to Help Guide Anti-Racist Conversations in the Classroom**	**The Brown Bookshelf**
From Culturally Responsive Leadership; forty-three key books on antiracism for teachers and teacher book discussions.	BookSource Banter Blog; list with descriptions of each book; variety of grade levels.	Showcase of the best Black voices writing for young readers, elementary through high school levels.

Build Your Stack: Antiracist Books for Your Curriculum Today

Compiled for the National Council of Teachers of English by Lorena Germán, Kathleen Colantonio-Yurko, Felicia Hamilton, and Holly Spinelli; short list of recommendations for elementary, middle, and high school.

Do the Work: An Anti-Racist Reading List

By Layla F. Saad in *The Guardian*; reviews of four books on antiracism, for adults.

EmbraceRace book lists

EmbraceRace.org.; lists of books at various grade levels for exploring race and antiracism.

Videos

Black Feminism & the Movement for Black Lives

National LGBTQ Task Force. Panel discussion by Barbara Smith, Reina Gossett, and Charlene Carruthers on how Black feminism remains a foundational theory and practice guiding social justice movements for Black lives. (50:48)

Black Lives Matter Instructional Library

Google Slides deck of picture books in five categories, with YouTube read-alouds of excerpts from the books.

A Class Divided

PBS *Frontline* film on the troubling classroom activity in which a teacher divided her third-grade class into blue-eyed and brown-eyed groups to show them how discrimination works. (53:00)

The Danger of a Single Story (TED Talk)	The Difference Between Being "Not Racist" and AntiRacist (TED discussion)	Robin DiAngelo discusses *White Fragility*
TED Talk by Chimamanda Ngozi Adichie on how stereotyping derives from taking one individual's story as representative of a whole group. (19:00)	TED discussion led by Ibram X. Kendi with Chloe Shasha and Whitney Rodgers on how antiracism requires action, unlike passive "nonracism." (50:00)	Seattle Central Library. Reading and discussion by DiAngelo at the launch of her book in 2018 emphasizing the concepts of Whiteness and silence around racism. (01:00:23)
How Studying Privilege Systems Can Strengthen Compassion (TEDx)	Killer Mike: Speech on how to respond to the police killing of George Floyd.	The Path to Ending Systemic Racism in the US (TED panel discussion)
Talk at TEDx Timberlane Schools by author Peggy McIntosh, researcher at the Wellesley Centers for Women, on privilege and racism. (18:00)	Speech at the Atlanta mayor's press conference, May 29, 2020, on engaging in real antiracist change rather than destructive riots. (08:00)	TED discussion featuring Dr. Phillip Atiba Goff, Rashad Robinson, Dr. Bernice King, and Anthony D. Romero, in response to the killing of George Floyd. (1:06:22)
Yolanda Sealey-Ruiz: Featured Interviews, Speeches & Past Events	Yolanda Sealey-Ruiz: The Art of Culturally Responsive Education	Systemic Racism Explained
Short talks by Yolanda Sealey-Ruiz on aspects and developments around race.	Arts in Education Roundtable. Talk by Yolanda Sealey-Ruiz on culturally responsive/ sustaining pedagogy, March 17, 2020. (40:12)	Act.tv media company. Short video explaining redlining and implicit bias as key elements of racism; appropriate for upper elementary students. (04:23)

TED Talk Playlist: The Link Between Health and Racism	TED Talk Playlist: Talks to Help Understand Racism in America	Why Does Privilege Make People So Angry?
Nine TED Talks on the mental and physical impact of racism and what society can do "to heal and support the well-being of all"; includes brief summaries of each.	Twenty-five TED Talks covering a wide range of aspects of racism and how to undo it.	MTV News: Decoded. A lively explanation of how systemic racism creates race-based privilege and how to defuse angry responses to discussing it. (4:51)

APPENDIX 4

Important Books on Antiracism and Equity

Following are the books we've found most important and most helpful in developing racial literacy and learning how to act to interrupt inequities in schools. There are others that are valuable as well, and more being published at a great clip. Also refer to Appendix 1 and our references for additional resources. Our apologies for those we may have overlooked.

Ahmed, Sara K. 2018. *Being the Change: Lessons and Strategies to Teach Social Comprehension.* Portsmouth, NH: Heinemann.

> Provides teachers with tools and activities to help students make sense of themselves and the world as they navigate relevant topics in today's society.

Alexander, Michelle. 2020. *The New Jim Crow: Mass Incarceration in the Age of Colorblindness* (10th ed.). New York: New Press.

> Targeting Black men in the War on Drugs and decimating communities of Color in the US criminal justice system of racial control, which claims it is colorblind.

Angelou, Maya. 1984. *I Know Why the Caged Bird Sings.* New York: Little, Brown.

> Widely read autobiography about growing up overcoming challenges colored by racism.

Arnold, Jenna. 2020. *Raising Our Hands: How White Women Can Stop Avoiding Hard Conversations, Start Accepting Responsibility, and Find Our Place on the New Frontlines.* Dallas, TX: BenBella Books.

> A reckoning cry that asks White women to step up and fight against complacency—in their homes, behaviors, and attitudes.

Baker-Bell, April. 2020. *Linguistic Justice: Black Language, Literacy, Identity, and Pedagogy.* New York: Routledge.

> Ethnographic snapshots of how Black students navigate and negotiate their linguistic and racial identities across multiple contexts.

Baldwin, James. 1963. *The Fire Next Time.* New York: Dial Press.

> The personal impact of racial injustice, formatted as two letters written on the centennial of the Emancipation Proclamation, strongly advocating an attack on racism.

Boggs, Grace Lee. 2012. *The Next American Revolution: Sustainable Activism for the Twenty-First Century.* Oakland: University of California Press.

A guide to activism for social justice in politics, economics, and environment.

Collins, Patricia Hill. 2009. *Black Feminist Thought: Knowledge, Consciousness, and the Politics of Empowerment.* New York: Routledge.

Explores the words and ideas of Black feminist intellectuals and African American women outside academia.

Cooper, Brittney. 2018. *Eloquent Rage: A Black Feminist Discovers Her Superpower.* New York: St. Martin's Press.

Black women's anger as a powerful source of energy that can give people the strength to keep up their advocacy.

Culham, Ruth. 2016. *Dream Wakers: Mentor Texts That Celebrate Latino Culture.* Portsmouth NH: Stenhouse.

Teaching writing using children's books focusing on Latinx life and culture.

Delpit, Lisa. 1995. *Other People's Children: Cultural Conflict in the Classroom.* New York: The New Press.

On the variations of communication across cultures that create barriers students and teachers face.

DiAngelo, Robin. 2018. *White Fragility: Why It's So Hard for White People to Talk About Racism.* Boston: Beacon Press.

Best seller on how White people avoid discussing race, and thus the silence supports White supremacy.

Emdin, Christopher. 2016. *For White Folks Who Teach in the Hood . . . and the Rest of Y'all Too.* Boston: Beacon Press.

Advancing equity for students of Color through building their leadership in the classroom.

Hammond, Zaretta. 2014. *Culturally Responsive Teaching and the Brain: Promoting Authentic Engagement and Rigor Among Culturally and Linguistically Diverse Students.* Thousand Oaks, CA: Corwin.

Using neuroscience research to understand and implement culturally responsive instruction.

Jewell, Tiffany. 2020. *This Book Is Anti-Racist: 20 Lessons on How to Wake Up, Take Action, and Do the Work.* London: Frances Lincoln Children's Books.

Understanding identity, history, action, and solidarity as tools to encourage middle and high school students' antiracist reflection, thought, and action.

Katznelson, Ira. 2006. *When Affirmative Action Was White: An Untold History of Racial Inequality in Twentieth-Century America.* New York: Norton.

How the establishment of affirmative action in the 1930s and 1940s excluded people of Color.

Kay, Matthew. 2018. *Not Light but Fire: How to Lead Meaningful Race Conversations in the Classroom.* Portsmouth, NH: Stenhouse.

Explicit guidance on making difficult classroom conversations productive, with lively real-life examples.

Kendi, Ibram X. 2016. *Stamped from the Beginning: The Definitive History of Racist Ideas in America.* New York: Bold Type Books.

Award-winning history of racism in America, from the arrival of the first slaves to the present day, told through the lives of five famous Americans.

———. 2019. *How to Be an Antiracist.* New York: One World.

Detailed analysis of how racism manifests itself in multiple ways in US society and of the difference between being actively antiracist and claiming to be nonracist.

Kendi, Ibram X., and Ashley Lukashevsky. 2020. *Antiracist Baby.* New York: Penguin.

A picture book for parents and children on antiracism.

Kendi, Ibram X., and Jason Reynolds. 2020. *Stamped: Racism, Antiracism, and You.* New York: Little, Brown Books for Young Readers.

Version of the history covered in *Stamped from the Beginning*, written for young people.

Kinloch, Valerie, Tanja Burkhard, and Carlotta Penn, eds. 2019. *Race, Justice, and Activism in Literacy Instruction.* New York: Teachers College Press.

Addressing race, justice, and activism in teaching and learning critical literacy.

Ladson-Billings, Gloria. 2009. *The Dreamkeepers: Successful Teachers of African American Children* (2nd ed.). San Francisco: Jossey-Bass.

Culturally relevant teaching as reflected in the portraits of effective teachers, both Black and White.

Livingston, Robert. 2021. *The Conversation: How Seeking and Speaking the Truth About Racism Can Radically Transform Individuals and Organizations.* New York: Penguin Random House.

A consultant's account of how to connect with skeptical audiences on racism.

Lorde, Audre. 2007. *Sister Outsider: Essays and Speeches.* Berkeley, CA: Crossing Press.

Fifteen essays and speeches addressing sexism, racism, ageism, homophobia, and class, proposing that social difference leads to action and change.

Love, Bettina L. 2019. *We Want to Do More Than Survive: Abolitionist Teaching and the Pursuit of Educational Freedom.* Boston: Beacon Press.

Argues that rather than just talk about social change, educators must teach students about racial violence and oppression, and make change through active civic initiatives and movements.

Minor, Cornelius. 2019. *We Got This: Equity, Access, and the Quest to Be Who Our Students Need Us to Be.* Portsmouth, NH: Heinemann.

Focuses on equity strategies for teaching existing curriculum, including step-by-step guides to help teachers analyze what is and isn't working for students, and how to make changes to address their needs.

Moraga, Cherríe, and Gloria Anzaldúa, eds. 2015. *This Bridge Called My Back: Writings by Radical Women of Color* (4th ed.). Albany: State University of New York Press.

Forty-one short pieces on race and feminism.

Muhammad, Gholdy. 2020. *Cultivating Genius: An Equity Framework for Culturally and Historically Responsive Literacy*. New York: Scholastic.

Explores the previously neglected history of nineteenth-century Black literary societies and the equity education principles they developed, which provide guidance for today's equity education.

Nieto, Sonia. 2013. *Finding Joy in Teaching Students of Diverse Backgrounds: Culturally Responsive and Socially Just Practices in U.S. Classrooms*. Portsmouth, NH: Heinemann.

What it means to be culturally responsive, a pedagogy that recognizes the importance of including students' cultural references in all aspects of learning.

Nieto, Sonia, and Patti Bode. 2017. *Affirming Diversity: The Sociopolitical Context of Multicultural Education* (7th ed.). London: Pearson.

Explores the larger social, economic, and political factors that affect students' success or failure in the classroom.

O'Donnell-Allen, Cindy. 2011. *Tough Talk, Tough Texts: Teaching English to Change the World*. Portsmouth, NH: Heinemann.

Using books that challenge students' thinking about important social issues, and supporting thoughtful student discussions about them.

Oluo, Ijeoma. 2019. *So You Want to Talk About Race*. New York: Seal Press.

A widely read personal exploration of the nature of racism in America and how to be able to discuss it meaningfully.

Paris, Django, and H. Samy Alim, eds. 2017. *Culturally Sustaining Pedagogies: Teaching and Learning for Justice in a Changing World.* New York: Teachers College Press.

Chapters by many current educational equity advocates, providing theoretically grounded examples of how to support Black, Indigenous, Latinx, Asian/Pacific Islander, South African, and immigrant students through educational justice.

Price-Dennis, Detra, and Yolanda Sealey-Ruiz. 2021. *Advancing Racial Literacies in Teacher Education: Activism for Equity in Digital Spaces.* New York: Teachers College Press.

Strategies to increase educators' capacity to respond to inequities that plague our educational system, providing theoretical and practical ways to address race in the digital age.

Ritchie, Andrea J. 2017. *Invisible No More: Police Violence Against Black Women and Women of Color.* Boston: Beacon Press.

How women of Color are uniquely affected by racial profiling, police brutality, and immigration enforcement.

Saad, Layla F. 2020. *Me and White Supremacy: Combat Racism, Change the World, and Become a Good Ancestor.* New York: Sourcebooks.

For White people who want to challenge White supremacy but don't know where to begin; moves readers from their heads into their hearts and ultimately into their practice.

Sealey-Ruiz, Yolanda. 2020. *Love from the Vortex and Other Poems.* New York: Kaleidoscope Vibrations.

Charts her journey of finding and losing love, a universal take on what can happen when one seeks love and connection with others, and moves beyond these anticipated stages to moments of grace and beauty.

Sealey-Ruiz, Yolanda, Chance W. Lewis, and Ivory Toldson. 2014. *Teacher Education and Black Communities: Implications for Access, Equity and Achievement.* Charlotte, NC: Information Age Publishing.

Articles to stimulate thought and discussion among policymakers, practitioners, and educational researchers concerned about the performance of Black students, and to provide evidence-based strategies to expand our nation's pool of Black teachers.

Singh, Anneliese A. 2019. *The Racial Healing Handbook: Practical Activities to Help You Challenge Privilege, Confront Systemic Racism, and Engage in Collective Healing.* Oakland, CA: New Harbinger.

A practical guide to navigate racism, challenge privilege, manage stress and trauma, and begin to heal.

Singleton, Glenn, and Curtis Linton. 2014. *Courageous Conversations About Race: A Field Guide for Achieving Equity in Schools* (2nd ed.). Thousand Oaks, CA: Corwin.

Outlines essential conditions and agreements to enable people to discuss racial issues productively.

Stevenson, Bryan. 2015. *Just Mercy: A Story of Justice and Redemption.* London: One World.

A story of deep-seated injustice in the justice system, along with moments of human compassion, understanding, mercy, and justice that offer hope.

———. 2018. *Just Mercy (Adapted for Young Adults): A True Story of the Fight for Justice.* New York: Delacorte Press.

Delves deep into the broken US justice system, detailing from personal experience Stevenson's challenges and efforts as a lawyer and social advocate.

Tatum, Alfred. 2004. *Teaching Reading to Black Adolescent Males.* Portsmouth, NH: Stenhouse.

Making reading meaningful for young Black students, based on Tatum's work with them.

Tatum, Beverly Daniel. 2017. *Why Are All the Black Kids Sitting Together in the Cafeteria? And Other Conversations About Race* (Rev. ed.). New York: Basic Books.

Exploring young people's development of racial identity in a racist society.

Wilkerson, Isabel. 2011. *The Warmth of Other Suns: The Epic Story of America's Great Migration*. New York: Penguin.

History of the decades-long movement of Black Americans from the South.

———. 2020. *Caste: The Origin of Our Discontents*. New York: Penguin.

Best-selling book analyzing racism in America as actually a tightly structured caste system, with all the social trauma that entails.

References

Ahmed, Sara. 2018. *Being the Change: Lessons and Strategies to Teach Social Comprehension*. Portsmouth, NH: Heinemann.

Aldrich, Marta W. 2019. "Money over Merit? New Study Says Gifted Programs Favor Students from Wealthier Families." *Chalkbeat*, October 4, 2019. https://tn.chalkbeat.org/2019/10/4/21108935/money-over-merit-new-study-says-gifted-programs-favor-students-from-wealthier-families.

An, Susie. 2019. "Changing Classrooms: When Students Are Black and Teachers Are White." WBEZ, August 15, 2019. https://www.wbez.org/stories/changing-classrooms-when-students-are-black-and-teachers-are-white/dbac7063-8152-4d0f-91b3-14d0d67ffc17.

Anderson, Melinda D. 2015. "Why Are So Many Preschoolers Getting Suspended? The Frequency of Punishment Has a Troubling Racial Skew." *Atlantic*, December 7, 2015. https://www.theatlantic.com/education/archive/2015/12/why-are-so-many-preschoolers-getting-suspended/418932/.

Annie E. Casey Foundation. 2015. "Race Equity and Inclusion Action Guide." https:// www.aecf.org/resources/race-equity-and-inclusion-action-guide.

Arao, Brian, and Kristi Clemens. 2013. "From Safe Spaces to Brave Spaces: A New Way to Frame Dialogue Around Diversity and Social Justice." In *The Art of Effective Facilitation*, ed. Lisa M. Landreman, 135–51. Sterling, VA: Stylus.

Arundel, Kara. 2021. "Promising Practices: How a Network of Male Teachers of Color Expanded Leadership Opportunities." *K–12 Dive*, February 4, 2021. https://www.k12dive.com/news/male-teachers-of-color-expand-leadership-opportunities/594345/.

Bacher-Hicks, Andrew, Stephen B. Billings, and David J. Deming. 2019. *The School to Prison Pipeline: Long-Run Impacts of School Suspensions on Adult Crime*. Working Paper No. 26257. Cambridge, MA: National Bureau of Economic Research.

Bailes, Lauren P., and Sarah Guthery. 2020. "Held Down and Held Back: Systematically Delayed Principal Promotions by Race and Gender." *AERA Open* 6 (2). https://journals.sagepub.com/doi/full/10.1177/2332858420929298.

Barshay, Jill. 2018. "Teachers of Color Have Increased 162 Percent over the Past 30 Years, but They Are Also More Likely to Quit: New Data Paints a Picture of an Increasingly Unstable Teaching Force of Rookies." *Hechinger Report*, November 19, 2018. https://hechingerreport.org/non-white-teachers-have-increased-162-percent-over-the-past-30-years-but-they-are-also-more-likely-to-quit/.

Bednar, Steven, and Dora Gicheva. 2017. "Retaining Minority Teachers in Schools Where Most of Their Colleagues Are White." *Brown Center Chalkboard* (blog), August 2, 2017. https://www.brookings.edu/blog/brown-center-chalkboard/2017/08/02/retaining-minority-teachers-in-schools-where-most-of-their-colleagues-are-white/.

Bisplinghoff, Betty. 2004. "Inquiry Circles: A Protocol for Professional Inquiry." National School Reform Faculty. PDF document reached from https://nsrfharmony.org/.

Blake, Jamilia J., and Rebecca Epstein. 2019. *Listening to Black Women and Girls: Lived Experiences of Adultification Bias.* Washington, DC: Georgetown Law Center on Poverty and Inequality.

Brown, Erikca. 2019. "African American Teachers' Experiences with Racial Micro-Aggressions." *Educational Studies* 55 (2) 180–96.

Brown, Keffrelyn. 2011. "Breaking the Cycle of Sisyphus: Social Education and the Acquisition of Critical Sociocultural Knowledge About Race and Racism in the United States." *Social Studies* 102 (6): 249–55.

Camera, Lauren. 2019. "Study Finds That Schools Remain Largely Segregated by Race and Income." *US News*, July 25, 2019. https://www.usnews.com/news/education-news/articles/2019-07-25/racial-and-economic-segregation-reinforced-by-school-district-boundaries.

Chan, Carrie. 2018. "Stopping the School to Prison Pipeline." *Educate 78* (blog). June 2018. https://www.educate78.org/crunched-suspensions/.

Chang, Ailsa, and Jonaki Mehta. 2020. "Denver School Principal on How Black Students Led Swift Changes to History Curriculum." NPR, July 10, 2020. https://www.npr.org/sections/live-updates-protests-for-racial-justice/2020/07/10/889743843/denver-school-principal-on-how-students-led-swift-changes-to-black-history-curri.

Cherry-Paul, Sonja. 2021. Online discussion. National Council of Teachers of English, April 27, 2021.

Clay, Gregory. 2020. "A Black Epidemic We Don't Talk About." *Newsday*, January 30, 2020. https://www.newsday.com/opinion/commentary/suicide-teens-children-black-african-american-bryce-gowdy-1.41237747.

Coleman, Bonnie Watson, et al. 2020. *Ring the Alarm: The Crisis of Black Youth Suicide in America. A Report from the Congressional Black Caucus Emergency Taskforce on Black Youth Suicide and Mental Health.* https://watsoncoleman.house.gov/uploadedfiles/full_taskforce_report.pdf.

Coleman, Sherry, and Howard C. Stevenson. 2014. "Engaging the Racial Elephant." *Independent School*, *73*(4), 86–90.

Curran, F. Chris, Benjamin W. Fisher, Samantha Viano, and Aaron Kupchik. 2019. "Why and When Do School Resource Officers Engage in School Discipline? The Role of Context in Shaping Disciplinary Involvement." *American Journal of Education* 126 (1): 33–63.

Danowitz, Erica, and Carol Videon. 2010. "Native American Resources: Sites for Online Research." *College and Research Library News* 71 (8). https://crln.acrl.org/index.php/crlnews/article/view/8424/8636.

Diallo, Amadou. 2019. "Teachers Go to School on Racial Bias." *Hechinger Report*, April 29, 2019. https://hechingerreport.org/teachers-go-to-school-on-racial-bias/.

DiAngelo, Robin. 2018. *White Fragility: Why It's So Hard for White People to Talk About Racism.* Boston: Beacon Press.

EdBuild. 2019. *Dismissed: America's Most Divisive Borders.* EdBuild. https://edbuild. org/content/dismissed.

Edsall, Thomas B. 2019. "Separate Has Never Been Equal." *New York Times,* July 17, 2019. https://www.nytimes.com/2019/07/17/opinion/integration-politics. html.

Educational Leadership. 2019. "Research Alert: The Impact of Teacher Diversity." *Educational Leadership* 76 (7). http://www.ascd.org/publications/educational-leadership/apr19/vol76/num07/The-Impact-of-Teacher-Diversity.aspx.

Ferguson, Ronald F. 2016. "Racial Bias in Gifted and Talented Placement, and What to Do About It." National Association for Gifted Children blog, May 13, 2016. https://www.nagc.org/blog/racial-bias-gifted-and-talented-placement-and-what-do-about-it.

Ferlazzo, Larry. 2015. "Response: The Teachers of Color 'Disappearance Crisis.'" *Education Week,* January 6, 2015. https://blogs.edweek.org/teachers/classroom_qa_with_larry_ferlazzo/2015/01/response_the_teachers_of_color_disappearance_crisis.html?r=1658922548.

———. 2020. "Saying 'I Don't See Color' Denies the Racial Identity of Students." Five-part series. *Education Week,* February 2, 4, 6, 9, and 12, 2020. http://blogs.edweek.org/teachers/classroom_qa_with_larry_ferlazzo/2020/02/being_nice_is_not_enough_to_make_racism_disappear.html.

Finley, Todd. 2019. "A Look at Implicit Bias and Microaggressions: A Primer on the Impact of Implicit Biases in Schools and How They Can Be Expressed by Students and Faculty." *Edutopia,* March 25, 2019. https://www.edutopia.org/article/look-implicit-bias-and-microaggressions.

Flake, Sharon. 2000. *The Skin I'm In.* New York: Disney Hyperion Books.

Flitter, Emily. 2019. "This Is What Racism Sounds Like in the Banking Industry." *New York Times*, December 11, 2019. https://www.nytimes.com/2019/12/11/business/jpmorgan-banking-racism.html.

Gardner, Roberta Price. 2016. "Unforgivable Blackness: Visual Rhetoric, Reader Response, and Critical Racial Literacy." *Children's Literature in Education* 48 (2), 119–33.

Geiger, A. W. 2018. "America's Public-School Teachers Are Far Less Racially and Ethnically Diverse Than Their Students." Washington, DC: Pew Research Center Fact Tank. https://www.pewresearch.org/fact-tank/2018/08/27/americas-public-school-teachers-are-far-less-racially-and-ethnically-diverse-than-their-students/.

Georgetown Law. 2019. "Research Confirms That Black Girls Feel the Sting of Adultification Bias Identified in Earlier Georgetown Law Study." Georgetown Law, May 15, 2019. https://www.law.georgetown.edu/news/research-confirms-that-black-girls-feel-the-sting-of-adultification-bias-identified-in-earlier-georgetown-law-study/.

Gershenson, Seth, M. Cassandra, D. Hart, Joshua Hyman, Constance Lindsay, and Nicholas W. Papageorge. 2018. *The Long-Run Impacts of Same-Race Teachers.* National Bureau of Economic Research Working Paper No. 25254, November 2018. https://www.nber.org/papers/w25254.

Gershoff, Elizabeth T., and Sarah A. Font. 2016. "Corporal Punishment in U.S. Public Schools: Prevalence, Disparities in Use, and Status in State and Federal Policy." *Department of Health and Human Services Social Policy Report 30* (1). https://www.ncbi.nlm.nih.gov/pmc/articles/PMC5766273/.

Gewertz, Catherine. 2019. "Hiring Teachers of Color Is Just the First Step. Here's How to Keep Them." *Education Week*, September 25, 2019. https://blogs.edweek.org/teachers/teaching_now/2019/09/hiring_teachers_of_color_is_just_the_first_step_heres_how_to_keep_them.html.

———. 2020. "Police Shootings Lower Black and Latino Students' Grades, Graduation Rates, Study Shows." *Education Week*, June 10, 2020. https://blogs.edweek.org/teachers/teaching_now/2020/06/police_shootings_lower_students_grades_graduation_rates_study_shows.html.

Gewertz, Catherine, Sarah Schwartz, and Madeline Will. 2020. "Classroom Discussions on Race: Hear What 5 Black Students Say They Need." *Education Week*, July 31, 2020. https://blogs.edweek.org/teachers/teaching_now/2020/07/5_Black_students_say_what_they_need_from_class_discussions_about_race.html.

Gilliam, Walter S., Angela N. Maupin, Chin R. Reyes, Maria Accavitti, and Frederick Shic. 2016. "Do Early Educators' Implicit Biases Regarding Sex and Race Relate to Behavior Expectations and Recommendations of Preschool Expulsions and Suspensions?" *Child Care and Early Education Research Connections.* Yale University Child Study Center, September 28, 2016.

Ginsberg, Alice, and Eric Budd. 2017. *Mentoring New Teachers of Color: Building New Relationships Among Aspiring Teachers and Historically Black Colleges and Universities.* CMSI Research Brief. New Brunswick, NJ: Rutgers Center for Minority Serving Institutions.

Gorski, Paul. 2019. "Avoiding Racial Equity Detours." *Educational Leadership* 76 (7) http://www.ascd.org/publications/educational-leadership/apr19/vol76/num07/Avoiding-Racial-Equity-Detours.aspx.

Grissom, Jason, and Christopher Redding. 2016. "Discretion and Disproportionality: Explaining the Underrepresentation of High-Achieving Students of Color in Gifted Programs." *AERA Open* 2 (1): 1–25.

Harris, Adam. 2019. "The Whiter, Richer School District Right Next Door: Public Schools' Dependence on Local Property Taxes Means Some Districts Get Isolated from the Financial Resources in Their Communities." *Atlantic*, August 1, 2019. https://www.theatlantic.com/education/archive/2019/08/segregated-school-districts-trapped-their-borders/595318/.

Hawthorne, Michael, and Cecilia Reyes. 2018. "Brain-Damaging Lead Found in Tap Water in Hundreds of Homes Tested Across Chicago, Results Show." *Chicago Tribune*, April 12, 2018. https://www.chicagotribune.com/investigations/ct-chicago-water-lead-contamination-20180411-htmlstory.html.

Hazard, Gemayel. 2019. "I'm a Black Teacher Who Works for a Black Principal. It's Been a Game Changer." *Education Week*, July 23, 2019. https://www.edweek.org/tm/articles/2019/07/23/im-a-black-teacher-who-works-for.html.

Heath, Shirley Brice. 1983. *Ways with Words: Language, Life and Work in Communities and Classrooms*. Cambridge, United Kingdom: Cambridge University Press.

Horsford, Sonya Douglass. 2014. "When Race Enters the Room: Improving Leadership and Learning Through Racial Literacy." *Theory into Practice* 53 (1), 123–30.

James, Steve, director, producer, co-editor. 2018. *America to Me*. Ten-episode documentary series. Chicago: Kartemquin Films. Available through various streaming services.

Jewell, Tiffany M. 2020. *This Book Is Anti-Racist*. London: Frances Lincoln Children's Books.

Kay, Matthew R. 2018. *Not Light, But Fire: How to Lead Meaningful Race Conversations in the Classroom*. Portsmouth, NH: Stenhouse.

Kebede, Laura Faith. 2020. "As More Black and Hispanic Students Enter Memphis' Gifted Program, Here's How It Might Change." *Chalkbeat*, January 31, 2020. https://tn.chalkbeat.org/2020/1/31/21121140/as-more-black-and-hispanic-students-enter-memphis-gifted-program-here-s-how-it-might-change.

Kendi, Ibram X. 2019. *How to Be an Antiracist*. New York: One World.

Kimmons, Staci L. 2012. "Successful Schools for African American Children: A Case Study of Franklin Elementary School." PhD diss., Marquette University, 2012. https://epublications.marquette.edu/dissertations_mu/233/.

Klisz-Hulbert, Rebecca. 2020. "Fewer Black Teens Seek Treatment for Depression, Mental Health Issues Than White Counterparts." *Washington Post*, August 15, 2020. https://www.washingtonpost.com/health/black-youth-at-higher-risk-of-depression-mental-health-problems/2020/08/14/e28056ec-d66e-11ea-aff6-220dd3a14741_story.html.

Kotkin, Joel, and Erika Ozuna. 2002. *The Changing Face of the San Fernando Valley*. Davenport Institute Research Report. Malibu, CA: School of Public Policy, Pepperdine University.

Kowalski, Kathiann. 2020. "Study Links Racism with Signs of Depression in Black Teens." *Science News for Students*, February 5, 2020. https://www.sciencenewsforstudents.org/article/study-links-racism-with-signs-of-depression-in-black-teens.

Ladson-Billings, Gloria. 1994. *The Dreamkeepers: Successful Teachers of African American Children*. San Francisco: Jossey-Bass.

Lauterbach, Madison. 2019. "APS [Aurora Public Schools] Lauds Pilot Program Boosting the Ranks of Minority Students Tabbed as Gifted." *Sentinel*, June 28, 2019. https://sentinelcolorado.com/news/metro/aps-lauds-pilot-program-boosting-the-ranks-of-minority-students-tabbed-as-gifted/.

Leachman, Michael, and Eric Figueroa. 2019. "K–12 School Funding Up in Most 2018 Teacher-Protest States, but Still Well Below Decade Ago." Center on Budget and Policy Priorities. March 6, 2019. https://www.cbpp.org/research/state-budget-and-tax/k-12-school-funding-up-in-most-2018-teacher-protest-states-but-still.

Lewis, Sharon. 2009. *Improving School Climate: Findings from Schools Implementing Restorative Practices*. Bethlehem, PA: International Institute for Restorative Practices.

Lockhart, P. R. 2019. "High School Students of Color Are Protesting Racism and Inequality." *Vox*, April 2, 2019. https://www.vox.com/identities/2019/4/2/18287053/student-protest-charlottesville-fieldston-racism-inequality.

Love, Bettina L. 2020. *We Want to Do More Than Survive: Abolitionist Teaching and the Pursuit of Educational Freedom.* Boston: Beacon Press.

Lowe, Brendan. 2018. "40% of America's Public Schools Don't Have a Single Educator of Color. How the New Nonprofit BranchED Is Looking to Rethink That Minority Teacher Pipeline." *T74*, November 26, 2018. https://www.the74million.org/article/40-percent-of-americas-public-schools-dont-have-a-single-educator-of-color-how-the-new-non-profit-branched-is-looking-to-rethink-that-minority-teacher-pipeline/.

Lyiscott, Jamila. 2021. National Council of Teachers of English Assembly for Research online keynote presentation, January 30, 2021.

Mannie, Sierra. 2017. "The Only A-Rated, Majority-Black District in Mississippi—Racially Integrated Clinton Receives Top Scores." *Hechinger Report*, July 12, 2017. https://hechingerreport.org/rated-majority-black-district-mississippi/.

Martin, Carmel, Ulrich Boser, Meg Benner, and Perpetual Baffour. 2018. *A Quality Approach to School Funding: Lessons Learned from School Finance Litigation.* Washington, DC: Center for American Progress.

Massey, Douglas S. 2016. "Residential Segregation Is the Linchpin of Racial Stratification." *City Community* 15 (1): 4–7.

Matias, Cheryl, ed. 2019. *Surviving Becky(s): Pedagogies for Deconstructing Whiteness and Gender.* Lanham, MD: Rowman and Littlefield.

McFarland, Joel, et al. 2018. *The Condition of Education 2018.* Washington, DC: National Center for Education Statistics.

McNeil, Linda. 2000. *Contradictions of School Reform: Educational Costs of Standardized Testing.* Boca Raton, FL: Routledge.

Meckler, Laura, and Kate Rabinowitz. 2019. "America's Schools Are More Diverse Than Ever. But the Teachers Are Still Mostly White." *Washington Post*, December 27, 2019. https://www.washingtonpost.com/graphics/2019/local/education/teacher-diversity/.

Mezzacappa, Dale. 2019. "Hite Says New Budget Represents Stability, Progress, and Good Fiscal Stewardship." *Notebook*. Philadelphia Public Schools, March 28, 2019. https://thenotebook.org/articles/2019/03/28/hite-touts-new-budget-as-representing-stability-progress-and-good-fiscal-stewardship/.

Michigan State University. n.d. *MSU Libraries Research Guide*. https://libguides.lib.msu.edu/latino.

Minor, Cornelius. 2019. *We Got This: Equity, Access, and the Quest to Be Who Our Students Need Us to Be*. Portsmouth, NH: Heinemann.

Mitchell, Corey. 2019. "The Latino Teacher-Student Divide: 5 Steps to Close the Gap." *Education Week* blog, November 1, 2019. http://blogs.edweek.org/edweek/learning-the-language/2019/11/five_steps_to_close_the_latino_teacher_gap.html.

Morton, Karisma, and Catherine Riegle-Crumb. 2020. "Is School Racial/Ethnic Composition Associated with Content Coverage in Algebra?" *Educational Researcher* 49 (5).

Muhammad, Gholdy. 2020. *Cultivating Genius: An Equity Framework for Culturally and Historically Responsive Literacy*. New York: Scholastic.

Murphy, Justin, and Georgie Silvarole. 2019. "Fewer AP Classes, Suspended More Often: Black Students Still Face Racism in Suburbs." *USA Today*, February 4, 2019. https://www.usatoday.com/story/news/education/2019/02/04/black-history-month-february-schools-ap-racism-civil-rights/2748790002/.

NAACP Legal Defense and Educational Fund. 2017. *Locked Out of the Classroom: How Implicit Bias Contributes to Disparities in School Discipline*. New York: NAACP Legal Defense and Educational Fund.

National Center for Education Statistics. 2019. "Dual Enrollment: Participation and Characteristics." *Data Point*. National Center for Education Statistics, February 5, 2019.

National Education Association. 2011. "Race Against Time: Educating Black Boys."

National Education Association, February 2011. https://vtechworks.lib.
vt.edu/handle/10919/84028.

O'Donnell-Allen, Cindy. 2011. *Tough Talk, Tough Texts: Teaching English to Change the World*. Portsmouth, NH: Heinemann.

Oluo, Ijeoma. 2019. *So You Want to Talk About Race*. New York: Hachette.

Pack, Emilio. 2019. "What Really Keeps Girls of Color Out of STEM: In a Field Dominated by White Men, Racial and Cultural Isolation Is a Hidden Barrier." *Education Week*, April 23, 2019. https://www.edweek.org/ew/articles/2019/04/24/what-really-keeps-girls-of-color-out.html.

Painter, Nell Irvin. 2006. *Creating Black Americans: African American History and Its Meanings, 1619 to the Present*. New York: Oxford University Press.

Palochko, Jacqueline. 2020. "Black Lives Matter Movement Prods Bethlehem and Other Districts to Review How History Is Taught." *Morning Call*, July 12, 2020. https://www.mcall.com/news/education/mc-nws-bethlehem-schools-history-curriculum-diversity-20200708-4jfhkvbsjrcu3je2hnty2p666a-story.html.

Paris, Django. 2012. "Culturally Sustaining Pedagogy: A Needed Change in Stance, Terminology, and Practice." *Educational Researcher* 41 (3): 93–97.

Patrick, Kayla, Allison Socol, and Ivy Morgan. 2020. *Inequities in Advanced Coursework: What's Driving Them and What Leaders Can Do*. Oakland, CA: Education Trust.

Payne, Charles M. 2008. *So Much Reform, So Little Change: The Persistence of Failure in Urban Schools*. Boston: Harvard Education Press.

Pearman, Francis A., II, F. Chris Curran, Benjamin Fisher, and Joseph Gardella. 2019. "Are Achievement Gaps Related to Discipline Gaps? Evidence from National Data." *AERA Open*, October 16, 2019. https://www.aera.net/Newsroom/Are-Achievement-Gaps-Related-to-Discipline-Gaps-Evidence-from-National-Data.

Pollard, Nyla. 2020. "Black Boys Need the Guidance and Mentorship of Black Male Teachers: Why Do Black Men Comprise Just 2 Percent of the U.S. Teaching Force?" *Hechinger Report*, January 7, 2020. https://hechingerreport.org/student-voice-black-boys-need-the-guidance-and-mentorship-of-black-male-teachers/.

Price-Dennis, Detra, and Yolanda Sealey-Ruiz. 2021. *Advancing Racial Literacies in Teacher Education: Activism for Equity in Digital Spaces.* New York: Teachers College Press.

Prothero, Arianna. 2020a. "Mental Health in Schools: Black and Hispanic Students Say They Have Less Support." *Education Week*, January 23, 2020. https://www.edweek.org/education/mental-health-in-schools-black-and-hispanic-students-say-they-have-less-support/2020/01.

———. 2020b. "Survey: Teens Are Worried About Coronavirus, Especially Teens of Color." *Education Week*, April 10, 2020. https://blogs.edweek.org/edweek/rulesforengagement/2020/04/teens_are_worried_about_the_coronavirus_especially_black_and_latino_teens_survey_finds.html.

Quillian, Lincoln. 2017. "Neighborhood and the Intergenerational Transmission of Poverty." *Focus* 33 (2). https://www.irp.wisc.edu/resource/neighborhood-and-the-intergenerational-transmission-of-poverty/.

Renzulli, Joseph S. 2019. "What We're Getting Wrong About Gifted Education." *Education Week*, November 11, 2019. https://www.edweek.org/ew/articles/2019/11/11/what-were-getting-wrong-about-gifted-education.html.

Riddle, Allison. "When White Teachers Avoid Conversations About Race, We Marginalize Students of Color." *Education Week*, February 26, 2018. https://www.edweek.org/teaching-learning/opinion-when-white-teachers-avoid-conversations-about-race-we-marginalize-students-of-color/2018/02.

Samuels, Christina. 2019. "Racial Segregation Grows as Southern Communities Splinter into New Districts." *Education Week*, September 4, 2019. http://blogs.edweek.org/edweek/District_Dossier/2019/09/racial_segregation_in_new_southern_districts.html.

Schoenbach, Ruth, Cynthia Greenleaf, and Lynn Murphy. 2012. *Reading for Understanding: How Reading Apprenticeship Improves Disciplinary Learning in Secondary and College Classrooms*. San Francisco: Jossey-Bass and WestEd.

Schultz, Brian. 2008. *Spectacular Things Happen Along the Way*. New York: Teachers College Press.

Schwartz, Sarah. 2019. "Next Step in Diversity Training: Teachers Learn to Face Their Unconscious Biases." *Education Week*, May 14, 2019. https://www. edweek.org/ew/articles/2019/05/15/next-step-in-diversity-training-teachers-learn.html.

Sealey-Ruiz, Yolanda. 2019. "Education Equity Starts with Critical Love." Online interview. *Resilient Educator* blog, September 5, 2019. Portland, OR: Concordia University. https://resilienteducator.com/classroom-resources/ education-equity-starts-with-critical-love/.

Shapiro, Eliza. 2020. "New York City Will Change Many Selective Schools to Address Segregation." *New York Times*, December 18, 2020. https://www. nytimes.com/2020/12/18/nyregion/nyc-schools-admissions-segregation. html.

Skiba, Russell J., and Natasha T. Williams. 2014. *Are Black Kids Worse? Myths and Facts About Racial Differences in Behavior: A Summary of the Literature*. Bloomington: Equity Project at Indiana University.

Southern Poverty Law Center. 2019. *The Striking Outlier: The Persistent, Painful, and Problematic Practice of Corporal Punishment in Schools*. Montgomery, AL: Southern Poverty Law Center.

Sparks, Sarah D., and Alyson Klein. 2018. "Discipline Disparities Grow for Students of Color, New Federal Data Show." *Education Week*, April 24, 2018. https:// www.edweek.org/ew/articles/2018/04/24/discipline-disparities-grow-for-students-of-color.html.

Starck, Jordan G., Travis Riddle, Stacey Sinclair, and Natasha Warikoo. 2020. "Teachers Are People Too: Examining the Racial Bias of Teachers Compared to Other American Adults." *Education Researcher*, April 14, 2020, 273–84.

Strauss, Valerie. 2019. "7 out of 895—the Number of Black Students Admitted to NYC's Most Selective High School. And There Are More Startling Stats." *Washington Post*, March 21, 2019. https://www.washingtonpost.com/education/2019/03/21/out-number-black-students-admitted-nycs-most-selective-high-school-there-are-more-startling-stats/.

Substance Abuse and Mental Health Services Administration (SAMHSA). n.d. *Ready, Set, Go, Review: Screening for Behavioral Health Risk in Schools.* www.samhsa.gov.

Superville, Denisa R. 2019. "Districts Struggle to Hire Black Teachers. Is the Solution Hiring More Black Principals?" *Education Week*, May 31, 2019. https://blogs.edweek.org/edweek/District_Dossier/2019/05/black_principals_black_teachers.html.

Truss, Joe. 2019. "What Happened When My School Started to Dismantle White Supremacy Culture." *Education Week*, July 18, 2019. https://blogs.edweek.org/edweek/next_gen_learning/2019/07/what_happened_when_my_school_started_to_dismantle_white_supremacy_culture.html.

Ujifusa, Andrew. 2019. "Kids of Color Often Shut Out of High-Quality State Preschool, Research Says." *Education Week*, November 6, 2019. https://blogs.edweek.org/edweek/campaign-k-12/early-education/.

US Commission on Civil Rights. 2019. *Beyond Suspensions: Examining School Discipline Policies and Connections to the School-to-Prison Pipeline for Students of Color with Disabilities.* Washington, DC: US Commission on Civil Rights.

US Department of Education Office for Civil Rights. 2014. *Civil Rights Data Collection – Data Snapshot: School Discipline. Issue Brief No. 1.* US Department of Education Office for Civil Rights. https://eric.ed.gov-/?q=source%3A%22Office+for+Civil+Rights%2C+US+Department+of+Education%22&id=ED577231.

US Government Accountability Office. 2018. *Discipline Disparities for Black Students, Boys, and Students with Disabilities.* Washington, DC: US Government Accountability Office.

Washburn, David. 2019. "Budget Realities Challenging California School Districts' Restorative Justice Programs." EdSource.org, July1, 2019. https://edsource. org/2019/budget-realities-challenging-california-school-districts-restor- ative-justice-programs/614572.

Wilkerson, Isabel. 2020. *Caste: The Origin of Our Discontents.* New York: Penguin.

Wisely, John. 2019. "Michigan Schools Face Huge Racial Disparity—and It's Hard to Fix." *Detroit Free Press*, June 17, 2019. https://www.freep.com/story/news/ education/2019/06/17/racial-disparities-in-schools/1333607001/.

Index

Page numbers followed by *f* indicate figures.